ROOTED
IN DECENCY

Finding inner peace in a world gone sideways

Colleen Doyle Bryant

Published by LoveWell Press

LoveWellPress.com

Find free printable journaling pages and more at:
RootedInDecency.com

Print book ISBN: 978-0-9849056-6-9
ebook ISBN: 978-0-9849056-7-6

To G, U, and the Team

Contents

Introduction

What happened to people? When did this bizarro-world become normal? When I started researching this book during the tilt-a-whirl ride that was 2020, people would naturally ask what it would be about. I'd start my thirty-second pitch with, "It seems like a lot of people feel like the world's gone sideways." And that was as far as I'd get. They'd jump in, saying, "I know right?" or "Sideways? Try upside down!" Then they'd launch into a heartfelt argument about what was wrong with the world.

For each person, the hot topics were different. For some it was the lack of truth and respect being shown in politics; for others it was race relations or the gender identity debate. People vented about the state of protests and riots, mass shootings, cancel culture, the immigration crisis, the opioid crisis, the homelessness crisis, soaring mental health issues, and the throbbing vein of fear and frustration fed by the global COVID pandemic.

Despite the breadth of the issues that concerned people, I felt a common thread running through the conversations: No matter who was talking, about whatever issue concerned them, I heard *a sense of disappointment in their fellow humans and concern about a lack of stability at the very foundation of society.* They would wonder aloud, "How did things get to be so nasty and divisive? When did it become *normal* to behave so *wrongly* toward each other?" What I came to realize, and what really struck me though, is that one person's "bad" was another person's "heroic." One person's "right" was another person's morally, offensively "wrong." So I began to wonder, *Do we even share a common idea of right and wrong anymore?*

A search to make sense of it all

With this thought circling around in my mind, I couldn't help but start researching why people are disappointed and discontent with each other. I looked into the ways that modern society influences our feelings of instability and divisiveness. Eventually, I sought an answer to my most troubling concern—*Do we have common values that transcend our political and sub-group differences? Is there a path back to contentment and cooperation?*

As it turns out, there are some pretty interesting reasons that we're feeling so off-kilter. Soon after my research began, when people would ask me about the book, I'd drop a nugget of scientific, historical, or philosophical gold that I'd found, like these:

Did you know that when we think of someone we identify as a "them"—like a strong Democrat toward a strong Republican and vice versa—it activates the same part of our brain as when we smell rotten meat?[1]

Did you know every major world religion has a version of the "Golden Rule" which says to treat others as you would like to be treated?[2]

Did you know that childhood, income, marital status, occupation, neighborhood, religion, and various other life circumstances only impact 10% of happiness?[3]

Whether I shared an arresting bit of data from neuroscientists or happiness scientists; quirky facts from biology, social science, or history; or enduring ideas from Aristotle and Thomas Paine to Buddha and Jesus, the people I was sharing them with would pause. Instead of launching into their personal frustrations, they'd want to know more about that nugget. The conversation would turn toward curiosity, with a touch of hope, that they just might be able to make sense of things in our world today. Sure, the old frustrations were still there. But each nugget of knowledge changed the tone of the discussion—and opened the door to a fresh perspective.

A path forward

This book is a collection of those intriguing nuggets. Taken individually, any of the short chapters invites you to look at our modern existence in new ways. Taken together, they'll lead you on a path of discovery toward an inner peace that remains stable regardless of the tumult around us. And the more of us that start to make shifts in our perspectives and actions based on these ideas, the sooner we'll get to an inner **and** outer peace, with more stability and civility in our society.

Does this book cover every possible angle of every issue? No. It's intentionally brief so busy people can read it. But, just in case you find something that moves you and you want to learn more, I've cited sources that go deeper so you can go deeper.

Mapping the route

The journey starts with you, and then expands outward, so that's how this book is structured:

Part one looks to the personal self and why we feel off-balance. We'll look at how modern life contributes to feelings of personal instability and how intentionally minimizing extremes in the ways we think, feel, and find fulfillment can immediately help us feel more steady. In the end, we'll see that *being rooted in decency—living life in line with what you think is right—builds an inner self-respect that is not easily swayed by circumstance.*

Part two looks at how we're not just individuals, but individuals who live in a society. We'll look at why we voluntarily limit our own freedoms and control our own behavior in order gain the benefits of living in a group. The current culture of nasty divisiveness and self-absorption runs counter to our own best interest and to the evolutionary wisdom humans have gained about how to live well together. *We'll look at some of the biological and cultural reasons today's Us versus Them atmosphere is so powerful and we'll consider some ways to change it.* By the end of the section, we'll see how we don't have to be perfect, but by simply being decent, we can create ripple effects that come rolling back to improve our world.

Part three explores the question: What does it mean to be a decent person? In a time when so many people think they're "right" while so many others think they're "wrong," we'll look to history and world belief systems to *find common values* that have guided human behavior for thousands of years. We'll use those values to *create a moral compass, viewed through a modern perspective, that enables each of us to make decisions that are rooted in decency.*

Each short chapter within the three parts of the book should give you some good nuggets to weigh. At the end of each chapter there are optional journaling pages to prompt self-reflection or book club discussion. (If you don't want to write in the book, free printable journaling pages are available on our website, RootedInDecency.com.) If you read the chapters in order, they'll guide you through a process of discovery and the development of your moral compass.

A note about perspective

The book is written from an American perspective and primarily references American culture, yet many of the ideas will apply across world cultures, particularly other Western democracies where individualism is paramount. The terms liberal/Democrat and conservative/Republican are based on American definitions of those terms. The moral compass is based on global ideas of right and wrong, drawn from world belief systems, including Eastern, Western, ancient, and modern ideas about morality.

Who am I to write this book?

That's a fair question because I'm neither an academic nor a scientist. But there are lots of great minds who wrote lots of great books that most of us aren't going to pick up in our leisure time. As much as I loved Aristotle's *The Nicomachean Ethics*, it's not a beach read. So, my goal with this book is to make ideas from those brilliant minds accessible for a busy, general audience. And if you want to know more or to verify the facts contained within, I've included a thorough Notes section at the end of the book so you can access the works of scientists, philosophers, theologians, and other verified sources across the many disciplines that I explored.

I have a foundation in researching sources and analyzing societal behavior, starting with a degree in sociology from Duke University. At the time of the writing of this particular book, I've spent over a decade writing books and creating learning resources that are used in curricula around the world. My Talking with Trees series for young children and Truth Be Told Quotes materials for teens have been building social emotional skills and good character traits in the younger generations for years.

I find it a little odd how we recognize the importance of teaching our children to be honest, respectful, responsible, and compassionate, while we adults haven't been doing a very good job of practicing what we preach. This book is a reminder of the ways of behaving that we all know are valuable and necessary for our well-being, as individuals and as a society. Without further ado, flip the page and start your journey.

Who am I to write this book?

∽

Part One:

Looking Inward

Part One

Looking Inward

We started this journey with the idea that life seems to have gone sideways. Why do we feel so off-balance today? It would be easy to say, "It's people's obsession with social media!" or "Political divisiveness!", but it's not really that easy. Those phenomena show *what* people are doing, but they don't explain *why* they are inclined to behave that way in the first place. ***Whatever chaos is happening around each of us, we're the ones who choose how we engage with it. So, we need to start by looking at ourselves.***

Starting with your "self"

In this first section, part one, we'll look within, helping you consider ways that modern life influences the way we think, feel, and find fulfillment. We'll start with the quest for happiness and how people truly find a contented and meaningful life. (It's probably not what you think.)

Then we'll move on to see how thinking (mind), feeling (body), and connecting (spirit) are all essential in our lives, yet today, we are less active, fewer people are religious,[1] and we spend a lot of time alone in our own heads. So we'll see that mind-body-spirit isn't new-age stuff—we'll talk about core biology, psychology, and how to recognize some ways that modern life encourages habits and extremes in the ways we think (mind), feel (body), and connect (spirit) that are throwing us off-balance. And we'll talk about how to correct it.

Finally, we'll discover that there's a difference between self-esteem and self-respect. One of them creates a rooted inner stability that comes from living in alignment with what you know is right. (Which one do you think it is?) *By looking within, we'll see how, in a world full of extremes, finding more inner balance and living in alignment with ourselves leads to a stability that persists despite the chaos going on around us.*

Being out of balance causes pain

Buddha famously said, "Life is suffering"—which sounds fairly pessimistic from this great spiritual leader. But what Buddha really said was "Life is dukkha."

According to preeminent religious scholar Huston Smith, *dukkha* was a word used "to refer to wheels whose axles were off-center, or bones that had slipped from their sockets."[2] In his definitive classic, *The World's Religions*, Smith explains that "Life is dukkha" means that when life is "out of joint," there's excess friction, movement is blocked, and it hurts.[3]

So, even if life around you were all sunshine and daisies, being out of alignment with yourself would still cause suffering. On the flip side, if the world around you is chaotic, when you're balanced within yourself, you can roll through the ups and downs more smoothly. In part one, we'll look at a few ways that modern life is throwing us "out of joint" and how we can get back to a smoother, more balanced ride.

Up next

Let's start our journey within with a look at why people are unhappy and which behaviors truly bring lasting inner joy.

Chapter 1

Finding Lasting Happiness
Why happiness comes and goes, and how that's a good thing.

Two friends chatting over coffee:

Ash: You know, I thought when I finally bought this house that I'd be happy. Or that when I got married, I'd be happy. Or if I just got that promotion and made more money then surely, I'd be happy.

Forrest: You're not happy? With your new house, spouse, job, and bigger paycheck?

Ash: Sometimes it's great. But there's still all this stuff that's so hard. When will I *just* be happy?

Why aren't more people happy? I could cite statistics on how unhappy people are these days, but that would just be depressing. Instead, let's look at *why* people are struggling to find peace in their lives. In *The How of Happiness,* Sonja Lyubomirsky, a world authority on happiness research, suggests three forces behind today's high rates of unhappiness:[1]

#1- We expect a lot. We have higher expectations for our lives today than people in the past and we are "profoundly disappointed when reality doesn't meet or even come close to perfection."[2]

#2- We're isolated and self-critical. Our individualistic culture leaves us alone to deal with everyday stressors and encourages us to be overly self-critical of our perceived shortcomings.

#3- We lack connection. Without a strong sense of belonging in our families and communities, we struggle to find the support or meaningful connection that would help us through life's challenges.

But, I thought you weren't going to depress us?!? Don't worry, there's good news in this! Let's start with high expectations and our perceived shortcomings.

Looking for happiness in the wrong places

High expectations and the sense that we don't "measure up" leads us to think we can find happiness through *external* sources, like money and success. We turn to ideas like, "If only I had… then I'd be happy." But as the saying goes, money can't buy happiness. However, it can buy groceries. UC Berkeley psychology researcher, Dacher Keltner, in *Born to Be Good*, reports that researchers have asked millions of people about happiness. The results consistently show that more money helps the poorest people avoid the struggles associated with a lack of security, but for "those in the middle classes and above … the association between money and happiness is weak or nonexistent."[3] A study of lottery winners showed that a year after they won it big, the winners were no happier than people who didn't win at all. In fact, a year later, "the lottery winners mused that they now derived less enjoyment from day-to-day activities, such as watching television or going out to lunch, relative to the nonwinners."[4]

Focusing on "If only I had…" is generally not helpful in a quest for happiness—and neither is wishing that the past had happened differently or waiting for a better future. Lyubomirsky's research shows that the events that shape our childhoods; significant events in adulthood; marital status; occupation; income; neighborhood; ethnicity; age; gender; and religious affiliation—only account for about 10% of happiness! She says,

> So, although you may find it very hard to believe, whether you drive to work in a Lexus hybrid or a battered truck, whether you're young or old, or have had wrinkle-removing plastic surgery, whether you live in the frigid Midwest or on the balmy West Coast, your chances of being happy and becoming happier are pretty much the same.[5]

Wow, right? How is this possible? Some of us are rethinking our whole life plan right now.

Happiness ebbs and flows

Here's what's going on. Once we achieve a level of core security, the things we think will make our lives better may give us a temporary boost, but the effect doesn't last as long as we think it will.[6] Thanks to a psychological concept called the *Hedonic Treadmill*, we quickly get used to what we have, and then we aspire to more. Even when we get more stuff to satisfy our material wants, a promotion to meet career expectations, or even plastic surgery to finally reach a beauty ideal, we may feel good for a little while, but then we adapt to the benefit and get used to the feeling of a "new normal." Remember those lottery winners from earlier in the chapter? A year after winning life-changing money, the happiness boost had worn off. Thanks to this hedonic adaptation, our happiness levels balance out to a steady state, and return to a base level, over time. *Some people have sunnier dispositions than others, but we all have a steady state that our bodies naturally return to.*

The upside of fleeting happiness

Before you decide the Hedonic Treadmill is the worst, know that our ability to adapt quickly to a new normal has an upside. When sad events and tragedies happen (and they will, because that's life), we are equally able to adjust and handle life's "down" moments. For example, when you get that new job, you might be ecstatic for a while, but then the feeling mellows to contentment—and that's a good thing! Because when you encounter new stresses later—like a difficult new boss—you figure out how to cope, and your tense frustration softens to acceptance. The flow of waves that carry us up toward joy, down into unpleasant emotions, and then back up to our baseline enables us to continually reset how much we need in order to feel satisfied, and it helps us find a level of contentment.

The first step in finding more happiness comes from recognizing that we won't ever "just" be happy; but that's okay, because the beauty of the Hedonic Treadmill is that *we're better able to appreciate the good and we're better able to recover from the bad.* We can persevere through the hard times because experience shows us that even the low points eventually level-out to something we can manage.

Lasting happiness comes from our own actions

The great news in all this is that our happiness is not at the whim of life's twists and turns. (*That's a relief!*) According to *The How of Happiness,*

> The key to happiness lies not in changing our genetic makeup (which is impossible) and not in changing our circumstances (i.e., seeking wealth or attractiveness or better colleagues, which is usually impractical), but in our daily intentional activities.[7]

We each have the ability to deliberately make changes to the way we think, feel, and engage with life to generate our own joy. So what do happy people do that's so special? Lyubomirsky analyzed her own and other researchers' studies and found some patterns in the way happy people think and behave:

Self-respect: Happy people have an inner sense of themselves and know their worth without comparing themselves to others. Thus, they're able to share in the joy of others' successes and recover from their own setbacks.

Flow: Happy people foster optimism for the future but are willing to flow with reality when things don't go their way. They savor the good times and express gratitude for what they have, and they show poise and strength when tough stuff happens.

Movement: Happy people take action to affect their lives and they use physical or meditative activities to help emotions flow, disrupting cycles of negative thinking.

Connection: Happy people have a sense of their impact beyond their finite selves. They value relationships and act to connect with other people and the world around them.

What promotes happiness?
Self-respect – Flowing through ups and downs –
Action and movement – Connection beyond oneself

Finding happiness amidst stress

Okay, so maybe that all sounds easier said than done. There's so much going on in the world that it may seem naïve to think circumstances could affect us to such a small degree. Psychologists Paul Napper and Anthony Rao have certainly seen an impact from what they call "The Age of Anxiety and Overwhelm." In their book, *The Power of Agency*, these doctors describe a pattern where patients were feeling overwhelmed by life, "stuck, adrift, or thwarted."[8] When they explored this further, they found that many patients felt a sense of insecurity or anxiety that didn't have a specific, identifiable cause. Many of their patients, mired in pressure and worry, were losing their ability to objectively evaluate what was happening in their lives and couldn't consciously make choices to direct their own outcomes. In psychology terms, this is called a loss of *agency*. The doctors explain:

> When you become too overwhelmed and lose your agency, you can no longer evaluate your circumstances, reflect on the challenges and opportunities you're confronted with, make creative decisions, and then act in ways that open up possibilities for a meaningful life on your own terms. In simpler words, agency is what humans have always used to *feel in command of their lives.*[9]

This pattern of overwhelming anxiety didn't fit all their patients though. When the doctors met patients who had a sense of control over their own lives—those who were connected to their sense of agency—those patients reported experiencing less anxiety, even during challenging situations. Here's where the proverbial light bulb went on above their heads: ***To find balance amidst anxiety, the answer isn't only to lessen the burden of the stressors, but we can also counterbalance the stressors with a healthy supply of agency.*** They found that having confidence in our ability to manage life can "actually *help keep stress away.*"[10]

With this new insight, the doctors developed seven principles around behavior and thought processes to help patients improve their sense of agency:

> **Behavioral Principles**– The first three principles help *reduce negative emotions* and provide a push to get patients to *take action* to affect their lives. They do this through controlling distractions, *connecting* with supportive people, and *moving* one's body.

Cognitive Principles– The other four principles help people change *how they think* and *how they deal with emotions*. They include being a learner who *improves oneself*, building a more *honest awareness* of oneself and one's environment, and *replacing impulsive reactions* with rational, informed decisions.

Just like with the happiness research, these practicing doctors found that we don't have to be at the whim of life's twists and turns. By intentionally changing the way we think, feel, and engage with life, we can find more balance and peace despite the many sources of stress in life today.

Transcendent happiness

But hey, who says we have to settle for finding contentment and managing stress? Maybe we want more. In *Transcend*, psychology researcher Scott Barry Kaufman explains how some people are able to elevate their lives "beyond stereotypical notions of happiness."[11] More than forty years of humanistic psychology research has shown that the secret to experiencing life in a fulfilled and vital way is through (*Yes, these are going to sound familiar given the paragraphs on happiness and stress*):

- **Managing emotions**– Feeling fewer negative emotions (like sadness and fear) while feeling more positive emotions (like joy and contentment) and finding more moments of awe, inspiration, and gratitude.

- **Competence and agency**– Knowing we are free to make choices and can affect the outcomes of our lives; knowing we are competent to manage the demands of life.

- **Personal growth**– Feeling a sense of physical health and energy; engaging with life; seeking to improve oneself.

- **Connection**– Enjoying positive relationships and feeling a sense of purpose and connection to something greater than oneself.

- **Self-worth**– Having a positive sense of one's worth which comes from knowing we're a "fundamentally good person" and knowing we are valued in our relationships with others.[12]

You may have noticed that there's nothing in there about money, possessions, beauty ideals, undoing the past, or eliminating unpleasant experiences. Kaufman explains that "Becoming fully human is about living a full existence, not one that is continually happy. Being well is not always about feeling good; it also involves continually incorporating more meaning, engagement, and growth in one's life."[13]

A path forward

What we see through all this research is that whether we're looking at happiness science, stress management, or living a full and meaningful life, the themes that arise are remarkably similar. Finding lasting happiness isn't about reaching an end state where we only feel good all the time. In fact, that force we saw earlier in the chapter, hedonic adaptation, makes sure that even if we did somehow experience joy-and-only-joy, then joy would become less satisfying. Instead, *happiness comes from how we choose to think, feel, and act as we flow through the ups and downs of life.*

If we put the research from this chapter together, we can summarize into four themes that we'll see again and again throughout this book.

The real secret to lasting happiness and well-being is:

- **Honest Self-Awareness**– When we accurately understand our own thoughts and feelings, and we accurately evaluate the world around us, we can consciously affect our lives for the better.

- **Appreciating the Positive**– When we look for opportunities to experience positive and awe-inspiring emotions, we can counterbalance the difficult ones.

- **Internal Self-Respect**– When we know we are a good person who has positive connections with others and makes an impact beyond ourselves, we develop an inner sense of worth that's not easily shaken by other people or circumstances.

- **Personal Responsibility**– By actively engaging with life, making the effort to improve ourselves, and taking ownership for creating our own outcomes, we build a sense of agency that gives us confidence to handle whatever comes our way.

Throughout the coming chapters, we'll get more specific about how the current culture works against these core means of achieving happiness and well-being that we just identified. To give you a small taste of what's to come, consider:

- How would a "post-truth" era affect our ability to accurately understand ourselves and the world around us?

- How would a culture of moral disgust and public shaming affect our sense of being good people?

- How would a culture of identity-based victimhood affect our sense of having control over our own lives?

The forces affecting us today go beyond mere tribalism. They hit at the very heart of how we find well-being and stability in life. As we journey through the upcoming chapters, we'll see that there are actions we can take right now to create well-being and stability for ourselves, and ultimately for society.

Journaling

What brings you happiness or joy? Is it things, experiences, relationships, etc.?

Have you ever experienced a difficult time that eventually got better? What changed?

Do you feel like you have control over your own life?

Up next

We saw in this chapter that we can influence our own happiness through the ways we think, feel, and are connected to the world, so in the next few chapters, we'll look at ways modern life throws our mind (*thinking*), body (*feeling*), and spirit (*connecting*) out of balance. And of course, we'll explore some actions we can take to get back to equilibrium.

Chapter 2

Mindless Thinking
How extreme thinking is knocking us off-balance

Two colleagues discussing a proposal

Ash: How can they think that? Clearly, they're all idiots. This whole thing is a disaster. If this goes through, life as we know it is over. They must think we're second rate. I feel like every time we do a deal with them, we never get anything we want.

Forrest: Hmm. When I presented the idea yesterday, they said almost the exact same thing about us.

Our minds are powerful, and they've helped our species survive for a long time. Humans have lived through wars, famines, and diseases while the effects of the Hedonic Treadmill (that psychological phenomenon from chapter 1) have helped us recover from devastating lows back to a steady state. We're incredibly flexible and adaptable when we think *mindfully*— meaning *we are aware of our surroundings, view situations from multiple perspectives, and adapt based on context.*[1] Harvard researchers Shelley Carson and Ellen Langer would tell us, when we're *mindfully* engaged, our responses "result in greater competence, health, positive affect, creativity, and reduced burnout."[2] But sometimes, we seek a false sense of stability by narrowing our thinking and we respond automatically, or *mindlessly*, becoming "trapped within a single perspective, oblivious to other ways of seeing the information."[3]

Human strength comes from *mindful* engagement with our world— evaluating, reasoning, and consciously choosing what to believe and how to react. Yet in the current environment, we may be caught up in an automatic way of thinking that's out of balance and leaves us feeling constantly out of sorts. Negative life events have always happened. So why, in today's times, are we so affected?

Flexible thinking versus automatic thinking

Let's start by looking at how we process negative thoughts and situations. *The Mindful Way,* written by a team of psychologists including Jon Kabat-Zinn and Mark Williams, explains that every day we have momentary negative thoughts that show up.[4] Take for example the thought, *I'm worried that this thing isn't going to go well,* and let's see the difference between *mindful* and *mindless* thinking:

> **In a mindful moment,** when the thought, *I'm worried,* arises, it sets in motion an effort to gather information, evaluate, consider alternate views, and decide on a course of action. So, we might ask ourselves: *What evidence do I have about whether this is true? Are there other ways I could be seeing this situation? Do I need to do something or can I just let this thought go?*

> **In a mindless moment,** we respond to the thought, *I'm worried,* automatically, limiting our perspective and accepting information without considering other ways of looking at the situation. We may also let negative filters, called *cognitive distortions*, reinforce our thinking. So, *I'm worried* may morph into: *I feel like it's going to be a disaster. I'm sure I know what he's thinking and it's bad news for me. I'm doomed!*

Danger lurks in automatic thinking

Thoughts can come and thoughts can go—unless *cognitive distortions* start meddling in your business. *Cognitive distortions are automatic ways of thinking that bend people's view of reality, often inflating their perception of negativity and hopelessness.* When cognitive distortions become habitual, they can turn passing sadness into a persistent unhappiness or depression by creating a *self-reinforcing cycle of negativity.*[5] To prevent cognitive distortions from inflating negative, mindless thinking, the first thing we need is to be able to recognize them. So, let's take a look at cognitive distortions and see if you've ever seen any of these thought patterns.

Forms of cognitive distortions:[6]

All-or-Nothing Thinking
Viewing people or situations only in terms of extremes without nuance or complexity.
Examples: This didn't go the way I planned so I'm a total failure. | This whole project is worthless. | You're either with me or you're against me.

Overgeneralizing
Seeing a single example and thinking it's a universal rule.
Examples: Everyone is always mean to me. | She hates everything that I stand for. | We never get what we want.

Negative Filtering and Discounting Positives
Only seeing the negative aspects of a situation or thinking positive aspects are not important when they conflict with the negative view you want to hold.
Examples: The one thing I got wrong is way more important than all the things I got right. | He hasn't done anything worthwhile for me in ten years!

Mind Reading and Fortune Telling
Assuming you know what someone else is thinking, or predicting what's going to happen without evidence.
Examples: He didn't respond so he must be mad at me. | They're all thinking about how dumb my ideas are. | She'll never like what we propose anyway.

Catastrophizing and Minimization
Grossly exaggerating or minimizing the importance of things.
Examples: This is the worst thing ever! | He thinks I shouldn't even exist. | This will ruin my life.

Emotional Reasoning
Deciding that because you feel it's true, it must be true.
Examples: I feel sad so the situation is hopeless. | This feels overwhelming, so it must be impossible to change. | It feels like you're out to get me, so I'm certain you are.

Should Statements
Holding unrealistic or unnecessary ideas of how things "should" be.
Examples: I should be able to be perfect at raising kids, being a spouse, having a career—and do it with a smile. | I should have had more time with him before he passed on. | They shouldn't do that; I wouldn't.

Labeling
Looking at one behavior or characteristic of a person and using it to define everything about that person.
Examples: I'm a loser. | She's a bitch. | He's a transphobe. | They're elites.

Personalization / Blaming
Assigning someone responsibility for a negative event that's not realistically their fault.

Examples: It's my fault my son didn't get an "A". | It's her fault that I keep getting into trouble. | I know they weren't even here when this whole thing started, but it's still their fault.

Cognitive distortions in action

Anyone who has spent time around teenagers is likely to have heard something like, "No one ever gets me!", "My life is ruined!", and "They're always so unfair to me!"; and as the adults in their lives, we often recognize these thought patterns for the exaggerations that they are. But what about us? It may not be so easy to recognize our own cognitive distortions. Yet, being aware of these patterns of thinking can help us break through automatic thought cycles that swing us to extremes. Using the opening dialog as an example:

"How can they think that? Clearly they're all idiots." — Here's some labeling and overgeneralizing. More likely, they have reasons behind their thinking that could be addressed rationally.

"This whole thing is a disaster. If this goes through, life as we know it is over." — Catastrophizing gets in the way of creating a reasonable action plan.

"They must think we're second rate. I feel like every time we do a deal with them, we never get anything we want." — Mind reading and emotional reasoning can create false assumptions that misguide our decisions.

Whether we're criticizing ourselves or interpreting other people's actions, *cognitive distortions make things feel worse than they really are, and they create a self-reinforcing negativity that makes it hard to find a way back to a positive state.*

A society lost in distortion

Usually, cognitive distortions are something we look at on an individual level, when repetitive negative thinking impacts someone's mental well-being. But, as you read the cognitive distortion examples above, you may have noticed that we're hearing similar patterns at a societal level today. When you listen to the news or read headlines, you'll likely see *catastrophizing*. Listen to political discussions and you'll hear *negative filtering* and *emotional reasoning*. And often it's wrapped in a package of *all-or-nothing* "us and them". **If cognitive distortions can lead an individual's unhappiness toward depression, what happens when a society surrounds itself with a constant stream of negative, catastrophized, overgeneralized, all-or-nothing thinking?**

In *The Coddling of the American Mind*, social scientists Greg Lukianoff and Jonathan Haidt reveal that exaggerating expectations for harm, relying on emotional reasoning, and Us vs. Them thinking (all fed by cognitive distortions) have created a number of problems in society. The researchers recount stories from university life where students feel that *hearing* something that makes them uncomfortable is the same as experiencing *actual, physical harm*. Students have argued that allowing speakers to present views they might not agree with is the equivalent of allowing "violence" on campus, so they feel they are justified in using physical violence themselves to protect their fellow students from hearing the words. We're not talking about abusive words; we're talking about academic discussions. In one example, students protested hearing a theory about how Black Lives Matter protests could cause police to be hesitant to engage in minority neighborhoods, which could negatively impact those neighborhoods. The topic was discussed nationally at the time, but instead of considering multiple perspectives, some students signed a letter of opposition stating that the speaker "would not be debating on mere difference of opinion, but the right of Black people to exist."[7] Lukianoff and Haidt explain:

This thinking is a form of *catastrophizing*, in that it inflates the horrors of a speaker's words far beyond what the speaker might actually say. The students also called [the speaker] "a fascist, a white supremacist, a warhawk, a transphobe, a queerphobe, [and] a classist." This is *labeling* running wild—a list of serious accusations made without supporting evidence.[8]

The Coddling of the American Mind explains that a culture that encouraged students to perceive life through cognitive distortions caused an increase in student anxiety, a decrease in free speech, and it led to a callout culture where a perceived slight could prompt a violent response.

Of course, catastrophizing isn't isolated to university students or liberal institutions. In *How the Right Lost Its Mind*, conservative commentator Charles Sykes offers this quote, made by the late conservative radio show host Rush Limbaugh, as evidence of a culture of exaggerated peril and all-or-nothing thinking during the 2016 election:

> We've got people coming at us that are gonna try to wipe us out and eliminate everything and pretend it didn't happen, corrupt, sabotage, undermine. ... you have no idea what's gonna be brought to bear! We're gonna need people with such backbone and guts and steel and iron to hold up and to withstand what's gonna come at 'em, you can't even imagine it.[9]

Despite being a political commentator, Limbaugh wasn't discussing policy issues or differences of opinion here. Catastrophizing and fortune-telling presented the 2016 election as a binary choice between survival and destruction.

Cognitive distortions on a national level encourage a sense that we're under a constant state of threat. *An exaggerated, overly negative thought cycle drives us to protect ourselves and to close ranks in solidarity with others like us.* Lukianoff and Haidt note that this type of distorted thinking is part of a cultural shift that drives a sense that, for many issues, everyone must be either a victim or an oppressor, an Us or a Them. This is the essence of the *all-or-nothing cognitive distortion,* and it affects our ability to see alternate perspectives—the *mindless* and limiting thinking described at the start of this chapter. (We'll come back to Us versus Them in chapter 8 with a dive into biology and the dangers of moral disgust.)

Clarity amid cognitive distortions

The good news is, we already know how to overcome cognitive distortions and how to start thinking in a more balanced, healthier way. Research shows that one of the most effective ways to interrupt a cycle of automatic negative thinking is with Cognitive Behavior Therapy (CBT). In *Feeling Good,* one of the leading resources for CBT, author David Burns, M.D., offers numerous self-guided techniques to help people think differently and create lasting changes to their outlook.[10] At the core of all CBT techniques is *the need to recognize when we're allowing cognitive distortions to influence our thinking.* Then, we can break the cycle by questioning those thoughts and choosing how to react.

To interrupt mindless thinking, ask yourself:

- What evidence do I have about the truth of this?
- How might cognitive distortions be impacting my interpretation?
- What are some other perspectives for looking at it?

Burns proposes the *triple-column technique* to get clarity on a negative thought. Each column helps us define the thought and the distortion, and then helps us propose some alternate ways of viewing it. Here are some examples of the triple-column technique in action:

Automatic Thought	Cognitive Distortion	Rational Response
This will ruin my life.	Catastrophizing	Which aspects of your life does it really affect? Which aspects won't it affect? How impactful will it really be? What are some things you could do to lessen the impact?
She hates everything that I am.	Overgeneralizing	Which specific attributes or actions does she object to? What other attributes do you have that she doesn't object to? Is this about you as a person or a specific issue?

The triple-column technique is one tool to clarify the situation and to reengage in mindful, rational thinking. If you're interested in more techniques used to address cognitive distortions in someone's personal life, the book *Feeling Good* is one of the best sources about Cognitive Behavior Therapy (CBT). Written by David Burns, a psychiatrist from Stanford University School of Medicine, the book contains explanations and practical exercises, and it has been shown in multiple studies to be immensely helpful for treating depression.[11]

A path forward

For eons, we humans have survived and thrived despite challenges by using our ability to evaluate, reason, and consciously choose how to deal with whatever comes our way. If we're aware of cognitive distortions, we might find that we can gain a more balanced perspective and we can step out of automatic over-reactions—whether we're hearing them from someone else or creating them ourselves. *When we mindfully choose how to view the world and respond to it, we take a big step toward feeling stability.*

Cognitive Distortions

All-or-Nothing Thinking

Overgeneralizing

Negative Filtering / Discounting Positives

Mind Reading / Fortune Telling

Catastrophizing / Minimization

Emotional Reasoning

Should Statements

Labeling

Personalization / Blaming

Journaling

Can you think of examples from your own life, your colleagues, or your family where someone was seeing a situation through cognitive distortions?

Can you think of something happening at a societal level that seems overly negative?

Choose one of the situations you thought of above and using the triple-column technique, what are some other ways to look at it?

Automatic Thought	Cognitive Distortion	Rational Response

Up next

We've seen that choosing to mindfully interrupt automatic thoughts and cognitive distortions can help us find more stability, despite the chaos around us. Next up, we'll look at the body and how noticing the signals our bodies send us is essential to a balanced foundation.

Chapter 3

The Body's Language
How there's a positive side to "negative" emotions

It's dark outside and you're walking by yourself. Suddenly you spy a person approaching you on the street. Your heart races and muscles tighten. You feel a pang of fear and then think about whether the person means you harm. Before you even know why, your muscles start relaxing and your sense of urgency is decreasing. Then you notice the smile that reaches their eyes, and you feel a gentle touch on your forearm. You feel relief and then joy as you realize you know this person. You just haven't seen them in years.

Put yourself in the scenario above. Really picture yourself there. Feel all the things that happen in your body as you transition from initial alarm to welcoming recognition. You didn't just think—you *felt*. The racing heart came before the thought, *Am I in danger?* You felt calmer before your mind even put a name to the person. Why? The mind and body are in a constant interplay that helps us evaluate the world around us—*and the body does way more than we usually think about.*

In modern life, how well do we pay attention to, and take care of, our bodies? We saw in chapter 1 that happy people make physical movement a regular practice, which helps them process emotions in a healthy way.

Yet, we're less active than we used to be. Instead of moving our bodies through the regular course of life, we have to make a point of exercising to stay healthy. Our hunter-gatherer ancestors didn't need to wear step counters on their wrists to make movement a part of their day. Despite all that they do for us, how much do we really notice our bodies, other than to complain of aches or to suppress pesky feelings that get in the way of the tasks we need to do?

The body and mind communicate all day

As we consider the "body" part of mind-body-spirit balance, it would be helpful to have a quick and hugely oversimplified understanding of how the body and brain interact.[1] One part of the human brain controls our automatic responses (we'll call this the *automatic* brain.) This part registers inputs very quickly and sends our bodies signals about what's going on in our environment. It catches a glimpse of a large, gray, furry creature and prepares us for fight, flight, or freeze—before we're even consciously aware of it. The more evolved part of our brain (we'll call it the *executive* brain) is a little slower in its operation than our automatic brain, but it's a lot more accurate. The executive brain takes raw signals and considers, *in what circumstances and to what extent might this situation be a concern*? It takes in the sight of the gray fur and your rapid heartbeat when you see that wolf, then clarifies that it's actually the neighbor's friendly husky escaped from the yard again, and tells you to shake off the fight/flight response that's coursing through your veins.

All day, it's this dynamic cycle between the automatic and executive brain functions and the body that helps us decide what action we think is right or wrong in a given circumstance. As neurology researcher Robert Sapolsky states in *Behave: The Biology of Humans at Our Best and Worst*, "you can't begin to understand things like aggression, competition, cooperation, and empathy without biology" because biological, psychological, and cultural aspects of behavior are "utterly intertwined."[2]

Feelings deliver important messages

We saw in the last chapter that exaggerating thoughts or *over*-indulging feelings is harmful. Yet *under*-indulging feelings—by denying or suppressing them—robs us of valuable information. Some people would say that feelings make you weak, are unseemly, or just get in the way of rational action. After all, "big girls don't cry," much less grown men. That perspective implies we shouldn't feel emotions much at all, or we should only feel the nice, pleasant ones.[3]

Avoiding so-called "negative emotions"—like fear, anger, sadness, and guilt—isn't the answer. Psychologists Jon Kabat-Zinn, Mark Williams and their colleagues note in *The Mindful Way through Depression: Freeing Yourself from Chronic Unhappiness,*

> The fact is that when emotions are telling us that something is not as it should be, the feeling is distinctly uncomfortable. It's meant to be. The signals are exquisitely designed to push us to act, to do something to rectify the situation.[4]

In a sense, trying to avoid uncomfortable emotions is like turning against our own warning system. While over-indulging fear isn't a good idea, it would be foolish not to pay attention if the fear really was about a wolf and not the neighbor's husky. Pretending you're not sad doesn't make the sadness go away. And sometimes anger is absolutely appropriate and will keep you from being taken advantage of. That doesn't mean it's a good idea to unleash your anger on the clerk at the coffee shop or to break down sobbing in a board meeting. But, *instead of seeing emotions as "getting in the way," we can view them for the helpful signals that they are, and let them flow in a healthy way, back to balance.*

Helpful messages hidden in so-called "negative" emotions

In *The Language of Emotions*, self-help author Karla McLaren offers an insightful view of the information some "negative" emotions offer when we let them flow in a healthy, productive way.[5] For example,

Fear *signals that something might be harmful and that we might need to take action.* In its healthy flow, fear gives us clarity, focus, and the vigor to do something.

Anger *signals that you, or someone you care about, are not being treated rightly.* Anger handled in a healthy flow gives us strength to set boundaries and the conviction to protect ourselves and others.

Sadness is a process of *honoring and grieving something that has been lost.* When healthy sadness flows through us, it helps us to release and ultimately revitalize after a loss.

Guilt is about *recognizing our own responsibility for an outcome and the need to make it right.* The anticipation of guilt helps us choose the right action even when we're faced with a more tempting option.

From this perspective, denying ourselves the messages that these emotions deliver makes no sense at all. Letting even "negative" emotions flow in a healthy way, without distortions, offers us powerful guidance.

Here's the next big moment to sit up and pay attention: ***Being out of touch with the sensations our bodies are sending us also limits our ability to revel in POSITIVE emotions like compassion, gratitude, and awe***—experiences that researcher Dacher Keltner explains are the very substance of a fulfilling life. In his book, *Born to Be Good: The Science of a Meaningful Life*, Keltner reveals that the body feeds us lots of little moments of joy that remind us life is worth living.[6] (More on this in the next chapter.)

> Being in touch with the signals our bodies send us offers valuable information and more opportunities for joy.

Feeling emotions like one of the five senses

Hopefully our discussion has made it clear that emotions in and of themselves are not the problem. The issue is when we over-indulge them without checking their validity or suppress them to avoid the discomfort that comes along with the signals they're sending. The answer *lies in a balance where we receive the signals that emotions send, decide what if anything we need to do, and then let the emotions flow, bringing us back to equilibrium.* One way to get closer to this type of balance is to treat emotions like some of our other senses: sight, smell, touch, and sound.[7] When you hear thunder, for example, you notice the sound, close the windows, and call the kids inside—then you let it go; you don't criticize yourself for hearing the thunder. If we can meet our emotions with the knowledge that they are delivering a message, we can appreciate the message and then let the emotions flow as we return to a state of balance.

How to let emotions flow in a healthy way

So how do we let emotions flow in a healthy way? Flow is **not** about indulging in a public catharsis that damages your relationships or gets you fired. Healthy flow is about recognizing the body's signals, taking in the messages, and letting the emotion go.

Physical movement

One way to encourage healthy emotional flow is through *physical movement*. We saw in chapter 1 that happy people move their bodies physically. It's no surprise that, according to Harvard Health, exercise "reduces levels of the body's stress hormones, such as adrenaline and cortisol. It also stimulates the production of endorphins, chemicals in the brain that are the body's natural painkillers and mood elevators."[8] Movement doesn't have to be formal exercise though: going for a walk, showing off your old high school dance moves—there are lots of ways to move and break up stagnant emotions. One person's yoga is another person's hike to a fishing hole.

Mindfulness techniques

Another way emotions flow in a healthy way is through *mindfulness techniques* that help you feel emotions without automatically turning away from unpleasant sensations. Kabat-Zinn and colleagues, in *The Mindful Way,* explain a technique called the *Three-Minute Breathing Space*, which they say is a good first step to respond to challenging situations and feelings that arise. They advise that the technique can be used anytime for a few breaths or a few minutes, particularly when we "notice unpleasant feelings or a sense of 'tightening' or 'holding' in the body."[9]

Three-Minute Breathing Space Technique

Step 1: Intentionally change position to sit or stand in a dignified posture. Bring your awareness within and ask yourself:

- What thoughts am I having?
- What feelings are here?
- What body sensations are here right now?

Step 2: Feel yourself breathing in the belly, expanding out and in. Be present.

Step 3: Expand your awareness to the rest of your body, posture, and facial expression. If you feel discomfort, breathe into those places. If you want to, consider saying on the outbreath, "It's okay… whatever it is, it's already here: let me feel it."

The Three-Minute Breathing Space Technique can help us pause automatic thoughts and feelings, giving us space "to steady ourselves," to see clearly what is happening in the here and now, and to more mindfully choose what to do about it.[10] (If you'd like to explore this more, *The Mindful Way* includes a more detailed explanation of this technique as well as numerous other mindfulness practices.)

A path forward

We're talking about feeling out of alignment in a topsy-turvy world. If we want to steady ourselves, the first thing we need is internal balance. Modern society can be dominated by thinking and doing. But being— noticing the signals our bodies send us—is essential to a balanced foundation. Being in awareness of our own bodies is an integral part of how we understand and respond to the world around us. *Pausing to notice thoughts, feelings, and body sensation offers a grounding in the here and now and the freedom to choose how to engage with anything coming our way.*

Journaling

Are there any emotions you think are "bad?" Any that are "good?" Why?

Think of a time you felt fear, anger, sadness, or guilt. Using the descriptions of the emotions on the previous pages, what message did the emotion deliver?

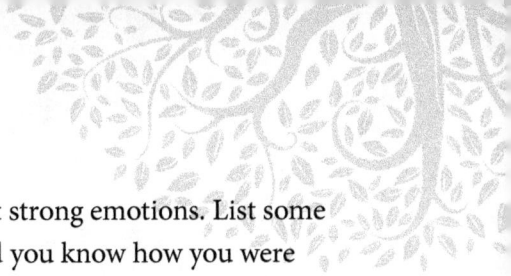

Picture yourself in a situation when you felt strong emotions. List some sensations you felt in your body that helped you know how you were feeling.

Up next

We saw how we can't deny the body's role in finding a balanced sense of stability. Next, we'll look at the role of spirit and the ways modern life gets in the way of the sense of fulfillment we're seeking.

Chapter 4

Spirited Connection
How feeding your spirit includes a side dish of happiness and meaning

---

A couple, dining out on a terrace overlooking the ocean.

"Wow. Honey, do you see this sunset? It's stunning. The way the light glistens off the waves. The sky and ocean seem to go on forever. You have to see this."

"What? Oh, nice. Hey, you have to see this TikTok. It's hysterical. Look, I'll show you."

We've seen that our minds and bodies are constantly communicating. But what of spirit? Where does it fit in the balancing act? Spirit shows us that all the ups and downs of life are worthwhile. It's an essential element in happiness because spirit gives us inspiration and courage to keep going when things are hard, and it raises us up to revel in the moments when things are going well. Spirit helps us find meaning and purpose through our connection to something greater and more enduring than our finite selves.

In the past, religion and the divine were a significant source of spirit in people's lives. They brought with them a sense of community, connection to a greater purpose, and a bit of the supernatural awe that comes along with the powerful forces in the universe. But today, in the US, the percentage of people who identify as non-religious is increasing. According to Pew Research, as of 2019, 26% of American adults describe themselves as atheist, agnostic, or "nothing in particular," up from 17% in 2009.[1] At the same time, church goers attend services less often than a decade ago, with a majority reporting they attend just a few times a year or less.[2]

So where, outside of religion, do people find connection to something greater and more enduring than the self? We're all looking for something—some sense of fulfillment. But in modern life, we may be trying to fill our need for something more with something that's really something less.

The surprising truth about stress

Stress—that's the last thing you need, right? You might be surprised to learn then, that *humans love a certain amount of stress*. Seriously. Our bodies have evolved to respond rapidly to stressors and then return us to balance.[3] Way (way) back when we had to run away from a sabre tooth tiger, our stress response kicked in for a short burst, saved us from being lunch, and then flowed out of our systems. (*Thanks flight or fight response; you saved me again!*) The reason stress has a bad rap today, is because modern humans turn on our stress responses—and we leave them on. As neurology researcher Robert Sapolsky explains in *Behave: The Biology of Humans at Our Best and Worst,* "If you're stressed like a normal mammal in an acute physical crisis, the stress response is lifesaving. But if instead you chronically activate the stress response for reasons of psychological stress, your health suffers."[4] But here's where it gets even more interesting. *While too much stress takes a toll on our health, not enough stress leaves us bored.* Sapolsky explains:

We love stress that is mild and transient and occurs in a benevolent context. The stressful menace of a roller-coaster ride is that it will make us queasy, not that it will decapitate us; it lasts for three minutes, not three days. We love that kind of stress, clamor for it, pay to experience it. What do we call that optimal amount of stress? Being engaged, engrossed, and challenged. Being stimulated. … The complete absence of stress is aversively boring.[5]

Like watching horror movies? Trying bizarre foods? Traveling to new places with no itinerary? Those are all the good kinds of stress that we clamor for to keep life interesting.

Let's add to the mix that humans crave drama. We evolved from hunter-gatherers who developed an interest in gossip and dramatic stories because they were the only source of news and information about the world around them.[6] So what happens in a modern society in which most of us don't have to flee wild animals but we do have access to the world's information at our fingertips? We seek out a certain amount of stress and drama to fill a craving for stimulation.

Our frenemy, the dopamine loop

Enter the "infinite scroll," that technological innovation that allows us to swipe up eternally, seeking bits of input that engage or enrage. As we scroll and discover the next tantalizing tidbit, we trigger hits of dopamine, the brain's "feel-good" chemical. Dopamine makes us feel pleasure, so we think we're finding satisfaction. But the brain throws a twist into it—we get a bigger hit of dopamine from *seeking* than we do from *finding*.[7] **Each swipe up in search of new stimulation keeps us stuck in a state of wanting more. Swipe. Just one more post. Swipe. Just one more video. Swipe.**

Philosopher, Alan Watts, describes the constant distractions of modern life as a state of "orgasm-without-release" in which each partial gratification is replaced by a new desire.[8] Now let's add some more biology. Sapolsky, in *Behave*, explains that the "heart does roughly the

same thing whether you are in a murderous rage or having an orgasm."⁹
And so perhaps today, *as we endlessly scroll through sensational
headlines and hate-filled social media posts, are we trying to reach a
satisfaction through outrage, and are we inadvertently doing it in a way
that it continually renews our desire for more?*

What's exciting today is boring tomorrow

Thanks to our human ability to adapt to pleasure and pain, the media
headlines have to get more and more extreme and people's behavior has
to become more and more outrageous for us to find them compelling.
Neurology researcher Sapolsky explains, "An emptiness comes from
this combination of over-the-top nonnatural sources of reward and
the inevitability of habituation. … What was an unexpected pleasure
yesterday is what we feel entitled to today, and what won't be enough
tomorrow."¹⁰ Whatever it is we're looking for, we aren't going to find
fulfillment while we're connected, yet alone, scrolling from one transient
moment of drama-stress that endlessly triggers more desire for, well…
more.

Finding meaning and connection

So we've been talking about what *doesn't* fulfill us. Then what, in modern
life, *does* create a sense of meaning and connection to something greater?
In his book *Born to Be Good: The Science of a Meaningful Life*, researcher
Dacher Keltner proposes that the feeling of *awe* is one of the secrets to
finding connection beyond the self.¹¹ Awe helps us see the vastness of
what's possible. It forces us to reframe our perspective and to recognize
that *we are part of something greater and more enduring than our
individual, finite selves.* It helps us connect with our common humanity.

In early human life, the feeling of awe was reserved for divinity—
awesome god-like power and mystery. While many people still feel a state
of awe from the sacred, Keltner proposes that we can feel awe or a state of
elevation in many everyday situations flavored by four themes:

Beauty– Experiencing something in harmony, balance, or proportion such as a symphony, a field of sunflowers, or an infant's delightful little toes.

Threat– Experiences of fear or reassurance, such as a tornado, a charismatic leader, or a hug from your mom after a harrowing experience.

Ability– Encounters involving people or things with exceptional ability, such as Michael Jordan flying from the free throw line to dunk or a hummingbird hovering in mid-air.

Human Goodness– Encounters with people who sacrifice themselves or do something that restores faith in humanity, like a black protester carrying a white supremacist protester to safety, or a doctor who works among the contagious to save lives.

> **Look for sources of awe in:**
> Beauty – Threat – Ability – Human Goodness

Feeling awe in the body

Remember how we saw in chapter 3 that the body communicates with us all day? So of course, the body has ways of signaling that we're in awe—and chances are you're already familiar with them. As Keltner explains, the body can *expand beyond* the skin to feel connected to other group members using *piloerection*, otherwise known as *goosebumps*. (Yes, goosebumps may also happen when you're cold, but shivering feels different than being awe-struck.) Or how about that feeling of liquid warmth that spreads through the chest along with a lump in your throat? That's the vagus nerve and it generates feelings of social connection.

Discovering awe all around us

Modern technology isn't all bad—the extent to which it enables us to discover new things that give us goosebumps or leave us elevated in amazement can be a good thing. Scrolling and then pausing to savor the latest pictures from the Hubble Space Telescope or discovering a new musician on TikTok whose ethereal voice makes your heart swell—go for it. *What's even better, is that we don't need technology to experience the elevated states that come from beauty, threat/reassurance, ability, and human goodness.* They are happening in our everyday lives, right in front of us, if we look for them.

A path forward

Opportunities to find connection and feed our spirit are all around us in the elevating and awe-inspiring details of everyday life. *When we give our mind some empty space, allowing it to wander into new discoveries, we just might notice the body's signals of expansion and connection.* In recognizing awe, we foster the balance between mind, body, and spirit that is the first step toward inner alignment.

Journaling

What is something you saw or experienced recently that gave you a sense of awe?

Are there sources of psychological stress in your life that you could eliminate? What are they?

What are 3 things in your life that create the good kind of stress—being engaged, engrossed, and challenged?

Up next

The last step on our look within continues the idea of living in alignment with yourself. More specifically, we'll discover the stabilizing self-respect that comes from living in line with what you think is right and decent.

Chapter 5

Self-Respect vs. Self-Esteem
Why it's good to feel bad sometimes

Enter room and find 5-year-old sobbing and 9-year looking smug:

Me: What happened?

5-year-old: She hit me, and it hurts!

Me to 9-year-old: That's not nice. Apologize to your sister.

9: I don't want to.

Me: She's crying because you hit her. Your actions caused someone to be hurt, so you need to make it right.

9: Stop talking to me like that. You'll make me feel bad about myself.

Me: You hurt someone. You're supposed to feel bad.

9: That's not what they said at school. I'm supposed to feel good about myself.

The moment I realize it's time to throw self-esteem-based parenting theories out the window if I want my kids to have a conscience.

We all want to feel good about ourselves. In fact, social scientists will tell you that maintaining a positive sense of our "self" is one of our fundamental goals in life.[1] Isn't it true that we're constantly evaluating ourselves to decide if we can feel proud or if we need improvement? *Do I feel good about how I acted at that dinner party? Did I impress my boss with my brilliance? Does my butt look good in these jeans? (Don't answer that.)* The point is, when we don't meet our own standards, we feel shame, guilt, or embarrassment and then we seek to restore a positive sense of our "self."[2] This internal cycle—I notice I'm disappointed in myself, I change my actions, I restore my positive sense of self—is part of the process of developing self-respect. *This positive-negative-positive feeling cycle is how we manage our behavior so that we can be proud of who we are and the outcomes we cause.*

The self-esteem revolution

Experts in the 1970s had good intentions. Research at the time showed that children with high self-esteem performed better in school, sports, relationships, and behavior.[3] According to the bestselling book *NurtureShock,* by the 1980s, experts were focusing policies around eliminating anything potentially damaging to kids' self-esteem. Authors Po Bronson and Ashley Merryman state, "Competitions were frowned upon. Soccer coaches stopped counting goals and handed out trophies to everyone. Teachers threw out their red pencils. Criticism was replaced with ubiquitous, even undeserved, praise."[4] This emphasis on self-esteem turned self-evaluation into something that could be controlled from outside oneself. Protecting self-esteem became a mantra that directed parents and teachers to ensure children *only* felt good about themselves, turning guilt and embarrassment into something to be avoided—even if that meant turning a blind-eye to reality.

Self-esteem isn't as great as experts hoped it would be

By the 2000s, a team of researchers evaluated decades worth of studies to see if the focus on self-esteem was all it was promised to be.[5] Social psychologist Roy Baumeister, a lead researcher on the team, concluded: "These studies show not only that self-esteem fails to accomplish what we had hoped, but also that it can backfire and contribute to some of the very problems it was thought to thwart."[6] Baumeister reported that feeling good about yourself isn't what causes good outcomes. It's more likely that *the act of exercising self-control in order to achieve the good outcome— that's what makes you feel good about yourself.* After decades of inflating people's sense of self and telling everyone they are "equally great" regardless of the effort they put in, the data shows we would drive more self-worth by focusing on building skills, applying effort, and honestly evaluating behavior.

It's good to feel bad sometimes

It turns out that focusing on self-esteem, which has come to mean protecting people from "feeling bad," is hindering our ability to feel good. You can't fool yourself into believing you're behaving well when your reality tells you otherwise.

Researchers have shown that when people receive praise that they know they don't deserve, their self-esteem actually goes down.[7] Other studies show that children over the age of seven know when you're offering inflated praise with a hidden agenda.[8] Not only does it make them discount false praise, it makes them skeptical of real praise as well. Research cited in *NurtureShock* showed that by the age of twelve, children who have watched teachers dole out excessive praise think that praise is **not** a sign that you're doing well; it means you lack ability, and the teacher is offering extra encouragement.

> Just because someone doesn't want to *feel bad* about a choice, that doesn't mean it was a *good* choice.

The gift of listening to your conscience

As it turns out, our *conscience*—the internal guide that measures our behavior against our standards and principles—is not easily fooled. Your conscience sends signals to your heart and mind to let you know if you're measuring up to your own ideas about what right and wrong behavior is. On the one hand, your conscience makes you feel disappointed or remorseful for a bad choice you made. Like we saw in the opening story, you're supposed to feel bad sometimes. Just because you don't want to feel bad about a choice, that doesn't mean it was a good choice. In fact, guilt and embarrassment about a choice can be your allies, encouraging you to right a wrong.[9] And the sheer anticipation of your body contracting in on itself in shame can keep you from doing wrong again.

Your conscience also helps you feel your heart swell with joy or pride for a job well done. It's your mind and body working in harmony to reward you so you'll live in alignment with what you believe is a decent and valuable way to behave. *By paying attention to this honest internal evaluation, you can find a meaningful measure of self-worth.* Like we saw in the previous chapters, the mind and body work together to feed spirit.

Self-respect offers you peace and stability

If you want to find peace with yourself, you'll need to ditch the idea of protecting self-esteem and *only* "feeling good." *Instead, embrace the idea of feeling the full positive-negative-positive cycle that leads to self-respect.* (Of course, we saw in chapter 2 that cognitive distortions can lead us to inaccurate, and sometimes harmful self-assessments, so remember the importance of a true and balanced view of your own behavior.)

We learned in chapter 1 that happiness comes, in part, from having a realistic, positive sense of your own worth. Happy people can share in others' successes and recover from their own setbacks (the positive-negative-positive cycle.) And happy people are aware of how their actions impact other people and the world around them. *Self-respect is the essence of taking joy in your own and others' positives and course correcting from the negatives, all in the service of behaving in a way you believe is decent, right, and valuable.* It's an inner sense that doesn't need external sources to inflate it with false compliments. Self-respect is being at peace with yourself no matter what is happening around you.

How do you build self-respect?

Self-respect comes from honestly looking at your actions and deciding if they are in line with what you know is right and wrong. Having self-respect means you welcome the positive and negative feedback that your conscience sends you, using it to guide choices that define your character and conduct.[10] *Your conscience knows if you're being cruel or kind, and if you're doing the easy thing or the right thing, even when you may not want to hear it.*

Self-respect comes from owning responsibility for the good and bad outcomes you create. Ultimately, self-respect helps you feel that you are in control of your own life—that you have agency—because you are in full awareness that *your good and bad choices create corresponding good and bad consequences.*[11] The choice is yours.

Self-respect is created within; it doesn't depend on acceptance by others and it helps you recover from mistakes. When you have self-respect, you choose to do what is right and you take solace in this, leading to feelings of dignity and being principled.[12] *Even when there's a cost for having done the right thing, there is comfort and stability in knowing you made a choice you believe in.* Self-respect offers a path to recovering a positive sense of self-worth even after a mistake, through experiencing remorse and seeking to make things right.

A path forward

Self-respect is essential to creating a rooted stability that helps you look in the mirror each day and find peace, no matter what tumult rages around you. Letting go of the focus on self-esteem means we might need to feel bad sometimes. *But the gift of listening to your conscience is that for all the times it gives you the stink eye, there are equal opportunities for it to elevate you to joy and pride when you choose to live life in alignment with the way you think is decent and valuable.*

Journaling

Have you ever received praise that you knew you didn't deserve? What happened? Did hearing it make you feel good about yourself?

When is a time you did the right thing, even though it was hard? Was it worth it?

Are there ways that you are protecting yourself, or others, from the real consequences of their actions? Is this helping long term?

Up next

We've reached the end of part one. Throughout this section, we looked within and discovered that we're built for balance, with our mind, body, and spirit each serving a purpose toward our well-being. Intentionally finding more balance in the way we think, feel, and connect with others is the first step in feeling a sense of equilibrium in the world. We've also seen that being rooted in decency, by living in line with what we think is right, is an important part of building self-respect and finding the stability and happiness that come along with it. In the next section, we'll look outward and discover why being decent to others isn't just a nice thing to do, it's also in our best interest.

~

Part Two:

Looking Outward

Part Two:

Looking Outward

My son and I chatting at the dinner table

12-year-old: Mom, would you rather be a good guy who always loses or a bad guy who always wins?

Me: Wow son, moral philosophy?! What made you think of that?

12: Don't get too excited, Mom. I saw it on Instagram.

Me: Oh. Well, I would be a good guy who always loses. Because being good is its own type of winning.

12: But Mom, winning is its own type of winning.

What do you think? In a society full of competition and cooperation, would you rather be a good guy who loses or a bad guy who wins? It's not always easy to choose. Being good can be hard, especially when it comes at a cost. Of course, when you're a good person, you can always take solace in having done the right thing even when things don't go well. How many feel-good hero movies show a decent person at peace with their choices, despite the personal cost? By comparison, how many show a jerk basking in glory for how well they took advantage of people?

Popular culture makes it clear that society prefers a good guy who respects himself and his choices over a bad guy who wins at the expense of others. The way we choose to live our lives is rarely just about what each of us wants for ourselves because we're not individual loners living in isolation—we're individuals living in societies. Every one of us lives a dual existence as an *individual* and as a *group member* who competes and cooperates with others. **The quality of our lives is impacted not only by the ways we treat ourselves, but also by the ways we treat each other.**

Here in part two, we'll look at how group life affects us. In this time when individual desires and self-expression seem so important, we'll look at whether each of us is better off looking out for number one, or whether something's to be gained by being a decent member of society.

What's in it for me?

Humanity has been debating the value of being a decent person for eons. The "would you rather…" quote at the start of this chapter that my son saw on Instagram is a modern version of a dialog from Plato's *Republic*, written by the Greek philosopher in 375 BCE, in which he debates whether being a good person is worthwhile. On one side, the dialog argues that morally bad people are more likely to get ahead in life: "gods and men are said to unite in making the life of the unjust better than the life of the just."[1] On the other side, Plato argues that not only is having virtue better than focusing on worldly self-interest, being good is an essential part of being happy: "the just soul and the just man will live well, and the unjust man will live ill. … And he who lives well is blessed and happy, and he who lives ill the reverse of happy."[2] Throughout his writings, Plato argues that the path to the good life is rooted in being a good person.

Being good really is its own reward—the science proves it

In case ancient philosophy isn't your thing, modern science has a lot to say about why Plato was right about the value of being a good person. We'll see in the coming chapters that humans have evolved to be "anti-jerk." Psychology research shows that even from infancy, babies know the difference between kindness and meanness.[3] Children, by instinct and intention, dish out playground justice to shape cooperation and establish expectations for behavior. And by the time we reach adulthood, we're subject to both innate *and* learned rules about what it is to be a good member of society. *We've evolved to know that being a good person is a good idea.*

Up next

In the next chapter, we'll see why, despite our focus on personal freedom, we voluntarily control our own behavior because we gain something by living and playing well with others.

Chapter 6

You Be You—Unless You're a Jerk

Why we voluntarily give up some freedoms to be part of society

Unwritten Rules

A Reddit user posed the question, "What is one "unwritten rule" you think everyone should know and follow?" Selected answers, in random order:[1]

Don't leave your shopping cart in the middle of the grocery aisle.

Don't propose at someone else's wedding.

Don't ask for something if the person only has one left (gum, cigarette, piece of cake, etc.)

Don't look through the ... gap of the bathroom stalls.

In a society that emphasizes individual freedoms, why do we have unwritten rules like the ones starting off this chapter? I'm sure you could think of many more, but here's what flashed into my mind:

- Don't talk on speakerphone in public.
- Wait your turn.
- Only take one free sample at the bakery.

There are lots of ways we voluntarily modify our behavior for the sake of others. *If we're so focused on our individual life, liberty, and pursuit of happiness, why do we choose to limit our freedom like this?*

Our ancestors learned the benefits of cooperation

People naturally look out for their own self-interest, but unwritten rules are evidence that we humans aren't purely self-serving. Early humans figured it out—groups that cooperated, divided responsibilities, and traded with fairness and reciprocity were more successful than groups full of individuals who were all out for themselves.[2] Darwin and modern social scientists have theorized that over the course of human evolution, people learned to limit selfish desires for the sake of security and an ability to thrive *together*. So while each of us *could* choose to say and do whatever we want without concern for how it impacts others, usually, we don't.

In *Born to Be Good,* UC Berkeley researcher Dacher Keltner reveals that it isn't the "domineering, muscle-flexing, fear-inspiring, backstabbing types who gain elevated status in the eyes of their peers."[3] (Sure, there have been prominent exceptions to this. But we can debate whether the tyrant CEOs and dictators of the world truly have "elevated status in the eyes of their peers" and we can definitely debate whether the societies they oversee are in a state of well-being.) Instead, Keltner argues that the people who naturally rise in social hierarchies are:

- the people with skills to bring people together
- those who can diffuse tension or discourage inappropriate behavior without resorting to violence
- the ones who can soothe others in times of distress

Over the course of human development, the people who could get along and promote group welfare were rewarded. Groups comprised of people who acted with a combination of self- and group-interest thrived, creating the next generation who could do the same. As we evolved into modern humans, society became decidedly… "anti-jerk."

We gain something by coming together

As much as we treasure our freedom to live life the way we choose, we know that we gain something by putting aside selfish impulses to come together into a society. Theorists like John Locke and Thomas Paine, who inspired Western ideas about inalienable rights and liberties, based those ideas in the reality that *humans need each other*, and that people find happiness by establishing ways of living together. Around the time of the American Revolution, Thomas Paine wrote in *The Rights of Man*:

> As Nature created him … she made his natural wants greater than his individual powers. No one man is capable, without the aid of society, of supplying his own wants, and those wants, acting upon every individual, impel the whole of them into society, as naturally as gravitation acts to a centre. … she has implanted in him a system of social affections, which, though not necessary to his existence, are essential to his happiness.[4]

What Paine recognized was that we need individual freedom and dignity, but we need it at the root of community. ***Without community, we don't thrive.***

The myriad ways we create community

Every day we come together in countless ways, for example:

- as extended families, coworkers, neighbors, and friends
- in softball leagues and book clubs, at drinks with colleagues, through hobbies
- in ethnic, religious, professional, and identity-based organizations
- through volunteering, service organizations, and political and social activism

In Bowling Alone: The Collapse and Revival of American Community,
Harvard researcher Robert Putnam calls these types of relationships *social
capital* and he divides them into two types:

> **Bonding social capital** brings people together who share *similar*
> characteristics or interests—from church groups to cosplay
> conventions. People find *solidarity* with people who are like them
> and they form strong ties that offer mutual support and promote
> common goals.

> **Bridging social capital** brings people together from *different* social
> backgrounds—from rights activists to professional networking
> groups. With bridging social capital, the ties are less strong, but
> people are better able to share information, establish reciprocity, and
> *get things done* more easily.

Putnam clarifies the distinction this way: "Bonding social capital
constitutes a kind of sociological superglue, whereas bridging social
capital provides a sociological WD-40."[5]

Through community, we join forces to create goodness for ourselves
and others. We can find people who understand our human experience
or want to do the things we like to do. We find purpose and meaning
in shared goals. We establish ground rules for behavior, finding people
we can trust and people we can do a favor knowing they'll do one
for us when we need it. With bonding and bridging, through formal
organizations and informal gatherings, we establish connections that
enable us to reach beyond our own resources to help each other. *Whether
it's finding comfort after a long week or using our contacts to help
someone's kid find a job, community helps us live better than we can do
alone.*

The benefits of a shared existence

Our social side is so important, it produces measurable benefits for society. Putnam shows that in communities with high social capital—where people trust each other, join organizations, volunteer, vote, and socialize—children flourish and crime is lower. Economically, social capital can improve home values, produce economic growth, and can even create transformative opportunities for the entire community.[6]

In terms of personal health, social relationships are so powerful, the "more integrated we are with our community, the less likely we are to experience colds, heart attacks, strokes, cancer, depression, and premature death of all sorts."[7] The *positive* effects of social relations are as strong as the *negative* effects of "well-established biomedical risk factors like cigarette smoking, obesity, elevated blood pressure, and physical inactivity."[8] Harvard medical researcher Robert Waldinger echoes these ideas in his Ted Talk, *What makes a good life? Lessons from the longest study on happiness.* The talk is based on results from one of the longest running research studies on human lives that observed over 700 men, rich and poor, over the course of 75 years. In the end, the study showed that:

> Social connections are really good for us, and that loneliness kills. It turns out that people who are more socially connected to family, to friends, to community, are happier, they're physically healthier, and they live longer than people who are less well connected.[9]

The isolation we experienced during the COVID-19 pandemic helped us recognize how important social interaction is for our well-being. Yet we still may not notice how much we help each other—not just in times of crisis, but in the course of everyday life. We tend to focus on the exceptional circumstance or the single, self-sacrificing individual while taking for granted **how often, we are all each other's heroes**. Psychology researcher Jonathan Haidt, in *The Righteous Mind*, said it well:

Our ability to work together, divide labor, help each other, and function as a team is so all-pervasive that we don't even notice it. You'll never see the headline "Forty-five Unrelated College Students Work Together Cooperatively, and for No Pay, to Prepare for Opening Night of Romeo and Juliet."[10]

Social goods are the gift that keep on giving

All around us, these moments of shared life help us to be part of something greater than ourselves, and they can be a source of inspiration and comfort. In *Morality*, rabbi and philosopher Jonathan Sacks describes the benefit of sharing social goods—things like friendship, knowledge, and love: "These are goods that have a moral or spiritual dimension, and they have this rare quality that the more we share, the more we have."[11] *When we expand beyond our lives as individuals, our resources, our impact, and our perspective grow as well.*

The Dalai Lama, Buddhist spiritual leader, and Desmond Tutu, Christian Archbishop and South African civil rights leader, put it another way in *The Book of Joy*. In the midst of suffering, they recommend expanding beyond yourself as an individual to think of others who are suffering too—not because someone else's suffering decreases yours, but because *somewhere, someone else understands how you feel.* Viewing yourself as part of the group means you are never alone.[12]

A path forward

In recognizing our dual existence as both an individual and as a group member, we open ourselves to a more complete, connected life. Part one showed that living a life rooted in decency enables us to build inner stability through self-respect. Here we see that being a decent human to our family and broader community also offers us a place in something that is greater than our lone selves. Why do we follow unwritten rules? Why do we voluntarily control how we treat people? Because part of us wants and needs to be part of something more than our own finite existence.

We walk a line between our individual desire to do whatever we want and the necessity that we moderate ourselves to be part of society. So go ahead and express yourself. You be you—unless you're a jerk.[13] That's not good for you or anyone else.

Journaling

What are some unwritten rules you think everyone should know?

Where do you find a sense of community? Have you benefited from bonding or bridging social capital?

Sometimes, do you really want to do something rude? What keeps you from doing it?

Up next

We've seen that we gain something by being part of a larger community and that being decent to each other is part of how we build that life together. But what if your idea of being decent is different than mine? Next, we'll look at how some people think they're doing what's *right* while at the same time, someone else thinks their actions are totally *wrong*.

Chapter 7

Competing Moral Priorities
Why people think they're "right" when others think they're "wrong"

A few moral dilemmas:

Adapted from *The Righteous Mind*, Jonathan Haidt[1]

A father, concerned about protecting his family from retaliation, does not call the police about a neighbor holding dog fights in his basement. Right or wrong?

Someone gets hurt at work because an employer didn't maintain safety standards. The law says they can collect government-funded assistance payments for six months for a work injury. Within one month, the employee is back at work but continues to collect the payments for the six months allowed. Right or wrong?

A grandmother dies. The family has all her teeth pulled out to give them to family members as memorial keepsakes. Right or wrong?

What do you think? In each of these situations, is the behavior right or wrong? If you answered, "That depends," you're not alone. As much as we might like to think that morality is a clear-cut black or white, often it's more shades of gray that are influenced by different values which compete for priority in our minds. Let's explore this by asking a few questions:

- In the first scenario, is the father right to prioritize the safety of his family or should he protect the abused animals and his neighborhood's security?

- In the second scenario, is the person wrong to keep taking the payments after they're back at work, or are they being helped fairly because they were hurt by the negligence of someone more powerful? If continuing to take the payments is the difference between their kids eating or going hungry, and the law says they can take them, would the person be irresponsible *not* to keep collecting the payments?

There's more going on in each scenario than we may initially realize and we can't assume that people in different circumstances will see the issue the same way we would.

What's the harm?

When we're deciding whether something is right or wrong, we often ask ourselves, "Is it hurting anybody?" but we'll come to see that people define "hurt" in more ways than we might expect. In *The Righteous Mind: Why Good People are Divided by Politics and Religion*, renowned social scientist Jonathan Haidt proposes that people weigh combinations from six moral foundations when deciding what's right and wrong. Not only can we physically or mentally harm an individual, but we can also cheat, betray, subvert, oppress, and degrade. People may feel it's morally wrong to do any of those things not just to a person, but also to a group, or to society at large. And to make it more complicated, we each prioritize the foundations based on our culture, personal views, and group affiliations. *So, if you've ever wondered how someone can think they are in the right when you think they are clearly in the wrong, it's likely you are prioritizing your moral foundations differently than each other (assuming neither of you is immoral.)*

Each of Haidt's Six Moral Foundations reflects a principle we turn to when we reason our way through moral decisions. So let's take a closer look at each foundation, identifying the moral principle it upholds, the types of questions we ask ourselves when considering each type of right and wrong, and some areas in modern life where these foundations tend to come into play.

Six Moral Foundations

#1: CARE/HARM

Principle: We should care for others' well-being and not intentionally or carelessly cause harm.

We might ask: Who or what is suffering? Do we have a responsibility to care for or to protect someone / something?

Situations: Child abuse prevention - Protecting a clean water supply - The need for community food banks - Requiring a test for competence to get a driver's license

#2: FAIRNESS/CHEATING

Principle: Relationships should involve give-and-take in equal measure.

We might ask: Is someone taking unfair advantage? Are they getting back proportionately to what they deserve / have earned? Is someone being denied equal treatment?

Situations: Negotiating for a "win-win" - Consumer protection laws - Controversy around welfare/public assistance - Equal pay for equal work

#3: LIBERTY/OPPRESSION

Principle: People should be free to choose how to live (within reason) while abuses of power should be prevented.

We might ask: When are limits on individual freedom necessary? Are dominant forces denying people their chance at life, liberty, and the pursuit of happiness?

Situations: Religious exemptions from laws- LGBTQ rights - Racial equality - Gun rights – Workers' rights

#4: LOYALTY/BETRAYAL

Principle: Group success requires shared responsibility and trust.

We might ask: Whose needs should be prioritized? How far does our responsibility extend—to family, group, country, all of humanity? Are you with us or against us?

Situations: Partisan politics - Cancel culture – Nationalism - Controversy around whistleblowers

#5: AUTHORITY/SUBVERSION

Principle: Maintaining social order is important.

We might ask: Does an act threaten important social structures like marriage, family, law and order, democracy? Does someone/something deserve hierarchical respect or obedience, such as elders, traditions, and people in authority?

Situations: Threats to "family values" - The right to peaceful protest - Respect for the legitimacy of the law and institutions - Doing one's duty

#6: SANCTITY/DEGRADATION

Principle: Some acts violate human or sacred dignity or invite harmful contamination.

We might ask: Does human dignity need to be protected? Is an act a desecration of something holy? Does an act encourage contamination, pestilence, plague?

Situations: Respect for the dead - Human rights violations - Protection of holy or world heritage sites - The darker side of "purity" and anti-immigration

What takes priority?

When we think about what's right and wrong in each of the moral foundations, we can see that "Is it hurting anyone?" is too narrow of a question. The decisions we make can cause harm not just to living people, but also to group cohesion, social order, companies, animals, the environment, beliefs about what is sacred... the list goes on. And the way we prioritize which type of potential hurt is "worse" than another varies by culture and group belief. Let's look at a few comparisons to bring this to light:

- If someone was raised in a culture that emphasized duty and respect for authority (for instance, in a family with ties to the military) they will likely have a stronger priority for the Authority side of the Authority/Subversion foundation than someone raised in a community that emphasized freedom of expression (such as in an artists' community.)

- Someone who feels a strong sense of group identity may put a lot of weight on the Loyalty/Betrayal foundation over other considerations.

- Someone with a strong religious background may emphasize the Sanctity foundation to protect what they view as sacred.

If you find someone you disagree with in your life, and look at the way their culture and circumstances affect their moral priorities—suddenly their feelings and reasoning might make a lot more sense.

Feelings forward

What makes understanding people's moral priorities (including our own) even more challenging is that we typically aren't *thinking* about the priorities—we're *feeling* them. When we're facing a moral decision, we don't start by mentally sorting through our foundations: "Hmmm, do

I prioritize the authority foundation or the sanctity foundation in this situation?" This is something no one has thought at the onset of a moral crisis. Haidt explains that moral decisions are **emotional** first. We *feel* as if something is right or wrong, and *our body chimes in* its support perhaps with a twist in the gut or by physically leaning toward or away from the thing we're contemplating.

You may not really want to, but think of the grandmother's teeth from this chapter's opening moral dilemmas and see what your body does as you consider: Is it right to extract a deceased grandmother's teeth and distribute them to her family as keepsakes? When I asked people this question, most twisted their faces as their bodies pulled backwards and away from the idea. Then they decided that even if it was "Grandma's dying wish" or a cultural tradition, pulling and distributing her teeth was "disgusting" and they wanted no part of it. In my unscientific sampling, disgust (*sanctity* principle) clearly won out over respect for elders and tradition (*authority* principle), but no one phrased it in those terms.

Haidt's research shows that our initial *feelings*, with our *body's urging*, lead us toward or away from what we think is right or wrong, and only then do we try to come up with a rational explanation for it. ***Couple these powerful feelings with our desire to be in agreement with others in our group, and it can blind us from seeing alternate perspectives.*** As Haidt explains, "team membership blinds people to the motives and morals of their opponents."[2] So let's turn toward group dynamics, which adds another powerful layer to how we decide right and wrong.

> If you are unwilling to see someone's point of view,
> how can you hope to change it?

Making sense of people with different moral priorities

We're so driven by our own biological instincts and the desire to stay in the good graces of our group that we can be baffled, even outraged, that someone doesn't see things "our way." Yet as Marcus Aurelius, one of Rome's greatest emperors and a Stoic philosopher, said:

> Whenever someone has done wrong by you, immediately consider what notion of good or evil they had in doing it. For when you see that, you'll feel compassion, instead of astonishment or rage.[3]

He makes an interesting point—someone you disagree with may have as intense an emotion and rationale about their opinion as you do about yours. *But getting through (and beyond) personal and group-driven bias is much more likely if you understand where someone else is coming from and can communicate your concerns in terms of things THEY care about.*

To help you put yourself in someone else's shoes, let's tackle a few tense and timely issues. Let's look at an American Conservative and an American Liberal view and transform the usual rhetoric into a sort of shared language based in the six moral foundations.

A conservative perspective:

> If you ask a conservative about immigration, they might say they CARE about the humans who are suffering at the border and don't want to cause them HARM. But in the face of limited resources, it's their responsibility to CARE first that their fellow Americans (LOYALTY) won't be denied what they need to thrive (HARM) because those resources are being used to help people who haven't yet contributed (FAIRNESS). In particular, those people who are entering the country illegally are CHEATING and to reward that is to support a lack of FAIRNESS for those who follow the rules (AUTHORITY).

A liberal perspective:

> If you ask a liberal about equal rights, they might agree with
> conservatives that individuals should be free to live life and pursue
> their goals as they choose (LIBERTY), as long as they aren't doing
> HARM to others. They might argue that it's society's responsibility to
> look out for all its members (LOYALTY), so we need to take action
> when someone's rights are being abused (OPPRESSION). Ensuring
> FAIR access to opportunities and equal treatment may disrupt the
> social order for a time (AUTHORITY), but only because there are
> times the social order needs to be adjusted to protect those being
> treated in an OPPRESSIVE or degrading manner (SANCTITY).

Looking at the issues through the six moral foundations instead of
relying on stereotypes and assumptions reveals that people of different
groups share more common principles than they generally realize.
And even if people don't agree with us or our group, the act of making
the effort to understand each other gives each of us a better chance of
being understood in return, which is the first step toward finding a
compromise, and some inner *and* outer peace.

A path forward

Understanding Haidt's six moral foundations can help us make sense of
how different people see the same situation, which offers us a way to see
past our own moral blind spots so we can address the emotionally driven
root of the issue. We each may feel passionately that our concerns are the
most critical, and that our priorities are the most pressing. But solving
tense societal issues is rarely possible without addressing competing
concerns. *Viewing issues through the perspective of moral foundations*
offers us a way of seeing people we disagree with not as "bad" people, but
as people with different priorities.

Journaling

Think of a moral issue you feel strongly about. Which moral foundations are you basing your beliefs on?

Six Moral Foundations

CARE/HARM | caring for, protecting, preventing physical/mental harm

FAIRNESS/CHEATING | people getting what they deserve/have earned

LIBERTY/OPPRESSION | people being free to choose how to live; or more powerful forces denying someone their well-being

LOYALTY/BETRAYAL | prioritizing group needs; or if you're not with us, you're against us

AUTHORITY/SUBVERSION | protecting social order, respect for tradition / elders / authority

SANCTITY/DEGRADATION | protecting human dignity or what is sacred

Think about someone in your life or on the news that you typically disagree with. Using the moral foundations as your guide, how might they look at the moral dilemmas at the start of this section?

What are some ways people misunderstand what matters to you?

Up next

We've skimmed the surface of how group identity affects our view of right and wrong. Up next, we'll dig deeper into Us and Them divisiveness and see how aligning ourselves into groups isn't necessarily a bad thing. It's how we go about it that matters.

Chapter 8

Us Versus Them

How group identity isn't the real problem

Sometime in the distant future, two friends discuss the government's call for unity

Ash: You want me to just forget about all the times they treated me like I wasn't one of them? Like I wasn't the right race or religion or gender or nationality or political party?

Forrest: Yesterday there weren't aliens hovering in the sky trying to colonize us Earthlings. Today, none of those differences matter. Today, we're united as humans.

Ash: A galactic common enemy? That's what it took?

We saw in the last chapter that we like to be aligned with others in our group, but those bonds that we cherish may also limit our ability to see points of view outside our own sphere. In this world gone sideways, it can feel like *group loyalty* is the source of a lot of our problems, as divisiveness breaks us into competing factions.

Yet we saw in chapter 6 that group life is a good thing. Group unity is what would give us a fighting chance if we really were staring at a sky teeming with alien marauders. But forming groups isn't just about defeating a foe, it's also about feeling camaraderie, cooperating toward shared goals, and finding purpose and strength in the face of life's challenges. So group orientation in general can't be the problem. There must be something in the way we're going about group life in today's times that is creating this divisive atmosphere.

The biology and allure of group identity

To understand the power of group identity, we need to take a short side trip into biology. In *Behave: The Biology of Humans at our Best and Worst*, Neurology researcher Robert Sapolsky explains that without even thinking about it, we constantly look for group markers and we'll sort ourselves based on anything we find in common.[1] Interestingly, we don't restrict ourselves to "big" categories like race, religion, or political affiliation. We can unite on any number of factors, like our favorite sports team, the company we work for, our favorite brand, the age of our children, and whether we think Superman is cooler than Batman (*He totally is.*)

The great thing about this, is that we can *quickly* shift our group orientation based on a different aspect of ourselves. For example, in one moment we're focused on being a loyal company employee in a competitive negotiation, but that can change the moment we discover the person we're negotiating with is a loyal fan of an underdog sports team, just like we are. *Go team! Let's make this deal happen.*

We also see this more poignantly when people from different backgrounds instantly come together as rescuers to help a stranger in distress. We're not locked-in to any one group, or even to learned social biases. ***All we need is a common goal, a common enemy, or another common characteristic to render other biases unimportant in the moment.***

My group's better than yours

Given how important group life has been to our survival, it's not surprising that our brains have adapted to identify Us and Them, and to quickly form bonds that favor "Us." A brain chemical called oxytocin helps people feel more caring, trusting, and empathetic toward each other while mirror neurons in our brains help us to feel each other's joy, pain, fear, and excitement. But when we're with group members, the effects of oxytocin and mirroring are amplified. They influence us to care, trust, and empathize even more with in-group members so we can cooperate more quickly and form stronger attachments to get us through challenges.[2] Remember the aliens in the opening dialog? Standing side-by-side on Earth against a common enemy, we would feel each other's emotions and oxytocin would help us trust each other and care what happens to each other.

No matter how we define the "common ground" we quickly develop a rosier picture of what it is to be one of "Us." A great example of this is the study of the reds and the blues, where preschoolers were put in either red or blue t-shirts for a few weeks. In the best-selling book *NurtureShock: New Thinking about Children*, the authors describe how, without the influence of any value judgments from their teachers, the children quickly developed bias for other kids who wore the same color t-shirt they did. Within weeks, the children didn't show hatred toward the kids in a different color t-shirt, but when asked about the groups, the preschoolers answered that those in the same color t-shirt—the Us-es—were better and nicer. They said that some of the children in the other color t-shirt—the Thems—were "mean, and some were dumb," but none of the Us-es were.[3]

Just like those preschoolers, we adults inflate our perception of the core values of someone we perceive as an Us. Sapolsky explains, in *Behave*, that we assume that our in-group is more "correct, wise, moral and worthy."[4] We act more trusting, generous, and cooperative with in-group members while we view Thems as more "threatening, angry, and untrustworthy."[5] Remember though, often these judgments aren't based on any meaningful measure. The color t-shirt a child wears doesn't have anything to do with how trustworthy and wise they are. We develop bias toward an Us simply because they're an Us and we develop bias against a Them simply because they're a Them.

Making it a moral issue

Focusing on who is better, more trustworthy, or more deserving of empathy and respect—that means we're into moral territory because we're judging based on virtues like trustworthiness and respect. Now let's bring the brain back into it. When we see a Them as *morally offensive*, the same part of our brain activates as when we're smelling rancid food.[6] Yes, you read that right. It's called the gustatory response, and it's that automatic sense of disgust that pulls us back and away in order to protect us from things that would cause us harm, like eating spoiled food or picking up germs from garbage. Moral disgust toward a Them affects our brain in the same way as things that cause physical disgust. Neurology researcher Sapolsky explains:

> The insula activates when we eat a cockroach or imagine doing so. And the insula and amygdala activate when we think of the neighboring tribe as loathsome cockroaches. As we'll see, this is central to how our brains process "us and them."[7]

He goes on to note that the amount the brain is activated for moral disgust toward a Them "predicts how much outrage you feel and how much revenge you take."[8] *This biological response reinforces our sense that Thems whom we feel morally offended by are an actual threat to our well-being, just like rancid food would be,* even if there's no real-world evidence to support it.

Leveraging the sense of moral disgust

So what do you suppose would happen if our sense of moral disgust was constantly activated against Thems? Well, we're seeing the effects of moral disgust in our political divisiveness today. One of the ways we got to the state we're in was by normalizing extreme behavior in politics, including the use of *extreme words that light up our moral disgust response.* As historian Julian Zelizer explains in *Burning Down the House*:

> An entire generation of Democrats and Republicans came of professional age watching a brutal style of political warfare in the 1980s and 1990s that spared nobody. The kinds of political fights that were once associated with the extreme fringes of democracy entered the mainstream, where they would stay.[9]

One example of that escalation is a memo released in 1990 titled, "Language: A Key Mechanism of Control."[10] Inspired by politician Newt Gingrich's speaking style, the memo was distributed by GOPAC, an organization that develops Republican leaders. The memo advised: "The words and phrases are powerful."; "Remember that creating a difference helps you."; "Apply these to the opponent, their record, proposals and their party." The words to be used against the other party included:

Words that activate moral disgust, such as "decay", "sick", "waste", "disgrace", "shame", "betray", "traitors"

Words that represent immoral behavior, such as "lie", "hypocrisy", "greed", "corrupt", "cheat", "steal"

Words that create a sense of being under threat, such as "collapsing", "crisis", "destructive", "destroy", "endanger", "devour"

During this political era, words and behaviors that were so outside the norm that they had been viewed as *dangerous*—they became *the new normal*. I'm not blaming any one group—there's plenty of responsibility to go around. Zelizer, in *Burning Down the House*, and conservative commentator Charles Sykes, in *How the Right Lost Its Mind*, each offer detailed accounts of actions by multiple players—Democrats, Republicans, the media, talk radio, social media, and the public's willing embrace of divisive drama—that led to the state we're in. Zelizer explains, "Although politics was always rough in America … the overall level of respect for elected officials and governance rapidly diminished as a result of this era in congressional history."[11] Part of what changed is that *the tone of the debate between Us and Them took on attributes of moral disgust, feeding the idea that we're in a battle against something that can harm us.*

Feeding a tribal battle for survival

Consider some of the different ways politicians, pundits, and regular people alike talk about a new policy:

> **Stating Facts:** "Here's the new policy and here's how it may impact society, based on evidence."

> **Delivering Disgust:** "They should be *ashamed* of this new policy. What they're doing is *sick.*"

> **Inciting Outrage:** "This policy is a *betrayal* and it *threatens* to *destroy* us."

As the intensity increases toward inciting outrage, the language motivates people—and it drives clicks and viewership. So we can understand why so many panels, consultants, experts, activists, and anchors choose to go down this path.

We can see an example of this in the debate around Florida's Parental Rights in Education law, a measure forbidding instruction on sexual orientation and gender identity in kindergarten through third grade.[12] When critics, including the LGBTQ community, opposed the bill they called the "Don't Say Gay" law, some conservative commentators inaccurately started talking about the law using the word "grooming," a word associated with child sexual abuse, which is an act that incites tremendous moral disgust on all sides of politics. One conservative politician, reflecting the cognitive distortions we saw in chapter 2, amplified the false association, stating that anyone who opposes any bills like this one is "pro-child predator."[13] The issue became more divisive as moral disgust overwhelmed rational discussion. As neuroscience showed us a few paragraphs ago, *the more moral disgust is activated, the stronger the negative response, the greater the sense of threat, and the more potential that those who feel threatened will have a desire for revenge.*

> Instead of seeing our opponents as people with different views, moral disgust can make us see them as an actual threat to our well-being.

The issue with Us and Them isn't that they exist; the sense of community we gain from being an Us has clear benefits as we saw in chapter 6. The issue with Us and Them appears when we emphasize our differences to the point that they feed a tribal battle for survival. David Brooks, in *The Second Mountain*, describes the situation:

> Community is connection based on mutual affection. Tribalism, in the sense I'm using it here, is connection based on mutual hatred. Community is based on common humanity; tribalism on common foe. Tribalism is always erecting boundaries and creating friend/enemy distinctions. The tribal mentality is a warrior mentality based on scarcity.[14]

Reestablishing objectivity

So what can we do about it? How do we dial back the moral disgust that feeds outrage and divides us so that we can move toward cooperation?

Four Effective Ways to Diminish Divisiveness

1. Recognize our biases

First, remember that we're biologically driven to be biased toward our in-group. Knowing this, we can choose to turn on a mental *Check Accuracy Warning Light* that alerts us to the possibility that we're thinking automatically about Us and Them. Remember chapter 2, where we compared *mindless* (automatic) thinking to *mindful* (executive brain) thinking? When we pay attention to our *Check Accuracy Warning*, we can engage mindful thinking, bringing reason and evidence back into the picture; and we can reap the benefits of greater accuracy, competence, and adaptability.

Being aware of our biases may help us see that the out-group isn't as awful as our emotional reactions tell us they are. And maybe, that the in-group isn't as trustworthy and without fault as we'd like to think it is.

2. Raise our awareness of the use of outrage

Some people, groups, businesses, and politicians benefit from stoking outrage. Whether they're choosing words that activate moral disgust intentionally or not, we can recognize when they're doing it. So wherever you get your information, play a game I call *Outrage Word Bingo*, noting how often words that stoke outrage are being used. This will help shed light on whether you're hearing facts, opinions, or provocations. You can question the validity of extreme statements and demand more balanced language **by choosing where you tune in, how you click, and how you vote.**

If a manufacturer was producing their product in a way that caused harm to society, we would object. We wouldn't buy it. We don't have to buy the outrage people are selling either.

3. Bring balance to extreme thinking

It's worth noting that during the 1990s while divisive words and tactics increased in politics, political moderates were stepping out of participating in political communities at greater numbers than those with "very liberal" or "very conservative" views. In 2000, Robert Putnam wrote in *Bowling Alone,*

> Ironically, more and more Americans describe their political views as middle of the road or moderate, but the more polarized extremes on the ideological spectrum account for a bigger and bigger share of those who attend meetings, write letters, serve on committees, and so on. The more extreme views have gradually become more dominant in grassroots American civic life as more moderate voices have fallen silent.[15]

Another way to bring more balance to political discussions is for moderates to ensure their views are being heard alongside more liberal and conservative views in public meetings, local organizations, political parties, rallies, and other forms of civic life.

4. Emphasize our similarities

We've seen that we don't have to be locked-in to any single group identity. In fact, we're able to quickly shift our group loyalties simply by changing our perspective and finding something we have in common to rally around. In part three of this book, we'll see that we still have shared values. And we can rally together as decent humans, looking for reasonable and responsible solutions so we can live well together. Instead of emphasizing the differences that separate Us and Them, *we can find the common ground that helps all of us work toward a shared goal*, and that can help us get through a divisive time without damaging each other.

A path forward

Biology plays a powerful role in helping us bond with others to survive and to thrive, but it also can blind us to a complete perspective. When we question our assumptions, we give ourselves the chance to see a more accurate picture of reality, and we give ourselves the choice not to be fed outrage for someone else's gain. All of us—Us *and* Them—can take an active role in reintroducing balancing views to the public dialog and *we can find new common bonds that have the power to override old divisions that don't serve us.*

Journaling

When is a time you saw people come together quickly? Did they do so by finding a common goal, a common enemy, or a common characteristic?

What are some assumptions you make about people in your group—your Us-es? How about your assumptions about Thems?

What is something you would like to do differently, this week, based on what you learned in this chapter?

Play Outrage Word Bingo:

How many of these words do you use, or hear others use, when talking about political issues?

Sick	Lie	Steal	Mandate	Failure
Decay	Bizarre	Betray	Destructive	Urgent
Shame	Greed	Bingo!	Destroy	Traitors
Disgrace	Corrupt	Abuse	Endanger	Threaten
Waste	Cheat	Crisis	Collapse	Punish

Up next

Turning the tide of divisiveness seems like a pretty big task. What difference can one person make in a sea of negativity? In the next chapter, we look at why one person's efforts to be decent still matter even when it seems so many people around them aren't doing the same.

Chapter 9

The Contagion of Cruelty and Kindness
In a world with so much negativity, why bother trying?

When did it become fun to be mean? When did it become acceptable to degrade someone for our entertainment? Jimmy Kimmel has a regular bit on his late-night TV show called *Celebrities Read Mean Tweets* where celebrities read real tweets that were written about them by other people. If you watch any of these on YouTube, you'll see some celebrities laugh it off. But often, like in the episode recounted above, you'll see real, vulnerable humans who are hurt that people can be so nasty. Reality TV shows like *Real Housewives* and *Bridezilla* glorify people who say and do things that are cruel, selfish, and even violent. These days, we see frequent news reports of adults throwing tantrums in stores,[2] airlines disciplining unruly passengers,[3] and even public officials being threatened and attacked when people don't like the way they're doing their jobs.[4] In chapter 6, we saw that humans figured out a long time ago that being decent to each other is good for us as individuals and as group members. So what happened to common decency?

Bad behavior is contagious

Taken by itself, a single act of bad behavior may seem harmless. But a powerful psychological principle can make bad behavior contagious. Renowned social psychologist, Robert Cialdini, researched the forces that influence how people make choices. In his best-selling book, *Influence*, he describes one of these forces: *Social Proof*, or the principle that, "*We view an action as correct in a given situation to the degree that we see others performing it.*"[5]

Cialdini's research shows that people often base their actions, in terms of morality, criminality, health, and more, on what they observe other people doing—and the effect is stronger when there are *a lot of people* doing something or if *other people in our group* are doing it. In other words, we take our cues about how to behave from those around us. Sure, this is really helpful when we walk into a new situation or aren't sure which fork to use at a fancy dinner. But it's not so great when it comes to justifying bad behavior.

Ironically, even describing with disapproval that "A lot of people are doing something wrong or immoral!" encourages other people to do the same thing. In one of his studies, conducted in the Petrified Forest National Park, Cialdini put up a sign urging people not to steal wood with an image depicting three people stealing. The result—thefts nearly tripled. Why? Because people saw social proof that stealing was common.

In the same study, when his team put up a sign showing a single, loner thief—thus marginalizing the behavior instead of making it appear common—thefts declined. Cialdini notes that *if you want people NOT to do something, don't make it appear to be common or to be a norm that one's group often follows. Instead, make the behavior appear to be an unacceptable exception.*

Going from "bad" to "normal"

Over time, allowing small acts of bad behavior to happen regularly makes that behavior less exceptional (kind of like we saw with the use of extreme words that became the new norm in chapter 8.) Ethics expert Susan Liautaud, in *The Power of Ethics: How to Make Good Choices in a Complicated World*, states:

> Behavior spreads on its own to the point where it becomes normalized—to where even well-intentioned people who may never think of engaging in immoral or illegal acts begin to consider: *Everybody else does it, maybe it's not so bad.* Or *Everyone else does it, why shouldn't I?* As the contagion spreads and more people engage in the unethical behavior, it becomes "normal" or "standard practice."[6]

There's a danger in laughing off or condoning bad behavior—it encourages more bad behavior. *If we "shrug it off" when people consistently break the rules that keep society stable—like being respectful, truthful, responsible, and compassionate—we lose stability.* Eliminating norms and putting individual desires ahead of societal standards comes at a cost.

Individualism vs. self-indulgence

But wait, I hear you saying! *Some norms have to shift over time or we'd be stuck living with oppressive, outdated customs.* You're right. Rule-breaking and challenging the status quo are an important part of how society keeps up with the times. Where would we be without recent cultural shifts that pushed for individuals to be able to express themselves and to live more freely and fully? Political and cultural commentator David Brooks explains it well in *The Second Mountain: The Quest for a Moral Life*:

> The individualistic culture that emerged in the sixties broke through many of the chains that held down women and oppressed minorities. It loosened the bonds of racism, sexism, anti-Semitism, and homophobia. We could not have had Silicon Valley or the whole information age economy without the rebel individualism and bursts of creativity that were unleashed by this culture. It was an absolutely necessary cultural revolution. But many ideas become false when taken to the extreme.[7]

One aspect of individualism going to the extreme is today's culture where people can express whatever thought gets them some retweets, and where people are disrespectful and even violent, disregarding their impact on others. *Those individual behaviors aren't about living more fully or freedom of expression. They're about self-indulgence—putting personal pleasure or personal gain over the behavior standards that make life as a society possible.* Taking individualism to an extreme is creating a "new normal" where carelessly harming others can spread like contagion. (We'll see this topic again in chapter 17 on respect.)

The antidote to bad behavior

So, bad behavior leads to bad behavior—but wait, there's good news. *Good behavior is equally contagious.* In *Born to Be Good: The Science of a Meaningful Life*, UC Berkeley researcher Dacher Keltner reveals that even perceiving someone's smile, feeling a kind touch, or hearing about someone's kindness to others leads us to feel more trust and goodwill. Kindness and decency can spread like ripples, rolling outward in mere seconds to encourage both the giver and the receiver to feel good—and to want to pay it forward.[8]

Do you remember from the last chapter that we're able to shift in and out of our group identities quickly? Now think about what happens when someone does something kind for you. Even between strangers, that moment of decency can act like an instant group identifier, creating a connection based on mutual kindness. For example, someone runs to the parking lot to let another know they left their credit card in the store and is met with heartfelt gratitude, or when a mom sees a fellow parent struggling with their stroller at the park and asks if she can lend a hand. These small acts of kindness make a connection in that moment. *When we're kind to each other, we acknowledge, no matter how briefly, that we're both on Team Decent Human together.* And that amplifies goodwill and encourages us to do more acts of kindness—because that's what decent humans do. Conforming to group behavior norms like this can be a beautiful thing, indeed.

What's your *jen* ratio?

So what if you want to feel more of that joyful state of people being decent to each other? Keltner suggests using a concept called *the jen ratio—a way of looking at the balance of good and bad in your life.* Small events of positivity, such as offering a compliment to someone or laughing off a mistake, are on the top of the ratio. Small events of negativity, like yelling at someone in traffic or being sneered at judgmentally, are on the bottom of the ratio.

The result is a proportion that shows whether you have generally more positivity or negativity in your life. *To increase your jen ratio, you can either increase positivity (the top number) or decrease negativity (the bottom number) in the actions you observe in others and in the actions you do yourself.* For those of us who haven't worked with fractions lately, 5 positivity over 1 negativity (5/1) is a lot better than 1 positivity over 5 negativity (1/5).

$$\text{Jen Ratio} = \frac{\text{Moments of positivity}}{\text{Moments of negativity}}$$

But, is changing worth the effort it will take? Keltner explains that high jen ratios, where people help bring out the good in each other, lead to the release of feel-good chemicals in the brain, more positive relationships, and even more thriving societies. So for individuals, acting to increase your jen ratio—by doing things that are positive, kind, and compassionate—comes back around to you in the form of greater happiness and the sense of a meaningful life. At a national level, high jen ratios are "a hallmark of healthy societies" and as trust between citizens goes up, so does their economic fortune.[9] So yeah, it's worth the effort.

Increasing your jen ratio

To improve your personal jen ratio, a great place to start is by decreasing the negative part of the ratio—like keeping nasty comments to yourself and not throwing a fit at flight attendants when your flight's delayed. You get back what you put out, so while you may not be able to control what other people do to you, *you can influence it.*

5 Easy Ways to Increase Your Jen Ratio
Wave to a neighbor
Keep a criticism to yourself
Let someone go first
Check in on a friend or relative
Forgive a mistake

Increasing the positive part of the ratio can be surprisingly easy, like smiling at a stranger, letting someone walk onto the elevator first, or giving your partner the last cookie in the box. Keltner explains that these small gestures are such an important part of how we diffuse tension and build goodwill that we humans have a full repertoire of facial expressions and gestures that express kindness and compassion. There are myriad ways we can ease tensions and reduce conflict, like simple chuckles of laughter, a shoulder shrug with raised eyebrows, and playful teasing, to name a few. Showing mild embarrassment can bring people back together after a mistake. Or, you know that sheepish wave someone gives you from their car after they accidentally cut you off? That's a subtle show of respect so you can add that to the top of your jen ratio. And when someone needs comfort, a genuinely compassionate touch, like a hand on the shoulder, can go straight to the heart, bumping up their and your jen ratio.

Keltner's research suggests you don't have to be a global philanthropist to make the world a more positive place. *Small, everyday actions create ripple effects that raise jen ratios for both the giver and the receiver, and ultimately to society.*

Interesting origins

Keltner's jen ratio is derived from the ancient philosopher Confucius, who developed his teachings at a time when Chinese society had devolved into brutal in-fighting. According to historian and religious scholar Huston Smith, Confucius recognized the need to create something that would bring people together so that they wouldn't destroy themselves.[10] He based his teachings on *simple ideas that reminded people that they still held values in common.*

Confucius encouraged people to make a deliberate choice about which values were important to collective well-being and then to act intentionally so those values would reach into every aspect of life. The most important of those values was jen (or ren 仁),[11] which can be translated as *benevolence, humanity,* or *true goodness.*[12] Confucius' teachings, written about 500 years before the birth of Jesus, still ring true. Finding peace and meaning might well be found in deliberately choosing to live with shared values and a priority on true goodness. At the heart of those values is the simple idea:

> "What you do not wish done to yourself, do not do to others." – Confucius[13]

A path forward

Turning a blind eye, or encouraging bad behavior, well you get back what you put out. If you wouldn't like to read a mean tweet about yourself, don't send one; there's a difference between freedom of expression and self-indulgence. The good news is that expressing yourself with kindness has the potential to spread goodwill and encourage more kindness. Feel free to indulge in *that* all you want. ***You have the power to create ripple effects—and to be sure they are the kind you want spreading and rolling back to you.***

Journaling

Have you experienced a moment of shared kindness when you felt like you were on Team Decent Human with someone?

What are some sources of negativity in your life that you could decrease? What are some sources of positivity you could increase?

What small, kind gestures could you do today, starting when you set down this book?

Up next

We've seen that even small acts of decent behavior are good for the giver and the receiver. But being a good person all the time sounds hard, if not impossible. Do we have to be perfect?

Chapter 10

The Myth of Perfection

Why life is a series of moments for practicing who you want to be

---

Two friends chatting at the coffee shop

Ash: Last week, I decided it was time to get in shape. You know, it's important to have a healthy heart and I could lose a few pounds. So I started a raw, vegan diet and decided to run five miles every day. I figured I'd run a marathon later this year.

Forrest: Really? How's it going?

Ash: Oh, I quit. It was way too painful.

Forrest: Well, maybe you could start a little slower. Cut back on some junk food and go for some long walks?

Ash: Nah. If I'm gonna do it, I'm going all in. It's the only thing that'll make a difference. It's a marathon or nothing for me!

Forrest: So, it's nothing, then?

How do you create change in your life? If you can't do something perfectly or instantaneously, is it worth doing at all? Creating positive change can seem so overwhelming, sometimes it's hard to imagine that it's worth the effort. Yet we saw in the last chapter that individual actions matter. Each small act of kindness or cruelty creates a ripple effect. One act of nastiness replaced by one act of decency can set off waves that roll out and do even more good. But what if you don't act like a paragon of virtue all the time? What if you don't *want* to? An all-or-nothing commitment to change may seem admirable, but it's rarely sustainable. Like the characters in the opening dialog, you don't have to train for a marathon to be a little healthier. *And you don't have to be perfectly kind and moral in every moment for the times that you are kind and moral to do some good.*

Nobody's perfect

Christian Archbishop and civil rights activist Desmond Tutu was good friends with the Dalai Lama, the Buddhist spiritual leader. In their coauthored title, *The Book of Joy*, these two icons of humanity reveal they are delightfully human, laughing about how they can get frustrated and angry sometimes. (Although maybe they do this less than they used to since they've had so much practice at learning to be calm.) In the book, the Archbishop counsels that we don't need to beat ourselves up for being imperfect—that just adds to any frustration. He says,

> I mean, we are human beings, fallible human beings. ... Sometimes we get too angry with ourselves thinking that we ought to be perfect from the word go. But this being on earth is a time for us to learn to be good, to learn to be more loving, to learn to be more compassionate. And you learn, not theoretically. ... You learn when something happens that tests you.[1]

Tutu says annoyances and negative moments are a natural part of being human and are only made more intense by obsessing with guilt and shame for having them. Instead, we should strive for balance: Do our best but give ourselves a break for not being perfect. He and the Dalai Lama note in their book how even they have to remind themselves that *becoming the person we want to be requires practice.*

Mistakes are about growth

The essence of practice means that sometimes you do well and sometimes you see your own weaknesses. But that's okay; it's part of growth. *Sometimes to know who you are, you need to know who you are not—or more accurately, who you choose not to be.* Part of the process of finding peace with yourself is to be aware of all the good, bad, and ugly that you are capable of, and then choosing to be good. Bestselling-author Debbie Ford, in *The Dark Side of the Light Chasers*, says,

> We live under the impression that in order for something to be divine it has to be perfect. We are mistaken. In fact, the exact opposite is true. To be divine is to be whole and to be whole is to be everything: the positive and the negative, the good and the bad, the holy man and the devil.[2]

In the moments that we catch ourselves with a nasty thought, the desire to do something cruel or vengeful, or just the craving for some guilty-pleasure escapism, it's an opportunity to remember who we want to be and to choose a path that will steer us toward our goals.

> Right now is a great time to make a good choice.

Each moment is a moment to choose anew

If you made a choice five minutes ago that you aren't happy with, that doesn't mean you have to keep making similar choices now. You aren't locked-in to how you've done things before. Right now is a great time to make a good choice.[3] *That's because every moment is a great time to choose actions that serve who you want to be. And each moment is an opportunity to let go of habits that no longer serve you.* This idea can liberate you from the intimidating demands of perfection, and free you from the mistakes of the past. If you waver and step off the path, the next moment is an opportunity to step back onto it. Whether you reach the ultimate ideal or not, there's value in making the effort in this moment. And the next moment. And the one after that.

A path forward

Being a decent human doesn't require you or anyone else to be perfect. Each moment is a moment to choose how you act and how you respond to the actions of others. *We have the option in this moment, and every moment after, to choose a new way of being with ourselves, and of being with each other.* Mistakes and sidesteps are part of the process. Yet over time, the sum of our small, everyday choices can redefine who we choose to be.[4]

With that bit of encouragement, we'll step into new territory in the next section. We'll get into the details of how we can choose to live a good life. We'll dig into what it means to be a decent person, and we'll learn how to look at events today through a set of guiding principles that can help us choose a moral path that lifts each of us and all of us. But first, journaling.

Journaling

Would you rather be good at a few things or perfect at one thing?

Have you ever changed a behavior or created a new habit? How did you go about it?

Have you ever made a choice that led you away from your goal? How did you course correct?

Up next

As we end part two, hopefully it's evident by now that being rooted in decency, with ourselves and with others, is how we'll get to more contentment, more stability, and a kinder world. But we've seen that we're pretty divided and it can be hard to agree on what being decent means anymore. In part three, we'll discover which values humans from different times and places have held in common for eons (Spoiler alert—they're amazingly similar!) and we'll use that insight to create a modern moral compass that's practical for real-life decision making.

∾

Part Three:

Setting a Course

Part Three

Setting a Course

In the first two parts, we saw that being rooted in decency is good for each of us individually and it's good for all of us as a society. Even when the world seems like it's going sideways around us, we can feel more stable personally by living in line with what we think is right. But we aren't just individuals, we're also group members. We saw that we need each other, and as a society, we're happier and more successful when we treat each other with decency. So then the big question is, **what does it mean to be decent**? At a time when we seem so divided about what right and wrong behavior looks like, how do we find common ground about what it means to be a good person?

The way to common decency

In part three, we'll take a step back in order to take a step forward. First, we'll consider where ideas about right and wrong come from—is morality a personal decision as some people suggest? Then we'll explore which values the world's major religions and belief systems have in common, which will lead us to the discovery that we share a moral root system based on the needs of humanity, not any single person or religion. Our ideas about what it is to be a decent person aren't so different after all.

Next, we'll use those eons of wisdom to define four guiding points on a practical moral compass that can help us navigate the complex situations we're facing today. In her book, *The Power of Ethics: How to Make Good Choices in a Complicated World*, ethics expert Susan Liautaud advises that the first step in any ethical decision is knowing what your guiding principles are. She states,

> Our principles define our identity and tell the world what to expect from us, as well as how we expect others to behave. ... They are enduring guides that help us navigate complex problems so that we make consistent choices.[1]

So let's get working to define those guiding principles, and then we can consider some ways that today's culture is fighting against our ability to be grounded by them. By the end of this section, we'll have an actionable way to use guiding principles to start making a difference in our lives. So lace up your hiking boots, we have an exciting journey before us.

Chapter 11

Right and Wrong

Where do moral values come from?

A father talking to his daughters

I only ever loved you girls. I did my best to make sure you would succeed, to achieve your fullest potential and everything worked out. ... Elena, you went on to become the greatest child assassin the world has ever known. No one can match your efficiency, your *ruthlessness*. And Natasha, not just a spy, not just toppling regimes—destroying empires from within. ... You both have killed so many people. Your ledgers must be dripping, just gushing red. I couldn't be more proud of you.

—The Red Guardian, villain in *Black Widow*, a Marvel Movie[1]

Who decides what's right and wrong? In today's individualistic society, some people argue that it's impossible, and perhaps immoral, to judge someone else's moral code. David Brooks, author of several books on culture and character, explains in *The Second Mountain* that in America today, some people believe that it's not up to "schools or neighborhoods or even parents to create a shared moral order. [They think] it's something you do on your own, and who are you to judge if another person's moral order is better or worse than any others?"[2] By that standard, the villain in the opening quote would be right to praise his daughters for being murderers. His moral order values killing, and who are we to judge? Yet if that were true, we wouldn't call him a villain, would we?

Morality is about well-being

The idea of right and wrong as a wholly individual choice would mean we don't need to consider how our actions impact other people. But remember from chapter 6 that each of us is an individual **and** a group member, so realistically *we can't be solely focused on ourselves.* Instead, we constantly balance what we want with the benefit we gain by being part of society—and that's where morality comes from.

If we look backward through human history, morality emerged out of a need for ground rules that could govern how humans would live and cooperate together.[3] The moral values of a society are based on the behaviors its people think are valuable to the group's well-being, hence the word *values.*

> The traits or behaviors that *help* well-being—and thus are the ones we want to encourage—are *good* or *right* and become *virtues.*

> The behaviors that cause *harm* and diminish common well-being are *bad* and *wrong* and are considered *vices.*

Personal preference may influence *how you prioritize* competing moral demands. But if we look back in time to the origins of morality, we'll see that *our definitions of right and wrong are rooted in the common good.*

Time capsule: how (and why) humans created the rules

Let's pretend we're early humans and I want what you have. Is it right for me to walk up and take it for myself? In the days of early humans, if one person tried to take what wasn't theirs, someone was getting hit on the head with a rock. If you and I want to live together peacefully, you

need to be able to *trust* that I'm not going to take away the things you
need for your well-being. And sometimes, creating well-being is hard
to do by yourself. For example, perhaps we both want to take down that
nourishing woolly mammoth that's too big for just one of us. I'll help you,
if you help me, and we'll each take our fair share. **With early humans,
trust, fairness, and reciprocity were the foundation of their moral
behavior because it helped them thrive—together.**

Natural selection favored those individuals who knew how to be good
team members and it also favored groups who worked well together.[4]
Early humans figured out that their own well-being was linked to
their group's well-being, so they developed an internal guide—a moral
compass—that helped them make choices that balanced what they
wanted for themselves with the benefit they knew they would gain by
continuing to be part of the team.

> Right and wrong are rooted in the common good and serve
> our need for trust, fairness, and reciprocity.

Religion teams up with morality

In small hunter-gatherer groups, reputation, gossip, and the justice meted
out by a retributive rock to the head could keep people in line. But as
groups became larger in size and complexity, early humans needed to
extend expectations for behavior to people who didn't know each other
well. Renowned religious scholar and moral philosopher, Rabbi Jonathan
Sacks explains in his book, *Morality*, that early forms of spirituality
evolved into more formalized religions that enabled strangers to establish
trust and increase cooperation with one another. Of course, religion
brought more benefits than just social control. However, in a time before

wide-spread civic law and order, the moral codes and watchful gods of religion helped humans have confidence that people they didn't know would act reasonably and predictably. Rabbi Sacks goes on to explain one of the profound impacts the advent of religion brought about: "By creating the conditions for trust between strangers, religion allowed human beings to become the only species ever to have evolved from small, tight-knit groups to large, structured societies."[5]

Religion adds human dignity

Religion also contributed another dimension to morality, elevating it beyond the practical concerns of group dynamics. Two of the earliest enduring belief systems, Judaism and Hinduism, both declared the dignity of human life. The Bible tells people they are created in the image of God (Genesis 1:27) while the Bhagavad Gita of Hinduism says to see all living beings in God and God in all living beings (Bhagavad Gita 6.29).[6] These concepts establish an intrinsic worth in all people and declare that each should be treated with the respect due something that is from God. *Preserving human dignity became an essential part of morality.* In the words of Rabbi Sacks, "Morality and human dignity go hand in hand. Lose one, and we will lose the other."[7]

Do you need religion to be moral?

Morality has been tied to religion for ages, so much so, that some would argue you can't have morality without religion. A study from 2014 reveals that a majority of people around the world think a person must believe in God in order to be good.[8] Some conservative commentators argue that a society without a strong religious presence would fall to "anarchy," "crime," and "disaster."[9] And some studies show that people who believe in God would rather trust others who believe in a different or "the wrong" god than trust someone from their own culture who is an atheist.[10]

Yet despite the ties that exist between them, morality and religion are not inseparable. Let's consider a few reasons why:

- **Morality predates religion**– As we saw above, people behaved in ways that contributed to group well-being before religion formalized them into moral codes.

- **Secular organizations perform moral acts**– Plenty of non-religious organizations are guided by ethical standards and create programs to improve human well-being without a religious imperative. For instance, groups like UNICEF have a non-religious, humanitarian mission statement.

- **Religion can be used to justify immoral acts**– While it can be used to promote moral behavior, religion has also been used to justify acts that are clearly against the well-being of other humans, particularly those who are of a different religion. History is rife with crusades and holy wars.

- **Secular sources can motivate moral behavior**– In societies with strong institutions, where people are confident that contracts will be enforced, competition will be fair, and cheaters will be punished, research shows that people trust each other and cooperate more, while the role of religion in public life decreases.[11]

What morality without religion looks like

In *Society Without God: What The Least Religious Nations Can Tell Us About Contentment,* sociologist Phil Zuckerman holds Danish culture as an example of a society that a few generations ago was piously Christian while today, most Danes either don't believe in God or don't consider God to be well-defined, watchful, or particularly important in their lives.[12] Despite this decline in religiosity, Denmark didn't fall into anarchy, crime, and disaster. In fact, as of this writing, it has low levels of violent crime and corruption while it consistently ranks among the happiest and most well-developed countries in the world.

So then, what governs behavior in a society in which people don't have a strong relationship with God and don't believe in eternal punishment or reward? In interviews with Danes, Zuckerman discovered a pattern—The Danes valued moral principles rooted in *fairness, cooperation, respect, caring for others,* and *treating others as you would have them treat you.* While their faith and commitment to God and religion has declined, Danes still value foundational moral principles followed by their ancestors.

It's a good thing people can be moral without religion

This is good news for the quality of life all around the world, because there are a lot of people who don't turn to religion for direction about how to be good people:

- As of 2019, more than a quarter of Americans identify as atheist, agnostic, or "nothing in particular."[13]
- 40% of French and Germans are atheist or agnostic.[14]
- 53% of British, 56% of South Koreans, 80% of Japanese, 30% of Australians, and 20% of Latin Americans are not religious.[15]

But wait—I hear you objecting—*in those countries, their ancestors were often religious.* That's true, and we'll soon see that the core moral principles around trust, cooperation, and fairness are included in all the world's major religions. So we have a sort of cyclical progression here— moral principles that pre-date religion were woven into the moral codes of the world's religions / belief systems, and in turn, those founding moral principles persist even as people become less religious.

A path forward

Despite the rise in individualism in modern times, we still need a shared sense of morality that helps us find connection with each other, shows us purpose beyond ourselves, and binds us in a team effort toward well-being. *The way we define right and wrong isn't arbitrary—it's rooted in eons of wisdom about which behaviors help individuals and societies to flourish together.* The specific rules vary by time, culture, and interpretation. But the underlying values that define decent behavior persist, even as society and religion evolve, because our common need for trust, fairness, and reciprocity is universally human. At a time when society seems like it's gone sideways and people are divided against each other, we can learn from the ways humans have built trust and cooperation in equally divisive times of the past.

Journaling

How did you learn about what is right and wrong?

In your experiences, are religious people moral? Are non-religious people immoral?

How would you define your current moral code?

Up next

For all our perceived differences, we'll see in the next chapter that the moral codes of the world's different belief systems actually share many of the same core values.

Chapter 12

Shared Values

Which values do the world's belief systems have in common?

For the thousands of years that formal religions have existed, people have defined their relationship with a supreme being differently. The religions' rituals, rewards, and goals have varied. But if we isolate just the moral guidance in the world's major belief systems, we'll find their core values have a lot in common. Don't believe me? Read on and see if you don't find yourself thinking, *Wait... didn't I just read this?*

Seven of the world's enduring belief systems

Let's take a brief look at the core moral values in Hinduism, Judaism, Confucianism, Buddhism, Christianity, Islam, and Greek philosophy. Why these seven? Not only do these seven systems offer insight into global human thinking on morality, their impact endures today. As of 2015, more than three-quarters of the world's population identified as believers in one of these religions or belief systems.[1] As for Greek philosophy, it has influenced modern moral philosophy and its legacy lives on in our system of laws and justice, which is part of how we enforce what we consider *right* and *wrong* in modern society.

These belief systems (they aren't all religions) emerged between 2500 BCE (Hinduism) through the most recent in 600 CE (Islam) on the Indian subcontinent, the Middle East, Asia, and Europe.[2] We'll take our tour chronologically, but keep in mind that the tour isn't meant to be an exhaustive explanation of any of the belief systems nor does it address differing beliefs about a supreme being and religious practices. We'll only be looking at the guidelines on how humans should act toward other humans; because as we saw in chapter 11, a society encourages the behaviors it considers valuable for well-being and calls them *right* or *good*, and society discourages behaviors it considers harmful and calls them *wrong* or *bad*. And that's how we crack the moral code.

Timeline of World Belief Systems

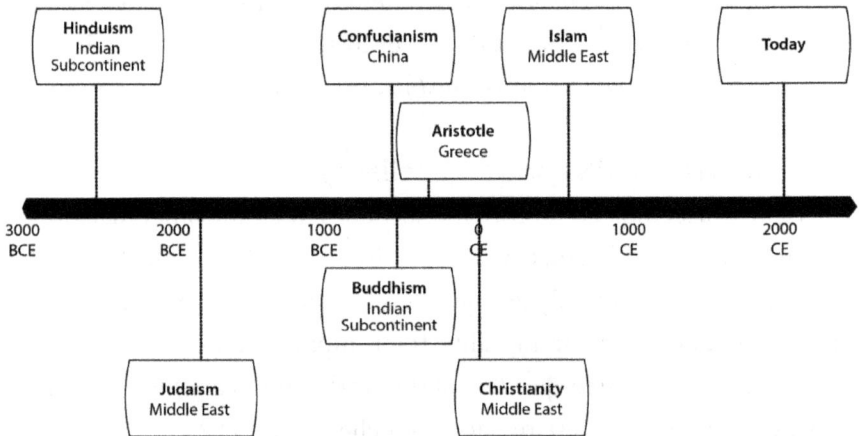

Source: Introduction to the World's Religions[3]

Hinduism

Hinduism originated on the Indian subcontinent around 2500 BCE and it teaches followers to live in accordance with *dharma*, the moral path.[4] As the Mahabharata, one of the sacred epic texts, states: "Dharma sustains the society. Dharma maintains social order. Dharma ensures the well being and progress of humanity."[5] Like ripples in a pond, individuals foster their own well-being while they also contribute to the betterment of families, societies, nations, and all humankind by living in line with dharma.

A central idea of Hinduism is the doctrine of *karma,* which means when someone does good deeds or bad, they will eventually get equivalent pleasure or pain in return. A combination of responsibility and empowerment, karma means each person can impact the quality of their own life by making good choices. Karma also ensures justice and fairness because over time, everyone gets what they deserve.

Truth and sincerity are also key principles in living the moral path of dharma, and this farewell address to students that is included in the Taittiriya Upanishad expresses some of the essential expectations for those who follow Hindu ideals:

> Let your conduct be marked by right action, ... by truthfulness in word, deed, and thought; by self-denial and the practice of austerity; by poise and self-control; by performance of the everyday duties of life with a cheerful heart and an unattached mind.[6]

Hindu ethics are based on the idea that everyone is connected so as Swami Bhaskarananda explains in *The Essentials of Hinduism*: "If I hurt anyone, I actually hurt myself. Therefore I must not hurt anyone."[7] The essential teachings of Hindu moral guidance emphasize ways to care for both oneself and others, including:

Self-care and improvement– Act with self-control and moderation. Maintain a pure mind and body. Study and improve yourself.

Responsibility beyond the self– Honor parents and respect the importance of family. Earn a living honestly and do service for the community.

Non-violence to all forms of life is a central idea, although it is not to be used to rationalize cowardice. Approach duty with courage.

Treating others with care– Act with gentleness, kindness, compassion, charity, and forgiveness. Renounce selfishness and be free from anger and malice.

Gratitude, contentment, and active enthusiasm– Appreciate what you have and how you live, but don't become selfishly attached to this. Long-term happiness is more important than temporary pleasure.

> One should not direct towards someone else what is unpleasant to oneself.
> (Mahabharata Udyoga Parvan 39.57)[8]

Judaism

Judaism began in the Middle East, around 1800 BCE in the time of Abraham, the common patriarch of Judaism, Christianity, and Islam.[9] The Ten Commandments in the Hebrew Bible are an outline of the moral principles of Judaism. Though there are actually 613 commandments that guide moral living in general, philosopher and theologian Rabbi Jonathan Sacks explains that the "Ten" lay the foundation for a just, functioning society.[10] Looking at the commandments that prohibit behaviors between humans:

You shall not murder: Establishes the sanctity of life and declares murder to be a violation of the dignity inherent in God's creation.

You shall not commit adultery– Affirms the importance of respecting marriage commitments because these unions are one of the core institutions that help keep society stable.

You shall not steal– More than banning theft, this commandment establishes property rights, which are essential to a free society.

You shall not bear false witness against your neighbor– Declares that a just society requires honesty. As Rabbi Sacks explains, "There is no freedom without justice, and no justice without each of us accepting individual and collective responsibility for truth-telling."[11]

You shall not covet your neighbor's house … wife … male servant … female servant … ox … donkey … or anything that is your neighbor's– This last commandment is much longer than the others because coveting is about envy, which is a potent desire that can drive people to violate the previous principles that are needed for an orderly society.

In addition to these ten foundational guidelines for how to create a good society, some central moral themes in Judaism emphasize:

Honesty and fair play– With friends, neighbors, and strangers, deal honestly and reliably.

Lovingkindness– Treat others with respect, care, and compassion, just as you would like them to treat you.

Responsibility beyond the self– Honor one's parents and take care of family. Scholar and acclaimed author Rabbi Joseph Telushkin explains that the word for helping those in need, *tzedaka*, comes from the Hebrew word for justice and "the Talmud taught, '*Tzedaka is equal to all the other commandments combined*' (*Bava Bathra* 9a)."[12]

Justice– Jews have a moral obligation to protect the vulnerable and not to stand idly by if injustice is committed against Jews or non-Jews.

> Love your neighbor as yourself.
> (Leviticus 19:18)[13]

Confucianism

Born 551 BCE, Confucius is known as a great teacher whose philosophy shaped generations of Chinese and East Asian thought.[14] During his time, rival groups fought constantly, and the conflict wore down societal norms. Individuals started thinking of themselves and held less concern for group well-being. Religious scholar Huston Smith explains that as self-interest took hold, "Proposals for action had now to face peoples' question, 'What's in it for me?'"[15]

Confucius' response was to teach the *Way*, a moral path, that would shape human nature and restore harmony between the individual, society, and the social order. He proposed that each person, with effort, could cultivate their character toward supreme goodness, or ren/jen.[16] The Chinese character for ren (仁) is comprised of two parts: the radical for person, and the radical for the number two. The presentation of the radicals together in the character symbolizes how true goodness could only be achieved with respect to how one behaved in their relationships with others.[17] Central moral ideas in Confucius' philosophy include:

Having respect for human dignity, including self-respect and benevolence toward others. Includes qualities of empathy, unselfishness, charity, and sincerity in your motivation to be moral, without ulterior motive.

Having qualities of a mature self, including graciousness, confidence and comfort with oneself, courteousness, even-temperedness, and realness.

Acting with propriety and being a model of how things should be done. Includes speaking with truth and accuracy, acting with traits in balance and not to extremes, acting responsibly within your relationships, and understanding how your actions impact others.

The power of moral example. Government leaders, in particular, must demonstrate high moral character to prompt moral behavior in the governed and to continue to be legitimate in their rule.

The importance of art (e.g. music, visual arts, poetry) in transforming human nature toward virtue. Includes the idea that culture can give evidence that a society has moral character and excellence.

> Do not impose upon others what you yourself do not desire.
> (Analects 15.24)[18]

Buddhism

Around 530 BCE, Buddha started teaching on the Indian subcontinent, spreading ideas that were derived from Hinduism, including dharma and karma. Buddhism[19] emphasizes that each individual has the power to end their own suffering through self-awareness and by being mindful of the forces that can pull one out of balance.

Living by the Buddhist Eightfold Path includes three components about how people treat each other: **Right Speech**, **Right Action**, and **Right Livelihood**. In *The Heart of the Buddha's Teaching*, renowned Buddhist monk Thich Nhat Hanh points out that the word *right* here is not an arbitrary standard: "Through our own awareness, we discover what is beneficial ('right') and what is unbeneficial ('wrong')."[20]

> **Right Speech–** This includes speaking truthfully and accurately; not saying one thing to someone and something else to another; not speaking cruelly; not making things sound better or worse than they are. Right speech with each other depends on deep and compassionate listening.

> **Right Action–** This involves upholding non-violence and reverence for life; cultivating compassion, generosity, and loving kindness toward the well-being of others; supporting justice, non-exploitation, and non-oppression; respecting the property of others; engaging only in sexual conduct that protects commitments, individuals, and society; bringing into the mind and body only that which is good for well-being.

> **Right Livelihood–** This involves earning a living in a way that doesn't require oneself, or encourage others, to violate Right Speech and Right Action.

This sutta, in the *Sayings of the Buddha*, offers advice on how to create well-being: "Generosity and kind words, helpful actions in this world,

And treating others equally in all matters and in all circumstances—Such kindnesses in the world hold the axle of its chariot as it moves."[21]

> Hurt not others with what pains yourself.
>
> (Udanavarga 5,18)[22]

Greek Philosophy

Living during the period of around 500 BCE to 300 BCE, Socrates, Plato, and Aristotle laid the foundations for modern moral philosophy and ethics. As the most recent of the trio, Aristotle's ideas on virtue ethics are the most detailed so we'll focus on them.[23]

One of the most common quotes we hear from Aristotle is that the purpose of life is "happiness," but he didn't mean the temporary emotion. The word he used was *eudaimonia,* and when you look at the Greek root words, *eu* and *daimon*, eudaimonia really means "flourishing" or "well-being."[24] So, the purpose of life is to achieve a state of well-being.

Aristotle explains that the way we achieve well-being is by living life in line with what is right—with good virtue. In *Nicomachean Ethics*, he explains that "Virtue, then, is a state of character concerned with choice" because in any situation we must choose, rationally and reasonably, which virtue is most important and how much of it we should employ—too little or too much of a virtue can become vice.[25] Aristotle wrote that applying virtue,

> … to the right person, to the right extent, at the right time, with the right motive, and in the right way, that is not for everyone, nor is it easy; wherefore goodness is both rare and laudable and noble.[26]

So being virtuous may not be easy, but with practice and experience, acting virtuously can become habitual and it can bring balance, inner peace, and well-being.

Aristotle's moral virtues in Nicomachean Ethics:

Courage– Facing fears and challenges, enduring hardship, and doing things that are difficult without being foolhardy.

Temperance– Enjoying healthy pleasures without being self-indulgent or giving in to excess.

Liberality– Dealing with money with responsible spending, reasonable generosity, honesty, and fairness.

Magnificence– Those with wealth shouldn't be cheap, but they also shouldn't be showy or tasteless.

Pride– Knowing one's own worth without being arrogant; Acting with self-awareness, honor, and truth.

Ambition– Pursuing success at a healthy level, from right sources and in the right way.

Good Temper– Anger is appropriate in the right amount for the right reason but not when overindulged or used to abuse others.

Friendliness– Being sociable while treating others with appropriate courtesy and respect.

Truthfulness– Representing oneself and one's motives accurately without exaggeration or boasting.

Wittiness– Enjoying a good time, being willing to take a joke, and being tactful in one's amusement.

Modesty– Engaging with life without being overly shy while also acting appropriately and not bringing shame on oneself.

Righteous Indignation– Strive for what is fair, but don't be envious or take pleasure in others' losses.

> Justice is often thought to be the greatest of virtues. ... It is complete because he who possesses it can exercise his virtue not only in himself but towards another also.
> (Nicomachean Ethics V.1)[27]

Christianity

Jesus, who lived from about 4 BCE to 30 CE, was Jewish, and his teachings reflect the moral code of the Hebrew Bible with an emphasis on living life with a selfless love for God and one's fellow humans.[28] When asked which of the commandments is the most important, Jesus made it clear that treating others with the care and dignity you'd like returned is essential to living a life in line with Christian principles:

> You shall love the Lord your God with all your heart and with all your soul and with all your mind. This is the great and first commandment. And a second is like it: You shall love your neighbor as yourself. (Matthew 22:37-39)

Jesus' focus on fairness and kindness to others wasn't new, but Jesus preached a radical inclusiveness that threatened the social order that existed in the culture of the time. Through his actions, Jesus showed that rich and poor, women and men, saints and sinners, strangers and friends were all worthy of love and respect. He taught that real goodness came from the heart; it was to be done with sincerity and not as a hollow observance of the rules. In addition to the ethical code in the Hebrew Bible described earlier, Jesus demonstrated moral behavior in the way he lived with moral themes that include:

Benevolence, concern for others, generosity, charity, service

Respect for all, humility, forgiveness, and mercy

Honesty in words and actions toward others (such as no deception, cheating, or gossip); and honesty with oneself (which includes not rationalizing or being hypocritical)

Self-control, including having perseverance and courage; and avoiding behaviors like arrogance, envy, greed, malice, and self-righteousness

> So whatever you wish that others would do to you,
> do also to them.
> (Matthew 7:12)

Islam

Around 600 CE, when the Prophet Muhammad began sharing the teachings of the Qur'an, a central religious text of Islam, the society around him was chaotic, plagued by blood feuds, thievery, and generally debauched behaviors.[29] At the time, the teachings of Islam prompted a social revolution that ultimately made moral behavior an encompassing way of life. Acting morally is integral to being Muslim.

Islam recognizes the Hebrew Bible and the Gospel of Jesus as part of a series that ends with the Qur'an as the culmination of God's teachings, therefore many of the moral themes in Islam are similar to those in the Bible. The teachings emphasize living life with self-control, sincerity, fairness, and compassion, while honoring relationships with family and the greater community.

In Islam, human nature is considered fundamentally good, but sometimes people forget their way; so Islam makes expectations and consequences clear which helps maintain peace, justice, and goodwill in society. For those who are sincerely remorseful, mercy and forgiveness go hand-in-hand with justice. Some other key themes in Islam include:

Justice and fairness are integral to Islam, including an obligation to share resources with the less privileged, to respect others' property, and to deal honestly and fairly. Despite cultural practices in some places today, Islam specifically elevated the status of women giving them rights and dignity in society. As the Middle East Institute notes: "Societies may erect barriers, but nothing in the spirit of the Qur'an subjugates women to men."[30]

Respect for all, based on character– The Qur'an encourages respect and equality among humanity, stating that character is more important than racial or religious differences. The Prophet Muhammad said in his farewell sermon: "There is no virtue of an Arab over a non-Arab, nor a non-Arab over an Arab, and neither white over black nor black over white, except by righteousness."[31]

Gratitude and responsibility– Islam encourages one to live in a continual state of gratitude and sense of responsibility for oneself, family, and the broader community. Everyday actions done with genuine goodwill become spiritually redeeming.

Sincerity– Dishonesty in words or deeds, as well as all wrong behaviors, reflect a lack of truth in honoring one's faith. An article from the Yaqeen Institute for Islamic Research states, "Right intention, which is sincerity, is the foundation of everything else we do in Islam."[32]

> None of you will have faith until he loves for his brother
> what he loves for himself.
> (The Prophet Muhammad)[33]

A path forward

Now that we've covered these seven enduring belief systems, did you notice some repeating themes? Even though the belief systems grew among people in different geographies, who lived hundreds or even thousands of years apart, they each describe many of the same behaviors and offer similar overarching ideas about how to promote individual and group well-being. In a nutshell, all teach:

Good values as a way of life– Hinduism and Buddhism called it dharma. Confucius taught the Way. Judaism's Ten Commandments defined the essentials of a just society. Each of the seven systems taught that embodying morality was good for the individual soul, and it was also the path to societal well-being.

It's all about you– Each system shows that individuals make their own choices and enjoy the benefits (or suffer the consequences) of their own actions. Each person is in charge of:

- what they do with their mind and body
- knowing their worth, living in moderation
- pursuing wisdom and self-awareness
- appreciating the good times
- having the courage to persist during the challenges

It's not all about you– In the highlighted section for each belief system, we see that they all express a version of the Golden Rule—to treat others as you would like to be treated. Each system's guidelines promote trust, fairness, and cooperation, through behaviors like:

- speaking and acting truthfully
- respecting others' property
- respecting life and human dignity
- acting with courtesy and benevolence
- honoring commitments
- showing compassion and mercy
- caring for family, community, and those in need
- justice and fairness—people getting the good and bad of what they have earned

So for all that we find that is different between us, we share a common humanity and a need for trust, fairness, and cooperation. Even in the modern world, these core behaviors around taking care of ourselves and treating others decently are still the path to well-being.

In the course of history, humans around the globe have interpreted this wisdom differently, sometimes at the expense of the wisdom itself. Yet if what's past truly is prologue, there's something to be learned from these recurring themes that appeared at times when humans needed clarity about what is right and what is wrong.

Journaling

Did any of the belief systems surprise you? In what way?

Which virtues or morally good behaviors were the most important to you personally?

Which virtues do we, as a society, seem to need more of right now?

Up Next

What can we do with this wisdom? In the next chapter, we'll organize the specifics, and pare it all down into four points on a moral compass—four essential common values to guide our actions toward our own and society's well-being.

Chapter 13

Defining a Moral Compass
What are your guiding principles?

Two friends hiking in the wilderness

Ash: I think we might be lost. Why isn't this on the map? Which way do we go?

Forrest: We're in uncharted territory but we have our compass to figure it out. That path there, that's definitely the wrong way. Between these other choices, the paths may not get us exactly where we want to be, but the compass says they're all heading in the right direction.

Ash: Okay, but if it seems like it's starting to go the wrong way, we'll need to course correct.

Day-to-day, we have countless occasions to ask ourselves, *What should I do?* Some situations are simple, so our choices in those moments are also simple. But you're not reading this book for those situations. We're here on this journey together because life is complicated and often, when we think, *What's the right thing to do?*, we find ourselves looking at alternate routes that each have tradeoffs. We may see multiple paths to the same destination, yet we'll probably get stuck if we insist on a "perfect" route to an "ideal" end point. Any journey starts with a step in the right direction, so before we venture out (and at each turn along the route) we need to check that we're heading the right way. We need a compass—in this case, a moral compass—that helps us have confidence that our choices are guided by our principles.

In the last chapter, we saw which principles humans, across time and geography, have agreed are good or right. They are the behaviors and traits that societies have valued because they help each of us and all of us on our quest toward well-being. It's great moral wisdom, but it's also a lot to take in. Let's start by organizing and distilling it down into something more manageable. Let's create a moral compass with four points that cover the essentials of human morality.

Creating a moral compass

If we went back to chapter 12 and created a list of the values and virtues that the world belief systems said make for a moral life, behaviors and traits like sincerity, trustworthiness, honoring relationships, moderation, fairness, personal accountability, lovingkindness, etc., then we took out duplicates and organized similar traits, we'd find that the common values can be grouped into four main moral categories. *Four!?! Seriously?* We'll get into the details of each value in the upcoming chapters. But for now, this handy infographic shows the overall logic for how we come to four direction points on our moral compass:

Truth — Respect — Responsibility — Compassion

The Moral Compass

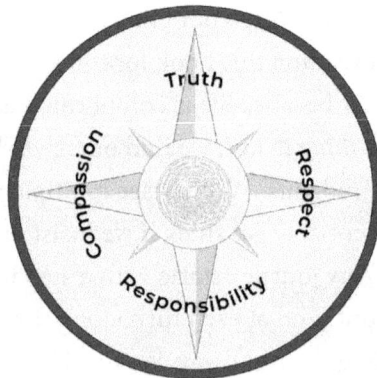

Defining a Moral Compass

Consolidation of Common Values

• truthfulness in word, deed, thought •
accuracy • sincerity • realness
• trustworthiness • earning a living honestly •
honesty in trade • ambition done rightly
• no stealing, cheating, lying, gossip,
false witness, hypocrisy, rationalizing

TRUTH

• respect for life & dignity • non-violence •
fairness • liberality • justice
• non-exploitation • non-oppression
• respect property rights • treat others as you
would be treated • even temper • wittiness
• courteousness • honoring parents • sexual
conduct that respects commitments •
self-respect • humility • poise • confidence in
oneself • appropriate pride / self-worth

RESPECT

• personal accountability • self-improvement •
caring for mind & body • self-control •
moderation • temperance • magnificence
• balance • courage • enduring hardship •
positive outlook • contentment
• avoiding arrogance, envy, greed, malice
• non-covetousness • being an example •
service to the community • caring for family

RESPONSIBILITY

• lovingkindness • gentleness • peace
• love • unselfishness • graciousness •
charity • caring for those in need • generosity
• benevolence • goodwill • friendliness •
forgiveness • mercy • empathy
• compassionate listening

COMPASSION

Why TRUTH:

Each of the seven enduring belief systems emphasized the importance of being truthful in words, deeds, and intent. We saw truthful behaviors repeated in multiple ways, such as:

- Being honest with ourselves about our motives
- Acting with sincerity
- Speaking truthfully and accurately
- Acting honestly in trade, in relationships, and with property

Morality grew from our need for trustworthiness, fairness, and cooperation, and truth is the foundation on which all of those are built. We can't cooperate without trust; and we can't trust without truth. We'll put TRUTH at true north on our moral compass because *without it the rest of our moral values are empty promises*. The upcoming chapters on TRUTH (chapters 14, 15, and 16) will reveal that despite predictions of a "post-truth" era, the truth still matters for our personal well-being and our group life.

Why RESPECT:

Respect is about treating people and principles with care, including treating others with the dignity and fairness we'd like in return. That reciprocity—I'll treat you the way I'd like you to treat me—is a key way we are able to cooperate and live peacefully in a society. In the belief systems, we saw specific behaviors that foster self-respect and respect for others:

- Self-care, self-worth, living in line with your own moral principles
- Respect for life and human dignity
- Treating others with courtesy and kindness
- Fairness and justice

We'll see in the upcoming chapters on RESPECT (chapters 17 and 18) that this value is about much more than courtesy and admiration. Respect is an essential rule of engagement for a stable, fair, and just society.

Why RESPONSIBILITY

A moral way of life is a life of responsibility. It's constantly being aware of how our actions create consequences and it's living up to the demands of both give-and-take in our relationships. To reap the benefits of being part of society, one takes on reciprocal responsibilities—because with rights come duties. The belief systems all included guidance on responsibility to oneself and to others:

- Developing oneself; Exercising self-control, balance, and moderation
- Taking care of others; Reciprocating with good will
- Personal accountability for your actions and consequences

In the chapters on RESPONSIBILITY (chapters 19 and 20), we'll see that even though responsibility may feel like a weight to carry, it also liberates us and empowers self-determination.

Why COMPASSION

Compassion is about connecting with each other as fellow travelers who are all experiencing the wonders and the tragedies that are part of being human. Each belief system includes themes around caring for others not just out of obligation, but with a sense of empathy and benevolence:

- Friendliness, goodwill, graciousness
- Forgiveness, mercy
- Unselfishness, generosity, charity

In the upcoming chapters on COMPASSION (chapter 21 and 22) we'll see that this moral direction point isn't just about relieving suffering.

Compassion requires us to find balance between competing needs and it encourages us to enjoy life together.

A path forward

There's a lot of great guidance in the world's belief systems, but it can be a bit overwhelming to sift through in the moment you're making a decision. To make it manageable, we've put four main points on our moral compass: TRUTH, RESPECT, RESPONSIBILITY, and COMPASSION. There may be more good traits we could choose from and there are overlaps and nuances among these traits. Yet in any given decision, these four can serve as a reminder about the core values we can all agree on. With our trusty moral compass in mind, we can consider different paths and know whether following them will take us in the right direction:

- *Is the path truthful?*
- *Is it respectful?*
- *Is it responsible?*
- *Is it compassionate?*

Still seem like it's too high level? I hear you. We just organized thousands of years of wisdom into four points, so next we need to learn how to use that compass in the context of modern life. One recurring theme in this book is that balance is essential for long-term stability. As Aristotle pointed out, being virtuous isn't just about having a lot of a good trait. He warned us that *you can, in fact, have too much of a good thing.* Is it possible there can be too much respect? Too much compassion? Too much truth or responsibility going on in society today?

To answer those intriguing questions, we'll get more in-depth with TRUTH, RESPECT, RESPONSIBILITY, and COMPASSION in the coming chapters, exploring what they are and how to live in balance with them.

Journaling

How does the situation in the opening quote reflect some of the big issues we face today? Do we always know how to solve a moral dilemma in an ideal way?

How does this moral compass compare to your current guiding principles? If anything is missing, where might it fit on this compass?

Do you tend to emphasize one point of the compass more than the others in your own choices?

Up Next

Who would've thought that we would ever need to debate what truth is and why it should matter? And yet here we are on the threshold of a "post-truth" society. In the next three chapters, we'll take a closer look at TRUTH and get some concrete definitions on the difference between honesty and deception—and we'll see why the difference definitely matters.

Chapter 14

What Is Truth?

Why we paint the truth in shades of gray

We all bend the truth sometimes. We spin a little to soften the hard truths; we embellish to make ourselves look better; we dramatize to capture attention. But when does bending the truth go too far? Few people would argue that malicious lies told to hurt someone are ever morally acceptable. Yet, how many of us actually expect to be told the cold, hard truth, all the time? Honesty may be the best policy, but there are a lot of gray areas around how much truth we choose to share. And today, a whole industry exists around selling us lies that we're all too eager to believe. In this age when people toss around the idea of a "post-truth" era, what even is truth and why does it matter? If truth is to take its place as a guiding direction on our moral compass, the first thing we need to do is establish what truth—and truthful behavior—are.

The Moral Compass- Truth

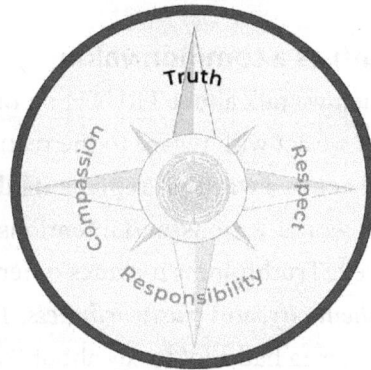

Truth

Compassion

Respect

Responsibility

Defining truth

The truth is factual and objectively accurate. It's the way things really are and the way they really happened, unaltered by spin, manipulation, or wishful thinking. If we're being honest with ourselves, we have to separate what we want to be true—what we feel should be true— from the actual facts that exist in reality. Real truth is based on reliable, accurate, relevant evidence.[1]

Here's the tricky bit: People can look at the same truthful information and see things differently. We can have different perspectives about the same facts. But as for the facts themselves—they're either accurate or they're not. *When people alter the facts for their own ulterior motives, they deceive us. When we deny facts we don't want to believe, we deceive ourselves.* In chapter 16 "The Post-Truth Con," we'll look more in-depth at deception and modern life. For now, we first need to recognize that truth is based in factual reality, whether we like the truth or not.

Truth as a common value

When we talk about TRUTH on our moral compass, we're talking about how we act with regard to the truth. **Being truthful means that we speak and act in a way that represents things as they are in factual reality.** Our words, actions, and intentions are genuine, free from falsehoods or deceit. Truthfulness includes other specific virtues like *honesty*, *sincerity*, *authenticity*, and *trustworthiness*. The world belief systems we saw in chapter 12 had a lot to say about truthfulness. Here's a quick summary:

True speech– Using words that accurately represent what we mean; not exaggerating or downplaying; not making false accusations or claims; not spreading false information. Lying, gossip, and rumor are forms of dishonest speech.

True intentions– Being honest with oneself and others about why we are doing something; being free of false pretense. Two vices that show a lack of true intentions are 1) *rationalizing*, which is when we create irrelevant or false reasons to justify choices and 2) *hypocrisy*, which is when we hold others to a moral standard that we don't live up to ourselves.

True action– Being honest about what we are doing. Our actions match our words. Deception, cheating, and manipulation are all forms of dishonest action. We can also deceive ourselves, particularly about our true intentions or the real consequences of our actions.

Truth telling in real life

I can hear you sighing. That's a pretty high standard for being truthful and frankly we're not living up to it. But realistically, can we? Should we, in all instances, tell the exact facts, as they happened, in their entirety? Maybe not:

> **Storytelling would be boring**– "To be honest, I caught an average-size fish and it required very little skill."

> **Social situations would be awkward**– "Truthfully, your husband is not funny; he's obnoxious. And I can't wait for you both to leave."

> **Negotiation strategy would become irrelevant**– "I'm truly desperate for you to make this deal, so just tell me what you're willing to pay and I'll agree to it."

Certainly, there are times when telling the-whole-truth-and-nothing-but-the-truth is the right and only option (like when we're under oath.) But the complete truth, all the time, in every situation? That's not how we really live. *Social niceties, white lies, and skillful deceptions are part of how we manage to cooperate and to compete while also being respectful and compassionate with each other.* The question is, where are the lines between bending the truth and committing a moral wrong?

The truth in black, white, and shades of gray

If the morality of truth telling isn't as simple as "always telling the truth" and "never telling a lie," then we need a different way to gauge whether we're being morally truthful. To echo Aristotle, **we need to know how to tell the right amount of truth, in the right way, for the right motive.** So let's take a cue from this ancient wisdom and put truth on a continuum that shows a full range of blacks, whites, and grays—from *too little truth* to *too much truth.* With a continuum, we take absolutes out of the picture and welcome the nuance that is real life.

> **We'll see what too little truth looks like–** What's the difference between a polite white lie and a morally wrong deception?

> **We'll see what too much truth looks like–** What's the difference between telling someone a hard truth they need to hear and selfish cruelty?

The truth continuum will help us navigate the gray areas where we balance being truthful with our concerns about treating people with respect, responsibility, and compassion. Sound confusing? Don't worry—we have infographics.

The Truth Continuum

Take a browse through the Truth Continuum. To help it make sense, think of the story of Goldilocks—some amount of truth is just right, but some amounts are too much or too little. Let's walk through it, starting in the middle of the continuum with morally good truth.

The Truth Continuum

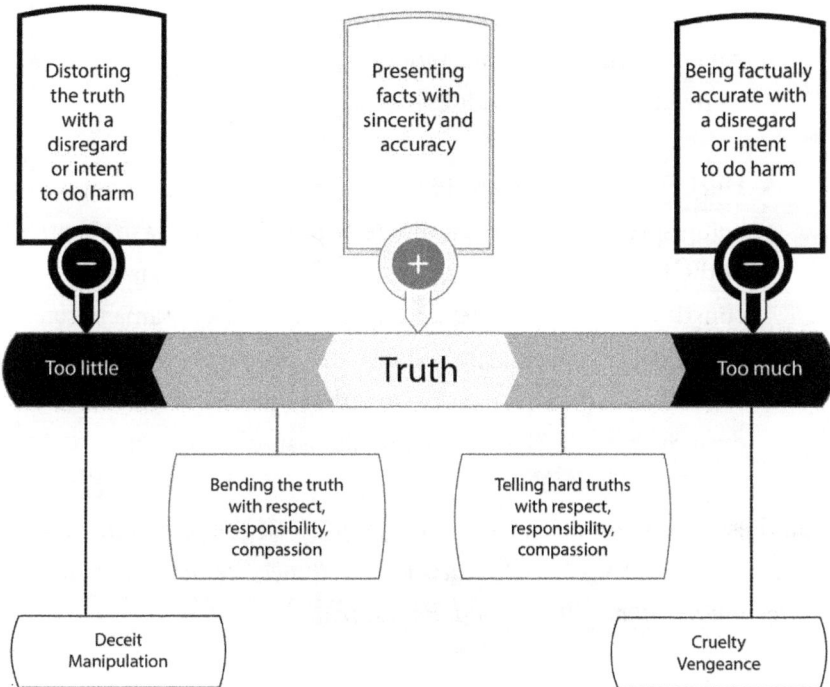

Distorting the truth with a disregard or intent to do harm

Presenting facts with sincerity and accuracy

Being factually accurate with a disregard or intent to do harm

Too little

Truth

Too much

Bending the truth with respect, responsibility, compassion

Telling hard truths with respect, responsibility, compassion

Deceit
Manipulation

Cruelty
Vengeance

THE GOOD, HONEST TRUTH

Looking at the middle of our truth continuum, we can see that morally good truthfulness is about *presenting facts as they really are, with a sincere intent to be accurate.* It's important to note that in morality, *intent* matters. If we truly intend to be accurate but accidentally get some information wrong, that's an honest mistake. Ideally though, we present information, ourselves, and our motives without exaggeration, downplaying, or deceit, even if sharing the truth comes at a personal cost. Let's look at some examples of good, honest truthfulness:

- Someone dents your car when you aren't around and leaves a note so you can contact them about repairs.

- An employee tells a boss about a problem with a product so it can be fixed before the product is sold to the public.

- During the 2008 US presidential campaign, false rumors were being spread that then candidate Barack Obama wasn't a citizen of the US. His opponent in the race, John McCain, faced a constituent who said she couldn't trust Barack Obama because she heard he was "an Arab." John McCain responded, "No ma'am. He's a decent family man, citizen, that I just happen to have disagreements with on fundamental issues."[2]

In all these examples, despite some negative consequences to themselves, *people chose to value truth while acting with respect, responsibility, and compassion for others. That's good, honest truth.*

TOO LITTLE TRUTH

Moving to one extreme of the continuum, we have *too little truth*—when someone **changes the facts, misrepresents the situation, manipulates, or intentionally withholds information, with a disregard for the harm it may cause.** Even worse, they may deceive with the intent to cause harm. For example:

- Someone dents your car when you aren't around and leaves a note with a fake phone number so onlookers think they're being honest, but you won't be able to contact them about repairs.

- An employee changes safety data to hide a product problem that ultimately harms consumers.

- Despite evidence that confirms the truth, a politician continues to spread rumors and distort facts to manipulate supporters into doing things that will serve the politician's purposes.

In each of these examples, not only did people act dishonestly by sacrificing truth, they also *acted with disrespect, irresponsibility, or a lack of compassion for the people they impacted. That's immoral lack of truth.*

TOO MUCH TRUTH

On the other extreme of the continuum, we have *too much truth*. When someone says, "Why's everyone so upset? I'm just saying what's true," they've **either shared facts they shouldn't have, or they could have told the truth more kindly**. For example:

- A mother, with vicious delight, tells her teenager, "You look ridiculous and you'll never get the job dressed like that. And by the way your brother is smarter than you and I like him better."

- Rather than share data about a product problem with his boss, an employee goes straight to upper management, hoping to get his boss fired so he can take her job.

- Someone reveals another person's sexual orientation or gender in order to damage them in a community or to incite a threat against them.

In these examples the information shared may have been accurate, but the person telling the truth had malicious intent and they may have acted with cruelty or vengeance. Telling the whole, accurate truth can be wrong when it's done for the wrong reasons, or in a way that's disrespectful, irresponsible, or lacks compassion.

Navigating the gray areas

In our look at the blacks and whites of truth telling above, you may have noticed two important factors that help us decide where the lines are between right and wrong.

   1) **INTENT**– Does the truth teller have good or bad intentions?

   2) **CONSEQUENCES**– How does telling the whole truth affect our ability to treat others with respect, responsibility, and compassion?

The morality of truth telling is based on a balance between *accuracy*, *intent*, and *consequences*. *The gray areas about how much truth to tell arise when we feel we have a good reason (intent) to sacrifice some truth (accuracy) in order to treat people with respect, responsibility, and compassion (consequences).*

Hard truths

The gray area between *good, honest truth* and *too much truth* has to do with telling people facts they may not want to hear, facts that may hurt their feelings, and facts that conflict with what they'd like to believe. But there's a time when telling a hard truth is the responsible thing to do. For example:

- An employee is being held back because their coworkers find them abrasive. When they ask their boss why they keep getting passed over for promotions, should their boss tell them the truth they need to correct the issue?

- Someone's beloved sister, who is hopelessly tone deaf, is planning to quit a good job to pursue a career as a singer. Should a caring and compassionate sibling respectfully tell her the truth about her chances at success?

In this gray area, the person hearing the truth may not like the news (especially if it's negative feedback.) But if they need the information to make informed decisions and to have a realistic view of themselves, the person who is denying them the truth, even when it's done with good intentions, may be acting *irresponsibly*.

Of course, being responsible and telling hard truths doesn't mean we should deliver the hard truth with cruel relish. It's not necessary to inform an employee that their social skills have all the finesse of a curmudgeon, nor should one tease their sister that she sings like a dying cow. While these descriptions may be creatively accurate, there's a respectful and compassionate way to deliver hard truths while softening the blow. And, telling hard truths is about being responsible, not about meddling where it's none of your business. If a stranger walks up to a family in a restaurant and volunteers, "Nobody asked me, but your child is a spoiled brat who needs to learn some manners," we may all be thinking it, and it may be undeniably accurate. But that doesn't mean it's our business (responsibility) to interfere.

> The morality of truth telling is based on a balance between accuracy, intent, and consequences.

Polite and skillful lies

Between *good, honest truth* and *too little truth*, is the gray area where we bend the truth, with good intentions, and minimal consequences. This is the land of white lies, negotiation tactics, and positive spin. The danger in this gray area is that there's a point where we can stray too far from the truth and we may be doing it for the wrong reasons—we can cross a line into manipulation and deceit. How do we know where that line is? We need to look to *intent* and the *consequences* we cause to respect, responsibility, and compassion. Let's use some scenarios to explore where the line is.

The Gift– A child tells their grandparent they like a present, even though they won't use it, in order to show compassion for Grandma's feelings. That's a white lie. But, if the child tells Grandma they can't use the gift because it arrived broken in the hopes that Grandma will send something else, that's manipulation.

The Ill-fitting Shirt– On the way out the door to a dinner party, a husband asks his spouse if his shirt is too snug (which it is). His wife says, "I think that fit is in style right now." That's spin. But, if the wife intentionally buys her husband clothes that are too snug with the hope he'll be encouraged to lose weight, that's manipulation. And if not telling her husband the truth will cause him public humiliation, that's a negative consequence that a responsible and compassionate wife would try to prevent.

The Deal– A salesperson accurately describes a product and then tells the customer how eager other buyers are, hoping to prompt the customer to make a decision (even though there's plenty of inventory.) The customer is making their decision based on accurate product data, with a push of urgency. That's a negotiation tactic. But, if the salesperson intentionally overinflates performance data or invents non-existent customers to steer the buyer's decision based on falsehoods, that's deceit.

In each situation we can see whether someone had good intentions that caused minimal consequences or we can see that they had ulterior motives which required them to trick someone in order to benefit themselves. *If someone is tricking or manipulating someone else for their own gain, that usually means they've crossed the line into an immoral wrong.*

The unintended consequences of white lies

The gray areas are gray because we come into them with good intentions, but even good intentions can have unintended negative consequences. When we hide or bend the truth, we're making a decision about how much information someone should have. In his book, *Lying*, best-selling author Sam Harris proposes that while we may think we're telling a white lie out of compassion, white lies can actually be disrespectful.

> When we presume to lie for the benefit of others, we have decided that *we* are the best judges of how much they should understand about their own lives—about how they appear, their reputations, or their prospects in the world. ... Unless someone is suicidal or otherwise on the brink, deciding how much he should know about himself seems the quintessence of arrogance. What attitude could be more disrespectful of those we care about?[3]

When we're considering consequences, we need to keep in mind that the person we think we're helping with a white lie might really have preferred the truth so that they would have a more realistic assessment of themselves. You may recall from chapter 5 that if we want to have *self-respect*, we need to take an honest look at ourselves, including the stuff we're proud of and the stuff we're not happy with, so we can choose how we want to live. White lies lead us to a false understanding of ourselves. They deny us information we need to control our own lives. And, they encourage us to live in an alternate reality—our own land of make-believe. If everyone else is living in reality, and we're living in a land of make-believe, we look the fool.

A path forward

In this age when people debate what the truth even is, we as a society must agree that the truth is about accurate facts that exist in reality. *Sometimes people won't like the facts, and that's why there are times, in order to cooperate and compete without harming each other, we present the truth in a way that also honors respect, responsibility, and compassion.* We navigate the gray areas around truth telling so we can decide when there is a time to speak up and a time to stay silent; when there is a time for the hard truth and a time for a softer, more polite version of the truth. But at the end of the day, we need the truth. We'll see in the next two chapters that the truth is essential to our well-being as individuals and as a society. Without it, we don't have a shared reality.

Journaling

Were any of the virtues and behaviors included in truthfulness surprising to you? (For example, sincerity and trustworthiness or not rationalizing or being hypocritical.)

Have you ever been told a white lie but wish you'd been told the truth? Why?

Are there any truths or lies you've told where you might need to rethink whether it was the right thing to do?

Up next

We've taken an in-depth look at what truth is and how we navigate moral choices around truth. In the next chapter, we'll ask ourselves, *Who cares?* Why does the truth even matter?

Chapter 15

Trust Me
Why the truth still matters

Ash: You know my boss, right? The one who tells each of us in the department different stories to get what he wants?

Forrest: Yes, you've mentioned how the whole department is looking forward to the day he gets what's coming to him.

Ash: Well, I asked him a question yesterday and he paused… I could see him thinking about which lies he had told so he could be sure he told me the right line. I knew then, it didn't matter what he said next. I wouldn't believe him.

There's a reason we don't like people who manipulate the truth—we can't trust them. Like the boss in the dialog above, people with a reputation for dishonesty threaten our ability to make smart choices and to predict what's going to happen next. Dishonesty makes life an unstable guessing game. Talk about feeling like life is off-kilter! Truth is as important today as ever because it's how we're able to trust each other—and civilized life doesn't work without trust. Let's see how playing with the truth takes a toll not just on society, but on each of us personally.

Good decisions depend on good data

Every day we make countless decisions. From small choices to life-altering moves, we depend on accurate information to make informed decisions:

- Which of these milk cartons is the lactose-free kind?
- Does this product really work?
- Is this person too good to be true?
- Is this cause worth my time and money?

Our ability to choose wisely depends on the information we use to guide our choice. People who are lactose-intolerant would be pretty upset if the milk company put false labels on the milk containers. That's a relatively small choice that could lead to an uncomfortable afternoon. For many of us, that level of deception would be bad enough. But how about when someone invests their heart, their money, or their life based on false information? Recently, we've seen deception lead people to make life-changing decisions. For example:

Ask the investors who lost hundreds of millions in the Theranos medical testing scandal, and the patients whose doctors adjusted treatments based on the company's blood tests, if they would have preferred that the CEO was more honest about product performance.[1]

Ask the people who stormed the Capitol building on January 6, 2021 if they would've liked to know that Sidney Powell, one of the lawyers who architected the 2020 election fraud cases, would later defend herself to the court by stating that given the "outlandish" nature of her claims about voter fraud, "reasonable people would not accept such statements as fact."[2]

Every day, reasonable people depend on accurate information from other presumably reasonable people to guide decisions. *If we look the other way and allow a culture of deceptions and outrageous claims to take root, we lose the ability to be reasonable.* Every one of us has a vested interest in a culture that is rooted in decency, with truth and honesty being the standard for individuals, companies, causes, our leaders, and society at large. We simply can't make informed choices and control our own lives with good judgment without it.

Society runs on trust

Truth is so important to daily life, we don't even think about it most of the time. Psychologists call this the *truth bias*, which means that rather than objectively analyzing everything we encounter in a day, we assume what we are seeing and hearing is true.[3] We assume we're able to trust that things, people, and situations are what they present themselves to be. For example, let's say you go to the coffee shop:

> You trust that when you order your dark roast, you'll actually get coffee, not some other brown-colored beverage. You trust it has been made as promised and is free from stuff that will make you sick. You trust that when you hand over your money, the clerk will reciprocate and hand back your coffee. When you get in your car and drive off, you trust that other drivers sincerely intend to obey stop signs and that bridge inspectors have honestly checked construction quality. Once you get to work, you do your job, trusting that the company has the genuine intention and legitimate financial resources to pay you in a couple weeks after you've already given them your time and effort.

But in a society where we can't know or believe what's true, we can't trust in each other or the processes that make everyday life possible. We'd have to scrutinize every decision, research every transaction, and doubt strangers, friends, and family. In her book, *Liespotting*, Pamela Meyer, a leading researcher on lying, states that without a truth bias,

> Our civilization could not survive. ... How could any normal human transactions and activities take place? Commerce would fail before it began; explorations and discoveries would founder; even normal parent-child relationships would be tangled by mistrust.[4]

Truth is the foundation of that trust. *Honesty, integrity, sincerity—these are the values that enable us to trust each other enough to cooperate. And you simply can't trust people who lie, manipulate, and deceive.*

Lying leaves a mark

If life were purely transactional, maybe we could get by with less truth. But life is built around relationships. We build rapport; we give people credit; we develop reputations; we establish reciprocity. That's why psychologist and researcher Robert Feldman says that all lies, even white lies, involve deception and a degree of victimization—and that leaves a mark. In *The Liar in Your Life*, Feldman reports that studies show how even small acts of deceit leave a "smudge" on the interaction.[5] Over time, we can accumulate a build-up of smudges and eventually the grimy finish can cause us to lose trust in one another and become cynical.

It's worse when we know we've been lied to out outright. Feldman reports that study participants who had been lied to "immediately formed a negative impression of the individual who had lied to them" and they saw the liar as "untrustworthy, unlikable, and generally more devious."[6] What's more, in future interactions, the person who had been deceived typically increased how much they lied to the original liar. When we play with the truth, we invite distrust and deceit in return. *In terms of dishonesty, it seems we really do get back what we put out.*

In contrast, in communities where people know they can trust each other, the "transaction costs" of everyday life are lower, which Harvard researcher Robert Putnam explains, improves our lives in unexpected ways.[7] In trusting communities, the background stress for daily life is lower, and this ultimately leads to greater life expectancy. Trust not only enhances life, it pays well. Economists have discovered that "trusting communities, other things being equal, have a measurable economic advantage."[8]

Lying costs us personally

Clearly lying costs us in the eyes of other people. But what does it do to our own sense of self when we choose to lie? Research shows that even for small lies, the liar can experience a "twinge of distress" that leaves them feeling a little worse than they did before lying, and the effects last even after the lie is over.[9] These twinges are what we talked about in chapter 5 on *self-respect*, which comes from knowing we are making choices that are in line with what we think is right. When someone lies, assuming they value honesty, those twinges impact their sense of self. *Lying costs us in the eyes of others and in our own self-reflection.*

> Our bodies help us to know we're lying,
> even when we don't want to listen.

A path forward

Truth and trust are as important as ever in our daily lives. We need accurate information to make informed decisions. We need trust to cooperate with everyone from the clerk at the coffee shop to work colleagues, government agencies, and our friends and families. A culture of truth and trust helps us live with each other, and it helps us live in a state of respect with ourselves.

Of course, we established in the last chapter that absolute truth all the time isn't really how we live. To cooperate and also compete with kindness, we adjust *how we tell the truth* so that we can preserve our other principles around respect, responsibility, and compassion as well. But that doesn't mean truth doesn't matter. It doesn't mean we should throw out our value for *all* truth just because *sometimes* it makes sense to be *polite* with the truth. What it does mean is that ***we need to have clear standards and expectations for truth, and we need to enforce consequences for the types of deception that undermine our ability to trust each other.***

Journaling

Have you ever made a decision and then found out you based your choice on false information? Would having accurate information have changed things?

Who in your life is trustworthy? How do they act?

Has anyone ever broken your trust? In what way? How did you treat them afterward?

Up next

If the truth and trust are so important, why is deception so prevalent? And why are people so willing to be deceived? In the next chapter, we'll look at these questions and discover insights that will help us reestablish our standards for truthful behavior.

Chapter 16

The Post-Truth Con

Why people lie and why we're willing to believe them

If a person gave away your body to some passerby, you'd be furious.
Yet you hand over your mind to anyone who comes along, so they may
abuse you, leaving it disturbed.

—Epictetus, Greek Stoic Philosopher[1]

Lies and deception undermine our ability to function as a society. We
saw in the last chapter that we all have a vested interest in maintaining
a standard for honesty in our words and actions. If the truth is so
important, why do people seem so willing to believe lies? In today's
"post-truth" culture, we not only allow misinformation to stand, but some
people embrace it, share it, and bond with others based on it.

Epictetus, the Stoic philosopher quoted at the start of this chapter,
presents an interesting perspective: *By allowing others to deceive us, we are
granting them the power to do us harm.* I don't know about you, but I just
got a lot less comfortable with allowing this "post-truth" era to continue.
In this final chapter on TRUTH, the first direction on our moral compass,
let's take a look at today's culture of rampant misinformation and take
charge of reestablishing a culture rooted in truth.

Defining post-truth

Today, falsehoods—and people's willingness to embrace them—are so common that a new term emerged to describe the phenomenon: *post-truth*. The word became the Oxford Dictionaries Word of the Year 2016 after its use rose dramatically during the Brexit and US presidential election campaigns.[2] The definition of post-truth is as an adjective describing circumstances where "objective facts are less influential in shaping public opinion than appeals to emotion and personal belief."[3] In his book, *Post-Truth*, philosophy and ethics researcher Lee McIntyre expands on this idea. He says,

> Many see post-truth as part of a growing international trend where some feel emboldened to try to bend reality to fit their opinions, rather than the other way around. This is not necessarily a campaign to say that facts do not matter, but instead a conviction that facts can always be shaded, selected, and presented within a political context that favors one interpretation of truth over another.[4]

Given our look at what truth is and why it's so important (chapters 14 and 15), it's not surprising that post-truth does not suggest that the truth doesn't matter or that facts are subjective. *What a post-truth era really represents is a climate where the truth exists, but people are willing to put it aside, to rationalize it, or to hide from it completely, so that they can choose to believe what they are comfortable believing.*

What makes this climate possible? A variety of industrial lobbies, politicians, radio/podcasts hosts, fake news creators, and biased news sources have earned a share of the blame for creating an environment in which facts are readily manipulated or selectively interpreted.[5] At the end of the day, each of those actors wants something—power, money, an audience—and they're playing with the truth to get what they want from others. But if we take a step back, that means *the people who believe their deceptions, they're the marks.* If we don't want to be conned, we should start by looking at how we are contributing to a culture of easy lies.

We train others to lie to us

Why do some people lie more easily and more often than others? One reason can be found in how we learn about lying when we're young. In *NurtureShock: New Thinking about Children*, Po Bronson and Ashley Merryman present data that shows how ignoring lies encourages more lying.[6] In studies, researchers found that when a child was caught lying to cover up a wrong-doing, 99% of parents only addressed the wrong-doing and ignored the lie meant to cover it up. Let's use a quick dialog to demonstrate:

> *A parent sees an empty bag of cookies and a child with cookie crumbs on their face.*
>
> Parent: Did you eat the cookies?
>
> Child: No.
>
> Parent: I told you not to eat the cookies. No dessert for you.

In this typical scenario, the parent knew the child was lying (the evidence being right there on the child's face), yet the parent ignored the lie and only addressed the original wrong-doing. What did the child learn?— That lies only have upside. Next time, the child can hope that the lie will work, but even if it doesn't, they know they won't lose anything for trying to deceive. In fact, studies that observed children's behavior over time revealed that after age six, a third of children who discover that lying is "a successful strategy for handling difficult social situations [will] stick with it."[7] *Ignoring lying, no matter the reasons for looking the other way, doesn't make people become honest.*

What really works to get a child to be honest is to teach them that you value honesty and that you'll reward honest behavior. One of the world's leading experts on children and lying behaviors, Dr. Victoria Talwar, found that if you want kids to tell the truth, you have to show them that you'll be happier if they tell you the truth than if they just tell you what you want to hear.[8] (If you want to know how to address this as a parent, check the notes section for an article about how to teach kids to be honest.[9]) From an adult perspective, the lesson we can take from this is that when we don't challenge lies, we send a message that people have nothing to lose by trying to deceive us. *If we want to prevent a culture of easy deceit, we have to value and reward honesty while we have consequences for dishonesty.*

We are participants in mythmaking

Another reason people lie to us is that we're all too willing to believe them. Your child, a friend, a politician, a salesman… sometimes we want what they're saying to be true. Pamela Meyer is one of the world's leading experts on lying. In her book *Liespotting*, Meyer points out an unpleasant truth about how we're deceived:

> The liar and the recipient participate in a fabric of mythmaking together. A lie does not have power by its utterance—its power lies in someone agreeing to believe the lie.[10]

Psychology professor Robert Feldman, in *The Liar in Your Life*, explains a similar idea: When we want to believe, both the liar and the target of the lie are "hoping on some level that the lie won't be revealed for what it is."[11] (*Really, I lost my charger so my phone wasn't working all those times you called.*) The fact is, we're often willing accomplices in the lies we're told. And sometimes, we're both the liar and the believer, convincing ourselves of what we want to be true.

Consistency beats truth

Why are we so quick to embrace convenient falsehoods? Sometimes, our minds and our bodies work together to motivate us to seek consistency over truth, thanks to a psychological phenomenon called *cognitive dissonance*.[12] As rational, thinking beings, we like our world to make sense. So when our beliefs, external information, or our own actions contradict each other, something feels "off"—our bodies feel a tension that psychologists call *dissonance*. Remember from chapter 3 that our bodies give us cues about what's going on in our world. Cognitive dissonance is a signal: *Alert! Alert! These things don't line up.* It feels uncomfortable, and we want to get rid of the nagging stress of dissonance.

To ease the discomfort, we try to get the beliefs, behaviors, or pieces of information (cognitions) to be less in conflict with each other. To illustrate how this works, let's use a sort of simplified mental equation (though we don't literally do this.) Our body tells us that Cognition A is not consistent with Cognition B, so to ease the discomfort we're feeling, we try to get A and B to be more in alignment with each other. Let's use a real-world example to clarify.

Cognition A	Cognition B
My doctor told me it's important to my health that I eat less sugar.	I am eating cake.

Our minds know that eating cake is not consistent with eating less sugar, and that makes us feel dissonance.

We can change side B and stop eating the cake.

Or, we can change our perception of side A to make it less of a problem: *The doctor is exaggerating the risk. How reliable is the science anyway? I know lots of people who eat cake and are perfectly healthy.*

Changing behavior is hard. Changing deep-seated beliefs is hard. But changing our attitude about information we don't want to agree with, that's pretty easy. One of the leading researchers in cognitive dissonance, Elliott Aronson, and fellow researcher Carol Tavris, explain that as soon as we make a choice, we begin to justify that choice in our own minds.

Over time, we believe that our mental reconciliations are the real, actual truth. And as decisions build on previous choices, people "find it harder to admit they were wrong at the outset. Especially when the end result proves self-defeating, wrongheaded, or harmful."[13] *We tell ourselves what we want to hear, and then become true believers in our own deceptions.*

> There's the easy way,
> and there's the right way.

We protect our self-image

The effects of cognitive dissonance are even more powerful when one side of the mental equation is about our self-image. Aronson and Tavris explain that dissonance is the most uncomfortable when it affects whether we can honestly see ourselves as "kind, ethical, competent, or smart."[14] This is an epic bit of insight.

> *Using this over-simplified mental equation may force someone into a corner where believing new information would mean they also have to believe they aren't as smart, moral, and capable as they thought they were.*

Cognitive dissonance can provide a powerful incentive to discount the truth in order to protect our self-image. Let's illustrate what's going on here.

Cognition A	Cognition B
I am smart, capable, and moral. Integrity matters to me.	A news source reveals that a politician I strongly support has been accused of doing something immoral.

Our minds know that these two cognitions don't match.

When we consider side A, we can take a hard look at ourselves: *If I'm smart and capable, how could I have chosen this crook? If I support someone who is immoral, what does that say about my morality?*

On the other hand, we can just change our attitude about side B: *The evidence isn't clear. The news source isn't reliable. What the politician did wasn't really that bad. Sometimes the ends justify the means. Have you seen the awful things the other party does?*

When facing contradictory beliefs, information, and behaviors, we can:

1) Do the hard thing and look for the truth, even if it means we have to change a behavior or see unpleasant facts about ourselves.

2) Do the easy thing and rationalize our way out of the contradiction.

Cognitive dissonance research shows that "human beings engage in all kinds of cognitive gymnastics aimed at justifying their own behavior."[15] There are plenty of excuses we can use to reconcile cognitive dissonance. To name a few, we can:

- discredit the messenger
- discount the facts
- turn blame in a different direction
- look for information to validate what we want to believe (confirmation bias)
- surround ourselves with people who agree with our views

The danger is that we become both the liar and the one being deceived. What's even more dangerous is when we rationalize away our own moral beliefs in order not to believe unpleasant truths. (*How important is integrity anyway? Look at how the other side acts. They started it.*) We may be embracing the all-too-appealing fantasy of our own rationalizations because it's easier than facing the truth.

Dealing with dissonance

Cognitive dissonance isn't a one-size-fits-all. Of course, different people will deal with dissonance in different ways. Some people are willing to look at hard truths and adjust their behavior. And yes, sometimes our rationalizations have an element of truth in them. Before you put this new information about cognitive dissonance into an over-simplified mental equation and decide you can dismiss the whole thing because you found one easy reason to discount it (*See what I did there? Wink.*), the point of recognizing cognitive dissonance is that *once we're aware of how people tend to deal with information that makes them uncomfortable, we can approach situations in a way that increases our chances of reaching the truth.*

4 Tips for Managing Cognitive Dissonance

1. Avoid making someone take a blow to their self-image in order to change their belief.

People feel more dissonance—and are more likely to defend themselves rather than accept new information—when their self-image is in the equation.[16] Don't try to convince them to believe the truth in a way that would make them question their own self-worth.

> *Don't say:* "The whole idea was stupid and immoral. How could you have agreed with it?"

> *Do say:* "I'm sure a lot of factors influenced your thinking. You might consider this information important too."

2. Allow people to accept new information without an accusation that they should've known better.

People feel less dissonance—and are less tied to defending their beliefs—if they could not have anticipated the current circumstances when they originally supported a belief.[17] Not surprisingly, "I told you so" doesn't win friends and influence people.

> *Don't say:* "Anyone could've seen how badly this would turn out."

> *Do say:* "You made a decision based on the information you had at the time. This new information may change your thinking."

3. Live with the dissonance instead of looking for a quick fix.

When we learn to live with the uncomfortable feeling of dissonance, we give ourselves the chance to self-reflect and we may find that contradictory beliefs, information, and action can co-exist. This is what cognitive dissonance experts Aronson and Tavris call the "Shimon Peres solution." They explain that former US President Ronald Reagan and former Israeli Prime Minister Shimon Peres were world leaders with a close relationship. When Reagan made a diplomatic visit that Peres was upset about, Peres had two cognitions to reconcile—a friend and an insensitive action. He could have downplayed the friendship or he could have downplayed the seriousness of the breach of friendship. Instead, Aronson and Tavris explain: "[Peres] did neither. 'When a friend makes a mistake,' he said, 'the friend remains a friend, and the mistake remains a mistake.'"[18] The way Peres handled the situation shows that we can stay in the dissonance; and rather than reacting automatically, we can give ourselves the time to respond more mindfully.

4. Change the equation

The over-simplified mental equation we use to weigh conflicting ideas is just that: over-simplified. We can recognize that issues, beliefs, and behaviors are complex. Sometimes, in our partisan culture with its amplified all-or-nothing thinking, we may feel like we have to reject anything that appears to counter our beliefs or is a threat to our identity as a loyal supporter of that belief. Yet we can remain a loyal supporter while we also consider other points of view or even refine our position.

- Someone can be a dedicated group member **and** disagree with some aspect of how the group wants to achieve its goals.

- Someone can be a supporter of a cause **and** be open to understanding other views.

Living with cognitive dissonance for a moment gives us the opportunity to expand our thinking beyond simple categories and easy answers. It helps us reengage the mindful thinking we saw in chapter 2 that has helped humans thrive through conflict and hardship. *Rather than narrowing our perspective to gain a false sense of stability, we can evaluate, reason, and consciously choose what to believe based on the whole truth.*

A path forward

It would be easier to blame the liars, deceivers, and misinformation generators for the poor state of truth in our culture. But this chapter was one of those hard truths we talked about in chapter 14—it's not pleasant to hear, but if we want an accurate view of ourselves, we have to be willing to look in the mirror.

The post-truth era is essentially culturally-condoned deception. It's an excuse to believe what we want to believe and to allow people to exploit us for their own gain. We have the power to take control. We can decide not to "hand over our minds to anyone who comes along" as Epictetus pointed out. *We can value and reward honesty while we criticize and enforce a consequence for deceit.*

Within ourselves, the drive to relieve the tension of cognitive dissonance with some quick mental compromises may be strong—but protecting our self-image short-term will cost us our self-respect long-term. *To be rooted in decency, and enjoy the stable self-worth that brings, we have to be honest with ourselves, and with each other.*

Journaling

Have you ever hoped what someone was telling you was true so much that you believed them despite your doubts? How did it turn out?

How did your parents treat lying? How did that shape your view of honesty?

Have you felt that nagging sense that two beliefs, actions, or new facts didn't match? What did you do about it?

Up next

We've explored TRUTH, the first point on our moral compass. In the next few chapters, we'll move on to RESPECT, the next guiding principle on our compass—what it is, why it's important, and what are some of the ways to live rooted in respect in today's culture.

Chapter 17

What Is Respect?

How too little and too much respect are destabilizing society

Let's take our moral compass back out of our pocket and check our bearings. We just explored TRUTH, so now let's change course to explore RESPECT. Ask any American about the state of respect in our culture today and you'll likely get an earful—"Social media is poison!"; "Politics is malignant!"; "Kids these days!" Okay, every generation since the beginning of time has said that last one. The point is, disrespect is everywhere and it's part of the reason we're feeling like the world has gone sideways, wondering what happened to people and what happened to society. So let's get to know RESPECT, and see how both too little respect—and too much respect—are putting our sense of stability off-balance.

The Moral Compass- Respect

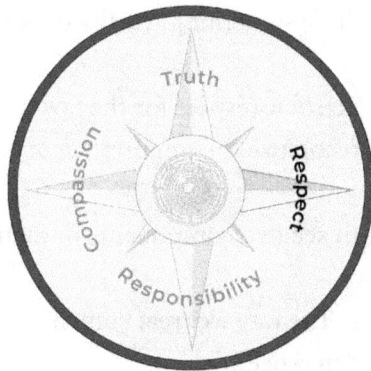

Defining respect

We talk about respect in different flavors, for instance: we treat someone with respect, we have respect for a person, we respect the law. On the surface, it seems like respect has several different meanings around courtesy, admiration, and deference. But underneath, there's a common thread that reveals the true meaning of respect, and it's tied to the fact that *we don't respect just anything*. Respect requires a reason—we're acknowledging something is worth paying attention to and worth altering our actions for.[1] When we use it as a verb, **respect is to take appropriate care with someone or something, because we feel it's important to do so.**[2]

> To *treat* someone with respect means we act courteously *because* we feel the person or the situation warrants it.

> To *have* respect for someone means we admire them *because* they've done something worthy of our esteem.

> To *show* respect for the law means we follow the rules *because* we recognize the importance of order in society.

We can see two components in each of these examples.

> 1) The way we treat someone/something (with courtesy, admiration, deference)

> 2) The reason we do it (because we feel it's worth our effort)

You might want to sit up for a second because these two little insights are a big deal. When you act with respect, *you* are choosing how *you* act in order to preserve something *you* value. Respect isn't simply about being polite or showing admiration; it's about **acknowledging the things you value and acting in a way that honors their worth.** Thinking of respect from this perspective helps human behavior make more sense:

Why treat a stranger we'll never meet again with respectful courtesy? We don't admire the person; we don't even know them. But we do recognize their value as a fellow human, and we recognize the value of maintaining a civilized society.

Why respect someone's freedom to express an opinion you don't agree with? Because we value the freedom to have an opinion—to have control over our own minds. And we value the importance of dialog in a society where we need to find peace between diverse views.

Why treat enemy combatants with a degree of respect? *Wow, that seems like an abrupt shift!* Stay with it for a second, because this example shows how we even have guiding principles of respect for our wartime enemies—people we don't agree with, who have tried to do us harm. Why do we ban abuse and degrading treatment even in war? Because at the heart of respect is our value for human life and dignity.

What these situations show us is that when we treat someone or something with respect, it isn't necessarily because we admire the person or the thing receiving the good treatment, but ***we do value the principle that people and things have worth and should be treated with appropriate care and dignity.***

> Respect doesn't require you to agree with a person to treat them with care and dignity.

Respect as a common value

Respect plays a prominent role in the world's belief systems that we saw in chapter 12. It's woven throughout the teachings not just in specific behaviors, but as an overarching theme that each person should treat others with care. In terms of specific behaviors, the belief systems weave respect throughout human interaction:

Respect for human life– We see this in guidance on not killing, non-violence, and taking action to protect the dignity and well-being of all people, particularly the vulnerable.

Self-respect with humility– The belief systems emphasize that each human should know their own worth but should live without arrogance and selfishness, being aware of their impact on others.

Respect through fairness and justice– All of the systems emphasize that each person should get the rewards they earn as well as suffer the consequences they bring upon themselves. We are personally responsible for the ways we impact others.

Respect in relationships– The expectation that each person should treat others with respect and work toward fairness and reciprocity appears in guidelines about:

- Behavior– treating others with courtesy, graciousness, and benevolence
- Sexuality– respecting commitments and well-being
- Family– honoring elders, caring for those who cared for you
- Property rights– not taking what belongs to others
- Business practices– prohibitions on exploitation and cheating

Finally, all the belief systems emphasize the need for balance and temperance, which is to say respecting boundaries and respecting the demands of morality.

Why respect is important

We saw in chapter 11 that moral values grew out of a need for ground rules that helped humans establish the *trust, fairness,* and *reciprocity* people needed to cooperate and flourish together. It's no surprise then that the world belief systems all included a version of the ultimate ground rule, a.k.a. The Golden Rule—to treat people the way you'd like to be treated. The Golden Rule is fair. It supports reciprocity. It invites trust. Communal life is possible when *we share an unspoken agreement to treat each other and our principles with the respect we'd like in return*:

> I'll treat you with the care and dignity that you deserve, and in return, I expect that you'll treat me with the care and dignity that I deserve. —*That's reciprocal respect for people.*

> I'll honor the ground rules that govern peaceful, cooperative existence, and in return, I expect you to do the same. —*That's reciprocal respect for principles, law, and order.*

> We'll each come into this arrangement of mutual respect with our human dignity, and over time we'll each get what we deserve based on the way we choose to live our lives. —*That's fairness and justice.*

Respect, which is treating people and things with care to preserve something we value (like civil society, law and order, fairness, and justice) is at the core of our ability to live peacefully and productively together.

Respect, fairness, and justice in modern democracy

Fast forward more than a thousand years and we see how these ideas continue to drive a modern democratic society. John Rawls, arguably the most important political philosopher of the 20th century,[3] states in *Justice as Fairness*, that we function as a society by recognizing and following shared principles that guide fair cooperation:

> Reasonable persons ... understand that they are to honor these principles, even at the expense of their own interests as circumstances may require, provided others likewise may be expected to honor them. It is unreasonable ... not to honor fair terms of cooperation that others may reasonably be expected to accept; it is worse than unreasonable if one merely seems, or pretends, to propose or honor them but is ready to violate them to one's advantage as the occasion permits.[4]

Respect is one of those essential ground rules for *reasonable* people who want to manage life among other *reasonable* people. Rawls explains that it may serve *rational* self-interest to take advantage of others or to ignore the rules for your own gain. But in terms of being part of society, it's not *reasonable*, and "common sense views the reasonable but not, in general, the rational, as a moral idea."[5] In plainer words, just because you can, doesn't mean you should.

We've been talking about why life seems off-kilter. People who act *unreasonably* throw a society off balance. *A culture of disrespect, where we can't expect people to treat each other or our governing principles with dignity, care, and fairness, is fundamentally unsettling—it destabilizes the rules of engagement.* Respect is a promise given and an expectation of return that enables us to trust and cooperate with each other in a stable, predictable, and just way.

The Respect Continuum

Now that we've established respect is so much more than being polite or admiring people, let's take a closer look at the degrees of respect. Like we did for TRUTH in chapter 14, let's put RESPECT on a continuum, from *too little respect* to *too much respect*, with a range of blacks, whites, and grays that show degrees of moral right and wrong. The Respect Continuum will show us that a lack of respect isn't just about insults.

Importantly, and perhaps surprisingly, it will show us that too much respect can lead us to blindly sacrifice our own moral principles.

The Respect Continuum

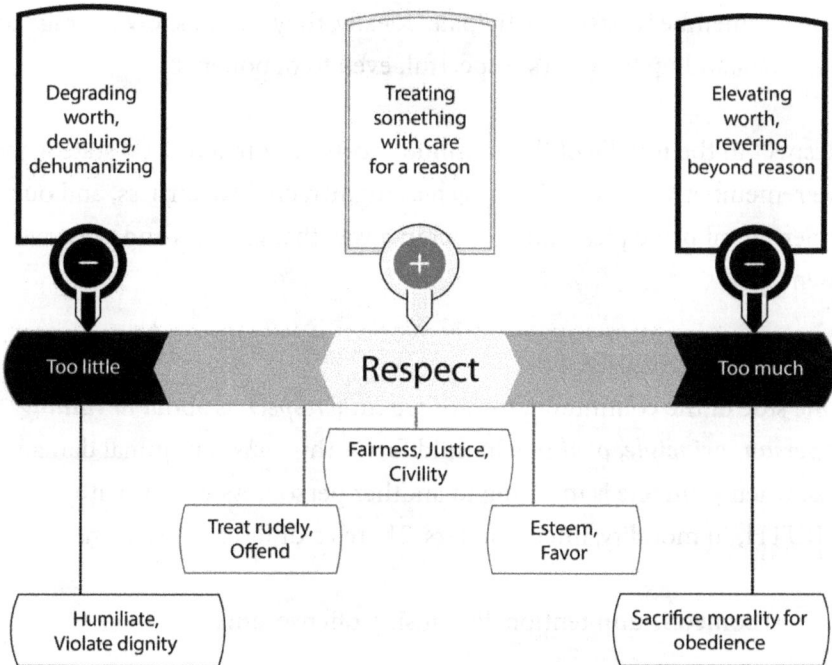

GOOD, MORAL RESPECT

Starting at the middle of the continuum, we have *good, moral respect,* where we **acknowledge the value of someone or something and act in a way that preserves its value.** Let's look at some examples of respect in real life:

- Throughout our day, we treat people with the courtesy and dignity we'd like in return.

- When people disagree with each other, they focus on the reasons why and don't launch into demeaning personal attacks.

- If someone's group wants to do something they would consider degrading if it were being done to them, at a minimum, the group member doesn't participate. Ideally, they would show courage to stand up for what's respectful, even to opponents.

Respect in the middle of the continuum comes from a neutral state where we remember what we value—such as dignity, civility, fairness, and our other moral principles—and we act in a way that protects and preserves them.

TOO LITTLE RESPECT

One side of the continuum, toward *too little respect*, is about **devaluing a person, principle, or thing**. In mild forms this causes minimal damage, like when someone is insulting to another person. As we saw with TRUTH, in morality, intent matters. There's a difference between:

1) someone unintentionally causing offense, and

2) someone intentionally being degrading.

For example, accidentally calling someone by the wrong name is more rude than immoral, while intentionally calling someone by the wrong name may be meant to degrade them.

If we flashback to chapter 2 where we talked about how cognitive distortions (like catastrophizing and labeling) are leading people to exaggerate or downplay harm, we may need to more carefully consider how we're assessing degrees of disrespect today.

When we treat an accidental or mild offense as if it's as bad as an act that demeans or humiliates—or on the other hand when we treat degrading behavior as if it's no big deal—that distorts our ability to fairly assess disrespect.

We need degrees by which we can accurately judge the gray areas. When everything is pronounced a catastrophe, it feels like nothing is that bad. When everything is dismissed, it feels like nothing is being acknowledged. We need balance in all our moral principles, including accuracy about the severity of disrespect, and compassion for those who cause unintended offense.

As we move even further on the continuum toward *too little respect*, the value of something can be dismissed completely. With people, this is the act of dehumanizing—stripping people of their worth and dignity. Renowned moral philosopher Jonathan Glover, in *Humanity: A Moral History of the Twentieth Century*, examines how people were able to behave with such cruelty and violence toward each other in recent history. He found that humans are able to suspend their morality and stop their natural aversion to cruelty, in part, by dehumanizing their victims. Regular people were able to violate, torture, and kill because they stopped seeing their opponents as people. A lack of respect for our principles around dignity, fairness, and compassion can lead to the guiding light of our humanity being extinguished.

TOO MUCH RESPECT

To the other side of the respect continuum, *too much respect*, we **elevate the value of something**. In healthy, moral forms, we acknowledge that someone or something is worthy of our admiration and we treat them with extra appreciation, like people who persevere despite challenges or people who accomplish something extraordinary. When we're compelled to respect someone for their moral goodness, kindness, or compassion, our bodies help us recognize it with a "warm, uplifting" feeling that social scientist Jonathan Haidt says "makes a person want to help others and to become a better person."[6] These are all examples of a positive state of respect, where we raise the value of something that deserves it.

Further down the continuum though, *too much respect can morph into something more dangerous, where we elevate a person or an idea until we judge it as having supreme moral value.* We may follow a person or commit to a cause and then give ourselves permission to sacrifice moral principles to protect it. For example:

> In the free speech debate on college campuses, students have protested speakers whose views, they feel, may be offensive to some students (such as the examples we saw in chapter 2.) The protesters are coming from a place of good intent to respect certain groups of people. But they're doing it by devaluing the rights of others— limiting free speech and preventing the dialog that's necessary to maintain peace in a society with diverse views. To protect dignity and justice for some people, students have shouted down speakers with demeaning and unjust accusations.[7] In the name of preventing the "violence" of hearing views they perceive to be demeaning, they've used physical violence and humiliated others.

Aside from the obvious hypocrisy, degrading one group as a method to protect the dignity of another violates principles of respect and compassion. A similar example can be seen in the January 6 attacks on the US Capitol Building.

> On January 6, 2021, a group of "patriots," in the name of respect for our country's founding principles, mobbed an honored government building, attacked fellow citizens who defended the building, even stabbing one with a metal fence stake,[8] and for hours "vandalized and looted the interior and ransacked offices as they searched for their perceived enemies in Congress."[9]

Were these people truly acting in the name of respect for our country, or were they relishing in disrespectful, irresponsible, and dehumanizing self-indulgence?

Of course, there's a time and place for elevating the worth of a principle and being willing to sacrifice for it. *But there's a way to go about promoting one principle, without rationalizing away our other principles.* Glover, in *Humanity* cautions:

> When terrible orders are given, some people resist because of their conception of who they are. But there may be no resistance when a person's self-conception has been built round obedience. ... A lot depends on how far the sense of moral identity has been narrowed to a merely tribal or ideological one.[10]

Too much respect can lead one to blindly follow orders, to get swept up in a group identity, or to devalue other humans and their own principles in the name of promoting a cause.

Navigating the gray areas

To keep ourselves on the moral end of the gray areas, we can ask ourselves some questions that get to the truth about people's motivations, the level of respect we're demonstrating, and whether we're being responsible and compassionate in how we treat other people.

- Are people being treated with dignity, care, and fairness? Would the action seem respectful if it were directed at me or my group?

- Are any cognitive distortions (chapter 2) or Us-and-Them biases (chapter 8) at work that might cause someone to over-inflate or downplay the harm that's being done?

- Is my response, or my group's response, being true to principles
  of respect for all people, even the ones we disagree with? Does
  the response work toward true justice and equality, or is there an
  element of vengeance to our actions?

A path forward

We have a common conception about what the right amount of respect is.
It starts with our fundamental obligation to treat each other with care and
dignity. The danger of too little respect is obvious—the worst atrocities
of our time were enabled by devaluing and dehumanizing. Yet today, too
much respect for tribal identities and causes is ironically leading to acts
of disrespect toward our principles and other people. *If we want stability,
we need to come back to our shared sense of who we are, not as tribal
factions, but as humans, rooted in decency.* We need to remember and
honor our unspoken commitment of respect for each other:

> I will treat you with the care and dignity you deserve, and in return,
> I expect you will treat me with the care and dignity I deserve as a
> fellow human.

Journaling

What do you respect? What are things you feel have value and should be treated with care?

Have you ever agreed with something because it was reasonable, even if it wasn't what you would have preferred?

Have you seen examples of people allowing their admiration for a person or cause to blind them?

Up next

Now that we've established what RESPECT is, in the next chapter we'll look at respect in modern life. We'll pull together concepts from a few previous chapters and see how respect with good intent has gone wrong.

Chapter 18

Working Against Ourselves

Why you can't disrespect someone into agreeing with you

Be wary of an age in which people find war a solution to the decadence of peace.

—Jonathan Sacks, *Morality*[1]

In the last chapter, we clarified that respect isn't just about being polite or admiring someone. Respect is so much more than that—it's the heart of an unspoken agreement between each of us that sets the rules of engagement for how we live and work together for mutual benefit. If respect is so important, what's with all the disrespect in our culture today? How did we get here and why is it so bad? The answer may surprise you. This chapter will reveal good intentions gone awry. We'll see how, in the name of respect, we've wielded shame as a weapon and created a climate of threat. Just as the opening quote cautions against, in the calm of peacetime, we've drawn each other into a "battle" which we've used to justify new and dangerous rules of engagement. All is not lost however. It won't all be doom and gloom. We'll also look at actionable ways to change the tone and reestablish our core agreement with each other—one that's rooted in respect.

Enter the arena

We've talked about the culture of disrespect in a few chapters now. We saw it in The Contagion of Cruelty and Kindness (chapter 9) where we looked at issues around people being nasty, rude, and even violent in very public displays. We saw it in Us versus Them (chapter 8) where we explored the dangers of stoking outrage against one's opponents by describing them in terms that activate moral disgust. Looking at those chapters now, through the filter of our Respect Continuum from the last chapter, we can see that these *forms of disrespect cause varying degrees of harm by decreasing the worth of something*—progressing from insulting to degrading to dehumanizing. We've also seen though that there is *danger in too much respect—when we elevate the worth of something*, progressing from admiration to reverence to blind obedience. Both of those forces are in play today, often at the same time, and it's turning life into a battleground where each side thinks they have the moral high ground.

In a diverse society, we're going to have groups with different views of how things should be done. It's not a question of whether we'll disagree; there's only the question of how we go about disagreeing. Just like in any conflict, the way we talk about each other and our ideas matters. *While disrespecting our opponents might be entertaining and it might satisfy our anger, it comes at a cost.* Let's take two examples, one from the political right and one from the left, and let's dig into just how dangerous this culture of disrespect can be.

The rules of war

In this first example, conservative commentator Charles Sykes, in *How the Right Lost Its Mind*, demonstrates the inflammatory tone of the 2016 US election by sharing a quote from another conservative commentator, Dennis Prager:

Leftism is a terminal cancer in the American bloodstream and soul.
… So our first and greatest principle is to destroy this cancer before
it destroys us. We therefore see voting for Donald Trump as political
chemotherapy needed to prevent our demise. And at this time, that is,
by far, the greatest principle.[2]

In fairness to Prager, in the original article where he wrote this, he was
arguing rationally about ideology.[3] Yet he chose to end the argument with
the sentences above, which degraded the entire set of leftist ideals (and
by extension those who believe them) to that of an insidious disease.
This is the type of language we talked about in chapter 8 that taps into
our disgust response, where our body reacts to protect us from sickness.
Prager is prompting his audience to pull back and away, as if leftism is
physically dangerous. He creates a battle for survival saying that this
"cancer" could "destroy" America. He justifies setting aside some of
his principles because protecting something he values is "the greatest
principle."

This sort of inflammatory language is playing at both immoral ends
of the Respect Continuum. It's leveraging respect for one's own ideology
to create a moral imperative that justifies immorality toward another. Let's
step back and see how this works:

Are there circumstances when immoral behavior is acceptable?

- Is lying okay? What if it's to save a life?
- Is killing okay? What if it's in self-defense?

*When we start framing political disagreements as a battle for survival,
we invoke the rules of engagement for self-defense or war, circumstances
when even normal, law-abiding citizens may feel justified in behaving
immorally.* Colorful analogies that stoke audience outrage aren't just
harmless entertainment. They can give people permission to suspend
their usual moral codes.

Attacking from the moral high ground

With a sense of moral superiority driving them, people justify all manner of immoral acts toward their perceived enemies. The left wields its righteousness just as much as the right. Sykes contrasts the inflammatory tone on the right with this example from the left, which describes the situation during protests over police brutality:

> During the campaign, commentators on the Left expressed (legitimate) concern that Trump was encouraging violence at some of his rallies. At the same time, conservatives were inundated with stories, links, and video clips of protesters chanting "What do we want? Dead cops! When do we want it? Now!" and "Pigs in a blanket, fry 'em like bacon." But on cable television, they watched their concerns about law and order denounced as racial "dog whistles."[4]

Here, protesters on the left say they are acting out of respect, in this case, for people who have been mistreated by the police. But with the battle lines drawn, protesters are suspending the very moral principle they say they are trying to uphold. Respect includes valuing life and dignity. Calling for "dead cops," equating them with animals, and worse yet, chanting about cooking them like food—that's dehumanizing. A group who is protesting in the name of fair treatment and equal justice is devaluing concerns about law and order and is throwing aside justice for all the cops who've done nothing wrong. Of course bad cops should be held accountable—that's fair; that's justice. But demeaning and dehumanizing a group of people in the name of respect for another? That's using respect to justify disrespect.

Shooting ourselves in the foot

Aside from the hypocrisy and immorality of disrespecting some in the name of respecting others, there's a practical problem with this approach. Have you ever had a disagreement about real issues when someone started insulting you personally? How'd it go? A quote on conflict resolution comes to mind:

In any conflict, be sure you know what you really want, and whether what you are doing is actually helping you get there.[5]

If our goal is to drive wedges between people and to feed hatred, then insulting and demeaning our opponents is exactly what we need. But, *if what we really want is to encourage respect between groups that ultimately will feed cooperation, fairness, and justice, then disrespecting our opponents is wholly counterproductive.* It's the rare person who will be openly degraded and then say, "You know what, you're right. I am as horrible and unworthy as you think I am. I'm going to overhaul my life and join your cause."

The shame game

While we're on the subject of working against our own interests, let's talk about shame. Have you noticed how often the phrase "should be ashamed of" comes up lately? A recent search on the Google news tab returned 130,000 news articles declaring that someone "should be ashamed" of themselves.[6] Apparently a city, a sports team, a world leader, some parents, an entire nation, prosecutors, and a judge should all be ashamed of themselves—and that was just on page one of the results. Public shaming is all the rage.

Taking shame up a notch, we find *cancel culture*: when a group calls for the public shaming of someone they feel has done something offensive. Canceling is an effort to ostracize someone and often includes stripping the person of their community, standing, and livelihood. Another form of shaming comes from groups, like social movements and political parties, who cast out those who don't tow the party line. For example, when Republican Liz Cheney stood against her political party to honor her principles around truth, she was shunned and stripped of her leadership position in the party.[7] Or in the case of protests in 2017 at Evergreen State College, when a student simply spoke to a professor who some students were trying to cancel, the protesters publicly humiliated the student, forcing her to read a declaration of her loyalty to the students' cause.[8]

Humans have used shame to influence behavior since we formed societies. Thankfully we're not locking people in a pillory in the public square anymore, yet public humiliation is still being used to enforce social norms. With the emergence of social media, shaming has given people without power a voice and a means to influence which behaviors are deemed acceptable. But good intentions don't always lead to good outcomes. *The frequency and magnitude of public shaming today isn't creating a well-behaved, cooperative society. It's often leading to the opposite result.*

The problem with shaming

Today, when people invoke shame, they may mean to say, "You did something wrong and you should change your ways." But that's not how shame works. According to psychology researchers, shame isn't about correcting specific behaviors. Shame is a criticism of the whole person.[9] It's right there in the words: you should be ashamed of your*self.* It's not about what you did; shame is a criticism of *who you are.*

Research shows that shame makes people feel small, worthless, and powerless. It sends a message that someone doesn't deserve to be part of the group and it leverages fear of losing connection, which we saw in chapter 6 is essential to our well-being as humans. Shame researcher Brené Brown, in *I Thought It was Just Me,* explains,

> When we are experiencing shame, we are steeped in the fear of being ridiculed, diminished or seen as flawed. We are afraid that we've exposed or revealed a part of us that jeopardizes our connection and our worthiness of acceptance.[10]

Notice the words here: *diminished, worthiness of acceptance.* **Shame is a way of demoting someone's worth and declaring them unfit for society.**

The difference between shame and accountability

If what we want is accountability, there are better ways to go about it than shame. Psychology research reveals that when we show someone how specific actions have caused real harm, it taps into our natural empathy and people typically want to fix the damage they've done.[11] On a group level we saw this at the start of the Black Lives Matter movement. Watching a police officer kneel on George Floyd's neck until he died brought people together in outrage and a sense of collective responsibility over the inhumanity on display. Someone's actions led to brutal consequences, and we had to heed the call of our own empathetic outrage.

That's not how people react to shame. Shame interrupts empathy and instead people will withdraw, deny, become defensive, or turn angry. To deal with the pain of being seen as defective or inferior, people being shamed will "lash out and blame others in order to regain a sense of control over their lives."[12] Casting someone out in shame pushes them away from their accusers and toward others who will help them deny the accusation and reclaim their worth. Liberal essayist Mark Lilla, in *The Once and Future Liberal*, points out how sentiment around the Black Lives Matter movement shifted once the movement voiced "a general indictment of American society ... and demand[ed] a confession of sins and public penitence."[13] Solidarity suffered once shame created separation and defensiveness.

When we see conservatives aligning together saying they feel their way of life is being threatened or when we see liberals rallying together saying that their right to exist is being denied, *it may well be a reaction to a culture of shaming that declares not that something is wrong with what they've done, but that something is wrong with who they are.*

> In any conflict, be sure you know what you really want,
> and whether what you are doing
> is actually helping you get there.

Shaming is social control gone wild

There's another problem with using shame as a means of social control. Society exists in a balance of power. The government (through laws) and society (through norms) share the power to control people's behavior.[14] The push and pull between the government and the people is how we keep the powerful from becoming oppressive. So what happens when the balance is thrown out of equilibrium and too much power is exerted?

> If a government, with little evidence and no trial could swoop in, take away your livelihood and destroy your standing in the community, we'd call that tyranny. *Yet what is cancel culture?*

> If the government could control your ability to think independently, to voice your concerns, or to act on your conscience, we'd call that oppression. *Yet social movements and political parties control their members in the same way.*

In this culture of public shaming, cancel culture, and casting out those who dare to even question their group's approach, society has become the despot.

Of course society must play a role in enforcing norms. Yet social control out of balance can become what authors Daron Acemoglu and

James A. Robinson in *The Narrow Corridor*, call a "Cage of Norms," where society suffocates liberty in a climate of fear and threat:

> Critically, liberty requires not just the abstract notion that you are free to choose your actions, but also the ability to exercise that freedom. This ability is absent when a person, group, or organization has the power to coerce you, threaten you, or use the weight of social relations to subjugate you. ... To flourish, liberty needs the end of dominance, whatever its source.[15]

Rampant public shaming limits our ability to think independently and to have open conversations that can resolve our conflicts. Through threat and dominance, public shaming replaces equal treatment before the law with mob rule.

That doesn't mean we should do and say whatever we want. Revisit chapter 6: You Be You Unless You're a Jerk for reasons why that's not a good idea. But *in a society that aspires to liberty, equality, and justice for all, we can't allow society to exert the same sort of excess force and control via threat we wouldn't allow from the government.*

4 Ways to Improve Respect in Society

There's something encouraging, even cathartic, in recognizing the problem. Living under a cloud of degrading language, a perpetual battle for survival, and the treat of public shaming is oppressive. If you've had enough, then let's turn toward what we can do to reset the culture toward mutual respect, fairness, and cooperation.

1. Decide what you really want

In any conflict, ask yourself what you really want and whether what you're doing will help you get there. Is this culture of disrespect and shaming really serving us? It can feel intoxicating in its drama. Yet if what we really want is a respectful, fair, cooperative society, we're going to need to take the less indulgent approach of acting with respect, fairness, and cooperation.

2. Put down the verbal weapons

We can act with passion while treating our opponents with dignity.
Framing our disagreements as battles for survival is allowing people to
justify degrading and even dehumanizing behavior. Starting right now, we
can choose words that respect the dignity of those we disagree with. We
can also question whether the people using inflammatory rhetoric really
have our best interest in mind. We have the power to change the tone of
the debate by choosing what to watch, click, and forward (or not watch,
click, and forward.)

3. Address actions and consequences

*People are more likely to want to right a wrong if they see how their
actions caused harm.* Talking about specific actions, policies, and
showing real world consequences prompts people to respond with
empathy. By sticking to the facts without the shaming, we can lead people
to see for themselves why we feel strongly about an issue. We can engage
in dialog, as opposed to sermonizing, that helps people understand what's
happening and why it's a big deal.

4. See the issues through a Veil of Ignorance

View both sides of the issue as if you don't know which side you're on.
John Rawls, the modern political philosopher we saw in the last chapter,
created a conceptual tool called the *Veil of Ignorance.*[16] The idea is of an
imaginary situation where the rules for society haven't been created and
the people creating the rules would do it from behind a veil of ignorance,
where they didn't know who they would eventually become in society.
They wouldn't know their socioeconomic status, gender, race, abilities,
natural assets, and so forth, so they would have to consider how a rule
could affect them if they entered society as anyone. Of course in real life,
we do know which groups we're part of and are likely to prioritize our
own interests. But the veil of ignorance is an interesting approach if we
want to think more objectively.

Considering another group's position or a policy from behind a veil of ignorance can make it easier to see other perspectives and have greater empathy for potential consequences. The veil of ignorance is the essence of putting yourself in someone else's shoes and making the effort to understand where they're coming from, so in that sense, it's not a new idea. But, if we could actually do it, the result would be the realization of the Golden Rule—to treat others as you would like to be treated.

A path forward

We started these two chapters on respect by recognizing that both too little respect and too much respect can be a problem. In fact, today, too much respect for one's own group or ideology is being used to justify disrespect—some people are elevating their own cause at the expense of others' dignity and well-being. Looking back to the roots of morality, respect is about fostering a climate of fairness, justice, and reciprocity. It's an essential part of the core rules of engagement for how we live with stability and predictability. It comes down to remembering that we are not just individuals out for our own self-interest, but we benefit from making the effort to understand others and treat them with the care and dignity we'd like as well. No matter how different someone may seem, we share a common humanity. Brené Brown suggests:

> I don't have to know "exactly how you feel"—I just have to touch a part of my life that opens me up to hearing your experience. If I can touch that place, I stay out of judgment and I can reach out with empathy. This is where both personal and social healing can begin.[17]

So let's put down our verbal weapons, decide what we really want, and step behind a veil of ignorance in an effort to treat each other with the respect we'd like to see in return.

Journaling

Have you ever been shamed? How did it feel?

Do you think cancel culture is about accountability, vengeance, or something else?

Think of an issue you feel passionately about. If you were behind a veil of ignorance, how might you see it differently?

Up next

We've looked at TRUTH and RESPECT now it's time to pull out our moral compass again and see how to navigate issues around RESPONSIBILITY. We'll look at what it is, why it matters, and how victimhood is messing with the empowering force of responsibility.

Chapter 19

What Is Responsibility?

Why responsibility is a blend of empowerment and justice

It's time to check in with our moral compass again to see where we're headed. We've journeyed through TRUTH and RESPECT; now we're venturing into RESPONSIBILITY. We've been talking about how we spend our days balancing what we want for ourselves with how our actions impact other people. That's because life runs on relationships—we may

The Moral Compass- Responsibility

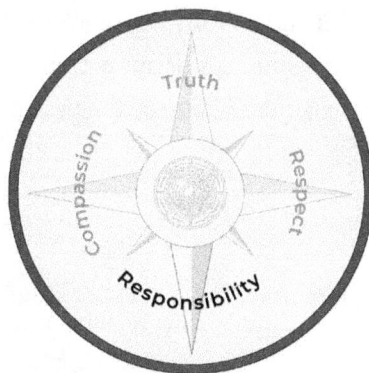

be someone's friend, spouse, coworker, neighbor, or fellow citizen, for instance—and you don't need a relationship self-help book to know that healthy relationships need a good balance of give-and-take. We'll come to see that responsibility is how we negotiate what we give and how we take. Where RESPECT for equal human dignity is *why* we have relationships based in fairness and reciprocity, we'll see in this chapter that RESPONSIBILITY is *how* we keep the relationships fair and reciprocal.

221

What is responsibility?

We talk about responsibility in a couple different ways—being responsible, having responsibility, taking responsibility—but they all come back to the same core idea. *Responsibility is about choosing to act in a way that promotes well-being for ourselves and for our relationships.*[1] Specifically:

Being responsible means we use self-control and put *boundaries* on our own behavior because it's good for us or good for the groups we want to be a part of.

Having responsibilities means we're trusted to do the tasks that maintain our own lives and our relationships. By reliably doing our *duties*, we earn the right to expect others to do their part in return.

Taking responsibility means that each of us is *accountable* for the consequences of our actions. If we do (or don't do) what's needed, we get the blame or the praise that we've earned.

> Responsibility includes
> setting boundaries on how we act,
> doing our duties, and being held accountable.

Responsibility within the rings of our relationships

If we imagine that each person is connected to the world around them in an expanding view of their relationships—from individual, to family, to community, to nation, and to humanity—we might picture something like this image of concentric rings. (Confucius and Hinduism each used symbolism like this to explain how morality and society work.[2])

Rings of Relationships and Responsibility

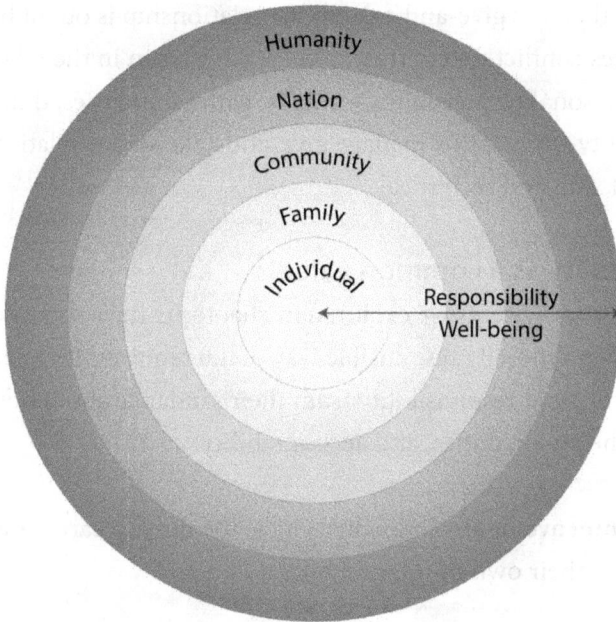

In each type of relationship, as a family member, a coworker, a citizen, etc.:

- We control how we act with each other. (Boundaries)
- We do what's needed for well-being. (Duties)
- We get the reward or punishment for how well we do our share. (Accountability)

We contribute to the well-being of others, and we expect our relationships to contribute to our well-being in return—because that's how a healthy society works.

But when people aren't being responsible, then they aren't keeping up their end of the relationship and the relationship breaks down. For example, if we're in a relationship where someone pushes for what they want for themselves no matter the harm they cause, or they don't do their share of the work, or they blame others instead of owning up to their own faults, then the give-and-take in the relationship is out of balance and it creates conflict. In contrast, when each person in the relationship acts with personal responsibility—that is, with boundaries, duties, and accountability—it helps us manage give-and-take so our relationships can be peaceful, fair, and reciprocal.

Responsibility as a common value

The world belief systems we explored in chapter 12 have some common ideas on what a morally responsible way of life requires. Let's see what we can learn about responsibility from their guidance about boundaries relating to behavior, duties, and accountability:

Self-improvement– Individuals have the duty to care for and develop their own minds and bodies.

Self-control– The systems universally encourage moderation and acting within the boundaries of truthfulness, respect, and compassion.

Service to others– An individual's responsibilities include duties to care for family, to do service for the community, to take care of those in need, and to help others become more able to care for themselves.

Rewards and punishment– Concepts like karma, eternal punishment/reward, and the ability to achieve higher purpose goals all depend on personal accountability. Each person pays the price or earns the reward based on the choices they make.

Why responsibility is important

Responsibility is how we manage actions and consequences with each other, knowing that each time we make a choice, it's like dropping a pebble in a pond—we create ripples that roll out to impact our own lives and the lives of other people. From that perspective, we're all incredibly powerful beings who can make waves that help or make waves that hurt.[3] Given our power to impact others, it's no wonder that being responsible is so important. Responsibility acts like a force that holds all the moral values in balance, so people make calmer, more helpful waves—instead of destructive tsunamis.

The (sometimes-overlooked) positive power of responsibility

Given our survival instinct to avoid tsunamis and other things that can either hurt us or get in the way of what we need, we humans are inclined to focus on the potential negative consequences more than the positive ones.[4] So we tend to think of responsibility in terms of preventing harm or holding people accountable for causing harm. But responsibility has two sides: the blame side and the praise side.[5]

When actions cause *negative* consequences, responsibility means someone gets the *blame, guilt, or punishment.*

When actions cause *positive* consequences, the responsible party gets the *praise, pride, or reward.*

So, while being responsible is partly about preventing negative consequences, it's also about having the power to create positive ones. The power is in each of our hands to choose how to act in order to create the outcomes we want.

Let's check our bearings for a second here, because what we just arrived at is that *having responsibility for your own life is empowerment.* Rather than feeling like we're at the whim of external forces, responsibility helps us know that no matter what happens around us, we get to choose how to act so we can be at peace with our own choices. And while we'll likely choose to do things we *want* to do, responsibility means that even when we choose to do something we *don't really want to do* (like being nice to our grumpy boss or paying our taxes) we're still *choosing* to do it—because it serves our bigger goals and overall well-being. That perspective shift is incredibly empowering. ***Being responsible puts us in control of our actions and it enables us to accept or enjoy the consequences we create for ourselves***—which is how we build the sense of agency, self-respect, and inner stability we talked about in chapters 1 and 5.

> Even when we choose to do something we *don't really want to do* we're still *choosing* to do it—because it serves our bigger goals and overall well-being.

Responsibility gives meaning and purpose

We've also seen throughout this book that people need a sense of meaning and purpose. When someone has responsibilities—to a family, at work, in the community—it means someone else depends on them to do their duties. Through our responsibilities, each person contributes something of value, regardless of their status or income. Let's use the staff at a hospital as an example: the surgeon does the operation, but the duties performed by the nurses, the operating room scheduler, and the cleaning crew all contribute to saving lives. ***Responsibilities connect people to a bigger picture that can give them a sense of worth, meaning, and purpose.***

Responsibility makes freedom and justice possible

As we extend outward into the rings of our relationships at a country-level, responsibility helps us find the balance between our personal interests and the ways we need to act to keep our nation healthy. In a free society, each citizen is expected to act with self-control—behaving within reasonable boundaries—because freedom is not a license to abuse others. And although we're free to make our choices and pursue our rewards, we rely on accountability to enforce justice when self-interest goes too far. To have all these wonderful freedoms and rights, we also have to do our duty to uphold the principles that make a free, democratic society possible. Even among people we don't know or don't like, we implicitly agree to be reasonable with each other, and to protect shared principles of freedom, equality, fairness, cooperation, and justice. The system works when each free and equal citizen acts responsibly, which is to say, each person balances what they want personally with what's reasonable for our shared well-being.

It's rather lovely there in concept and if it worked that well we'd be holding hands, waving flags, and singing in perfect harmony. In reality, a free society is a lot more messy, in part, because it's made up of citizens with lots of different viewpoints, who may not agree about what's reasonable. Yet a free society will always include different viewpoints, because forcing everyone to agree to the same ideology, religion, or way of life is the opposite of freedom. *The only realistic option is to work together to negotiate where the boundaries are for what's reasonable.* To help us find a common language as we talk through what would be a fair balance of boundaries, duties, and accountability, we can once again turn to a value continuum.

The Responsibility Continuum

If Aristotle is right, and the purpose of life is to create our well-being, then responsibility is one of the most important values for us to understand. When we put responsibility on a continuum, we can find the tipping points where we are doing too little, or too much, to support well-being. Since life runs on relationships, we can look to the responsibility continuum to help us find where the reasonable balance is between doing what we want for ourselves and what we need to do for well-being among other people.

The Responsibility Continuum

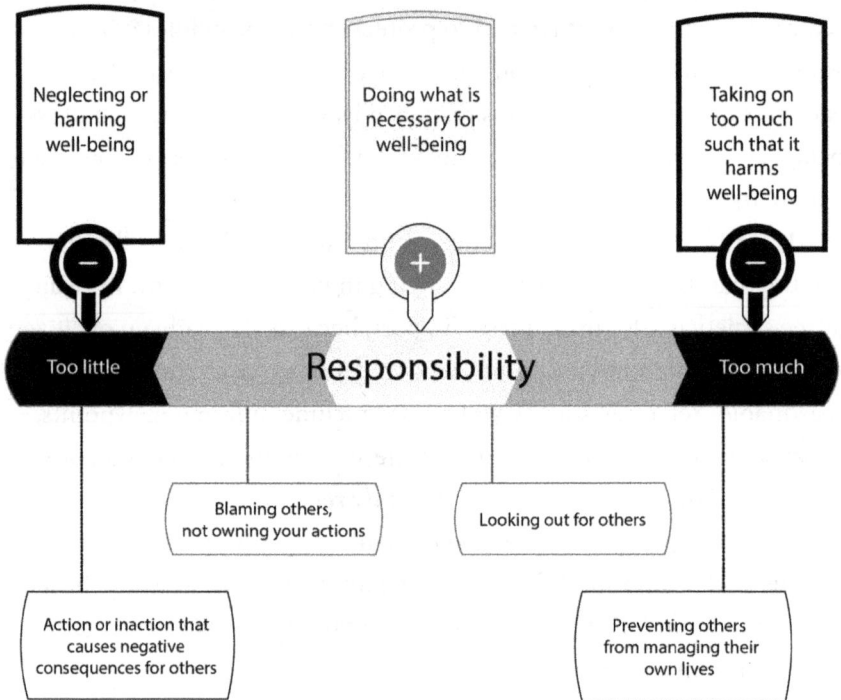

Neglecting or harming well-being	Doing what is necessary for well-being
	Taking on too much such that it harms well-being

Too little   Responsibility   Too much

Blaming others, not owning your actions

Looking out for others

Action or inaction that causes negative consequences for others

Preventing others from managing their own lives

GOOD, MORAL RESPONSIBILITY

Starting at the middle of the continuum, we have *good, moral responsibility* where we're **doing what is necessary for well-being and not doing that which harms well-being.** Let's explore some examples of good, moral responsibility in real life:

- We take initiative to care for and improve ourselves, like getting training that would help us get a new job. Or changing old habits that aren't good for us.

- We use self-control so we're being more helpful than harmful, like driving slowly through school zones to keep kids safe. Or not taking out our bad day on the cashier at the coffee shop.

- We do our duties within our close relationships and in the broader community, like getting our part of a job done so our colleague can get theirs done. Or making sure we're informed (with true facts) about public issues.

- We accept the blame when it's our fault and we don't blame others for what isn't their fault. We take the credit when it's our due, but we don't unfairly deny others what they're due.

That all seems reasonable, right? We're not talking about the controversial stuff here. This is day-to-day life for decent, responsible people.

TOO LITTLE RESPONSIBILITY

Moving to one end of the continuum, toward too little responsibility, we see areas where *people don't live within boundaries that promote well-being, don't do their duties, or don't take accountability where they should.* Intentionally causing harm to people or society is morally irresponsible. Yet being careless, reckless, or neglectful—where we don't consider the repercussions of our actions—can also create negative consequences. Let's explore some examples:

- The person who says it's always someone else's fault and won't admit how their own choices created the situation they're in.

- When someone pursues what they want in a way that they harm other people or public institutions, such as how some parents are increasingly confrontational and even violent at school board meetings, damaging community participation and democratic standards for cooperation.[6]

- When an employee doesn't maintain equipment, so chemicals leak into the public water supply. Or when a CEO uses the company to promote their own cause without considering how it could harm employees or shareholders.

- When people make statements that undermine public trust in our democratic institutions without evidence to support their claims.

With *too little responsibility*, people can cause harm to each other, to their groups, and to the stability of society. It's worth remembering from chapter 7 on Jonathan Haidt's Six Moral Foundations that people can cause harm in a number of different ways.[7] In addition to physical and emotional harm, actions and inaction can also cause harm to fairness, liberty, loyalty, social order, and dignity.

TOO MUCH RESPONSIBILITY

On the other end of the continuum, toward *too much responsibility*, people take on more responsibility than they should. They may have good intentions, but they **cause a negative consequence by imposing unreasonable boundaries on behavior, by taking on too many duties, or by holding people accountable when they aren't to blame.** For example,

- Taking too much responsibility for someone else's life can limit that person's ability to make choices and learn from consequences that would help them grow. Consider helicopter parenting, where parents with good intentions do too much and ultimately harm their child's ability to be a capable adult.[8]

- Someone may take on more duties than they can handle, like the person who adopts so many stray animals they can't humanely care for all of them.

- When people blame someone for something they didn't cause, or hold them accountable for acts done by other people who look like them. For instance, blaming all Muslims for the attacks done by a few people on 9/11.

Like we saw with TRUTH and RESPECT, *too much responsibility* can go too far. By being too responsible when it comes to what someone else should do, know, or experience, one person robs another of some of their agency and their ability to control their own life. In terms of duty, taking on so many tasks that they can't be done properly can ultimately harm well-being. And in terms of assigning responsibility and punishment, justice requires that we hold the right people responsible, based on a clear link to them having caused the consequence.

Navigating the gray areas

The gray areas around responsibility come up when we disagree about the right amount of *boundaries*, *duties*, and *accountability*. We may debate questions like:

- How much should people's freedom be limited for the sake of the greater good?
- What should people do by their own initiative and when should society intervene to help?
- What is a fair reward or a fair consequence?

In a society full of many viewpoints, it's unlikely we'll ever reach perfect consensus. As renowned political philosopher John Rawls wrote in *Justice as Fairness*, we can push the edges of possibility to try to achieve an agreement that is "realistically utopian," but we can count ourselves successful if we achieve something that's "reasonably just."[9]

The public justification

As we work out terms for what's reasonably just, we need passionate people with more extreme goals because that's who will push society toward change. But we also need the voices in the middle to cooperate as a stabilizing force, even if they don't agree on the exact outcomes, because *it would be irresponsible to change society so far and so fast that it does more harm than good.*

One way we can find middle ground is by talking about issues in terms of a *public justification,* another concept from Rawls. He explains that while we're entitled to our opinions, religions, and other personal viewpoints in our private lives, when we're talking about public policy, we need to relate what we want to public principles. By broadening our perspective to a public justification, we ensure there's balance between what people want personally and what makes sense in terms of shared ideals, like freedom, equality, fairness, cooperation, and reciprocity. Throughout this book, we've also seen that those political principles are made possible through shared moral values of truth, respect, responsibility, and compassion. *So to find the middle ground that most people can agree is reasonable, we need to step back from personal beliefs and instead explain what we want in terms of shared moral values and shared democratic principles.*

When and how much

Not surprisingly, we're likely to find that the answer to what's reasonable and responsible isn't black or white (these are gray areas after all.) As ethics expert Susan Liautaud says in *The Power of Ethics: How to Make Good Choices in a Complicated World*:

We often must replace questions like "*Should I or shouldn't I...?*" with the more open-ended and realistic question ...: "*When and under what circumstances should I...?*"[10]

We might ask for example:

- In what circumstances would it be fair? How much would be just?

- How true are our assumptions? How much is the approach based on personal belief as compared to a public justification?

- To what extent does this effort live up to our ideals about equality, cooperation, and reciprocity?

- Where is the tipping point when an effort to help the well-being of one group actually causes harm to another?

These are all questions that help us remember we're in a relationship based on fairness, freedom, equality, and cooperation. While each of us may passionately want to push forward our own preferences, the system simply doesn't work when we don't sincerely consider how other people in that relationship will be affected. Moderating voices can help society *look beyond the all-or-nothing choice of "should/should not" and instead encourage our fellow citizens to consider "when, how much, and in what circumstances."*

A path forward

Responsibility empowers us to have control over our own lives and to see how we connect and contribute to the lives of others. The tricky bit is that *responsibility is a package deal—personal empowerment comes with accountability. We can't have the power to self-determine without taking responsibility for the consequences we create*, because it's the balance between what we give and how we take that keeps our relationships working in a fair and just way. An ancient adage says that with great power comes great responsibility. Here we see that we *all* have power, which is why we *all* must act with responsibility.

While we work toward what's "reasonably just" we can take a little pressure off by realizing that we, as a society, are constantly adjusting the terms of how we live together. The difference in life from 1860 to 1960 to today is astounding. Each generation before us contributed to that evolution by debating behaviors, duties, and fair accountability. ***Today, the negotiation continues as we try to truly live up to our ideals. It feels tense and tumultuous because we're in the thick of it.*** We don't have it all figured out because we're still figuring it out as we go. The important thing is that we keep trying. And we'll likely find more success if we frame our debates in terms of a public justification as we explain when, how much, and in what circumstances an action would be reasonable, based on shared values.

Journaling

What are some responsibilities in your life that you feel like you *have to* do? What's in it for you to *choose to* do them?

Do you know anyone who takes on too much responsibility, either harming themselves or overstepping onto someone else's independence?

Is there an issue today where people have absolute stances about what should/shouldn't be done? If you reframed the conversation instead to "when and under what circumstances," how would it change the debate?

Up next

As we did for TRUTH and RESPECT, let's take a look at how this common value, RESPONSIBILITY, enters into the instability we're feeling in modern life. We'll focus on identity politics, where groups claim they have not been treated fairly. We'll see how the way we're handling this breakdown in our societal relationship is creating a vicious cycle that will only create more instability.

Chapter 20

Life After Victimhood
How to move society past a grievance state

To specify the idea of a fair chance we say: ... those who have the same
level of talent and ability and the same willingness to use these gifts
should have the same prospects of success.

—John Rawls in *Justice as Fairness: A Restatement*[1]

Since America began, we've looked to our ideals of equality, fairness,
and justice for all. Of course, at the time that the Founding Fathers
announced these truths they believed to be "self-evident," they were
revolutionary ideals, not realities; so subsequent generations have had to
do very real, and often painful, work to get closer to the vision of what
America should be. That's one of the reasons that we continually evolve
our ideas about responsibility, in terms of what the boundaries should be
on people's behavior, what our duties are to each other, and how we hold
each other accountable. Identity politics began as an effort to address our
responsibilities to each other and to get closer to our American vision
of fairness, equality, and justice. Over time though, identity politics has
morphed into something more like competitive victimhood between
factions on the right and the left. Given what we just learned about how

responsibility makes a free society possible, let's look at how identity politics is undermining fair accountability and personal responsibility, and how it's rattling self-respect.

From mobilization to a "blame game"

Identity politics is where people form groups based on a characteristic that they have in common, like race, religion, gender, etc., and then use that solidarity to push a political agenda based on the needs of their group. Identity politics started out with good intentions. As liberal commentator Mark Lilla, in *The Once and Future Liberal*, explains:

> Identity politics on the left was at first about large classes of people—African-Americans, women—seeking to redress major historical wrongs by mobilizing and then working through our political institutions to secure their rights.[2]

With the passage of time, identity groups on the left expanded to include ethnicities, LGBTQ+ groups, minority religions, and numerous subdivisions and intersectional identities. Eventually, as groups on the left gained focus toward their needs, groups on the right responded with identity politics of their own, calling attention to the concerns of white people, particularly poor and working-class whites and white Christians, who felt their needs were being de-prioritized and their identities were being attacked.[3]

Though identity politics started with the *intent to bring people together to work toward common goals* of fairness and equality, over time it changed direction. In *Political Tribes: Group Instinct and the Fate of Nations*, Yale Law School professor Amy Chua explains that in recent years, "A shift in tone, rhetoric, and logic has moved identity politics away from inclusion … toward exclusion and division."[4] It's turned groups in on themselves, focusing people on their own grievances, which typically center around how other people are causing them harm. The lens is aimed at how one group has been wronged, oppressed, or denied their freedoms, and it's someone else's fault. Ultimately, this blame aspect of responsibility (discussed in chapter 19) creates what Chua calls an "Oppression Olympics"—a competition over who is the most victimized and the most deserving of acknowledgment.[5] Mark Lilla adds that identity politics dismisses each citizen's responsibility to persuade people from different groups toward compromise, and instead encourages them to demand: "What does my country owe me by virtue of my identity?"[6]

Each identity group has their arguments as to how they are being treated unjustly, but we won't go into that because this chapter isn't about politics. We're talking about how *an approach that was meant to clarify our responsibilities to each other—in order to encourage fairness and equality—has ceased to be reasonable and helpful.* So let's focus on why and how we need to change this culture that over-emphasizes victimhood and oppression.

Seeking acknowledgment is understandable

We saw in the previous chapter, that we, the people in a society, are in an unspoken agreement with each other based in responsibility. When a group experiences a lack of equality, fairness, and reciprocity, the give-and-take in that relationship isn't working correctly—and it's reasonable to want that to be made right. Psychology researcher Scott Barry Kaufman explains that when someone's been wronged, it upsets their sense of how the world works.[7] Getting recognition that a wrong has been committed "can help reestablish a person's confidence in their perception of the world as a fair and just place to live," and it's "normal for victims to want the perpetrators to take responsibility for their wrongdoing and to express feelings of guilt," Kaufman explains. Each of us can likely relate to this: Acknowledgment goes a long way toward restoring a relationship when someone has done something wrong to us. But while it's reasonable to want wrongs to be acknowledged and corrected, *the way identity politics goes about getting justice thwarts its own aims.*

> When someone has been wronged,
> it upsets their sense of how the world works.

Casting blame in too-broad strokes

Identity politics today pits groups of people against other groups of people. When this happens, everyone in the opposing group is painted with the same brush and equally carries the blame for a perceived wrong.

- All black people are…
- All Republicans are…
- All Christians are…
- All transgender people are…

Are you offended yet? If not, just create a sentence where everyone in your group is characterized the same way or is blamed for some social issue. When someone says something like, "All [insert group] are responsible for [insert situation]," all people of that group are swept up in accusations of equal blame, regardless of their real actions. This is a big problem when we reflect back on the Responsibility Continuum in chapter 19, where we saw that applying blame in the wrong amount or to the wrong people, is well… wrong.

To further our insight, let's look at a controversial topic today to see why applying blame in broad strokes is such a problem. During an interview between best-selling author and psychologist Jordan Peterson (who is white) and the author of *Woke Racism*, John McWhorter (who is black), Peterson turned the conversation in this direction:

So I've been considering this proposition that's emerged from the woke end of the political spectrum … that "all white people are racist." And I think, *Okay, are all white people racist? What's the answer to that?* And the answer is: "Yes." And "No." And "How dare you frame the question like that?"[8]

Peterson and McWhorter explored the topic, discussing degrees of racism in society and that the way people notice or respond to race today is very different from the racism of the past. But they never got back around to Peterson's sense of insult when he said, "How dare you frame the question like that?" The answer to that will show us why casting blame in too-broad strokes is such a problem. Let's break it down:

- Saying that someone is racist today is an immense moral insult. It's a judgment on their character that carries a strong statement of moral blame. This is actually a really good sign for society because it shows that people broadly understand that racism is morally wrong. If people weren't insulted—if they were okay being a racist—we'd have a different issue.

- Grouping all white people into the single category of "inherently racist" casts all white people as *equally morally blameworthy*. It takes the degrees of behavior that Peterson and McWhorter discussed and lumps them all into the same bucket. It creates moral equivalence between, for example, 1) someone who has minor bias but treats everyone with equal respect and 2) a white supremacist who believes their race is superior and acts on that belief.

In each of the value continuums we've explored in this book—where we've compared what too little and too much of a moral value look like—both intent and degree have been an important part of the scale. *Casting blame at a group level assigns collective responsibility to all people in a group equally, no matter what their intent or real actions were.* This isn't just about white people being judged as a group. Reflect back to the statement you thought of about *your own group being blamed* for some problem in society, and then consider why collective responsibility is a problem:

- Accusations of equal blame may be inaccurate, and that's dishonest, based on the Truth Continuum (chapter 14).

- Accusations of moral blame that are inaccurate degrade someone's worth unfairly, and that's disrespectful based on the Respect Continuum (chapter 17).

- When accountability is applied to everyone equally, even if their actions didn't cause the same harm, that's irresponsible, based on the Responsibility Continuum (chapter 19).

Collective blame should send our moral compass into a whirring and buzzing alert mode.

Another problem with inaccurate blame is that with so many groups casting accusations against so many others, *many people are being caught up in a culture where they don't have control over how they're judged, and there's nothing they can do about it.* This robs people of their ability to control their own lives and to affect their own outcomes, which is a problem if they want to find self-respect and inner stability (chapter 5), happiness (chapter 1), not to mention if we want to maintain a free society (chapter 19). And one more thought: We saw in chapter 18 that shaming people isn't helpful for changing behavior. Collective blame is a way of broadcasting moral shame to allies and foes alike, which is more likely to create resentment and divisiveness than it is to rally people together to fix the injustice.

Speaking of taking away control of people's lives

We just saw that broad-based accusations are a problem for the accused (and under identity politics, nearly everyone is accused of some societal ill, it seems.) But what about the victims? Identity politics began because people who had been treated unfairly came together to find support among people who faced similar challenges—in order to change things. That sounds like positive self-determination and empowerment, right? But that's not where identity politics is today. In *Political Tribes*, Amy Chua describes it like this:

> Whites and blacks, Latinos and Asians, men and women, Christians, Jews, and Muslims, straight people and gay people, liberals and conservatives—all feel their groups are being attacked, bullied, persecuted, discriminated against. Of course, one group's claims to feeling threatened and voiceless are often met by another group's derision because it discounts their own feelings of persecution—but such is political tribalism.[9]

Rather than people being empowered by identity, groups are focusing on being the "voiceless" and "persecuted" victims of other groups. Identity politics today encourages people to structure their identity around *how they don't have control over their own lives and how they are at the mercy of what other people do to them.* This puts one's sense of control and worth outside themselves. So to sound like a broken record, this is not at all helpful for developing an internalized self-respect that leads to stability and long-term well-being.

The dangers of a victim mindset

Not everyone who has been a victim develops a *victim mindset*. Yet, we might find some interesting parallels if we compare the current climate of identity politics with these characteristics of someone who has developed a perpetual victimhood mindset, according to psychology researcher Scott Barry Kaufman:[10]

4 Characteristics of a Victim Mindset

1. Constant need for recognition– A perpetual need to have one's suffering acknowledged.

2. Moral elitism– A sense that one is more "immaculately" moral and that others are being immoral. Making accusations against others while denying one's own faults.

3. Lack of empathy– Being oblivious to or not caring about others' suffering. Feeling entitled to be aggressive or selfish because of what one has suffered.

4. Thinking about past victimization– A pattern of thinking and talking about the harm one has suffered without considering how to take action to resolve anything. This decreases motivation to forgive while it increases the drive for revenge.

Kaufman goes on to explain that once someone is in a victim mindset, they may develop *cognitive biases* that encourage them to perceive even minor offenses as a big deal, to assume people will be hurtful, and to feel hurt more intensely and longer. If the goal of identity politics was to **bring people together in solidarity toward changing a situation, it seems like encouraging a victim mindset would be rather counterproductive** to that aim.

On a group level, Kaufman draws parallels between an individual and a collective victim mindset by citing studies done in the Middle East. In the *European Journal of Social Psychology*, researchers from Tel-Aviv

University describe how a group can develop a collective sense of victimhood and can pass it on to future generations, where:

> Historical injustices incurred by the ingroup may have taken place many centuries in the past but still impact the attitudes, emotions, and behaviors of contemporary group members through the belief that past enemies are reincarnated in current adversaries. ... [The group comes to see itself as] being disposed or even destined to be victimized by others.[11]

So a collective victim mindset can be passed from person to person, generation to generation, creating a sense that one is destined to be perpetually victimized. This clearly works against identity politics' original intent, which was to pull people out of victimization, not lock them into a fate of inescapable victimhood. The current tone of identity politics described by Chua and Lilla is a warning bell that *while identity groups may have good intentions, they also may be causing more long-term harm than good with their approach.*

A healthier path

As we noted earlier, not everyone who experiences trauma or injustice develops a victim mindset. There are healthy ways to deal with it and plenty of people do. In *How to Be an Anti-Racist*, best-selling author and professor Ibram X. Kendi speaks in a similar vein when he states that there's a difference between experiencing victimization and turning it into a limiting characteristic:

> There is a thin line between an antiracist saying individual Blacks have suffered trauma and a racist saying Blacks are a traumatized people. There is similarly a thin line between an antiracist saying slavery was debilitating and a racist saying Blacks are a debilitated people.[12]

In *Morality: Restoring the Common Good in Divided Times*, Rabbi Sacks shares a similar idea when he describes talking to survivors of the Holocaust:

> There is a difference between being a victim and defining yourself as one. The first is about what happened to you. The second is about how you define who and what you are.[13]

Real injustices have happened, and people are reasonable to want that to be acknowledged and corrected. But if the goal is truly to reach our society's ideals for equality and fairness, *we need a different approach that doesn't wrap people's identities in a shared sense of suffering.*

The chasm in the common ground

At this point in the discussion, when we're looking at groups who are pitted against each other, we might be inclined to think we should reinvigorate people's shared sense of being American, with a heavy dose of nostalgia for the story of our nation's founding and its revolutionary ideals that all men are created equal. And there's logic in the argument. After all, America was founded on history-changing ideals of equality and fairness that inspired generations. But there's also a big flaw in a plan that asks people to rally around the idea of America's founding without acknowledging the reality of it.

For some groups, celebrating the story of America's founding, depending on how it's done, asks them to forego the acknowledgment they're seeking—that the American story wasn't one of freedom and fairness for everyone. In doing so, it also asks them to betray the memory of those who didn't enjoy the promise of what America was supposed to be. Nostalgia is not likely to be motivating for large groups of Americans.

On the other hand, for many Americans, the past decades of identity politics are not something they can rally behind. As Chua writes in *Political Tribes*,

> For tens of millions of white Americans today, mainstream popular culture displays an un-Christian, minority-glorifying, LGBTQ America they can't and don't want to recognize as their country—an America that seems to exclude them, to treat them as the enemy.[14]

If nostalgia for America's founding won't rally part of society and America's identity politics era doesn't rally another, what are we to do?

A path forward

Throughout part three of this book, we've been talking about values that we all can agree on—truth, respect, responsibility, and compassion. In particular, we've seen that

- Reinvigorating our commitment to respect resets the value we place on dignity and equality in the way we relate to each other.

- Reinvigorating our commitment to responsibility resets our core agreement on how we manage freedom, fairness, and justice.

These values and our democratic principles are still powerfully motivating. If we step away from both nostalgia and divisive victimhood, we might be able to ***create a new American story based in common values and shared democratic principles.*** We saw in the previous chapter that generations before us defined the standards during their time and it's now our time to define today's standards for what's reasonable and responsible. We can move our society forward, and we can do it by being rooted in core principles of truth, respect, responsibility, and compassion—and by extension, dignity, fairness, reciprocity, and justice. At its core, our society can likely still can agree with the quote from John Rawls that opened this chapter:

> To specify the idea of a fair chance we say: … those who have the same level of talent and ability and the same willingness to use these gifts should have the same prospects of success.

We may not have lived up to those ideals in the past, but the elements of mutual respect and self-determination in this quote might remind us of the beauty of our shared values, and *how we have the freedom to chart our own course in a new American way*.

Journaling

What groups do you identify with? What are their goals?

Have you ever felt like you were being held responsible for the actions of people who had the same race, religion, gender, etc. as you? Have you blamed someone else in that way?

Do you know anyone who has been a victim, but doesn't have a victim mindset? How do they act?

Up next

As we leave RESPONSIBILITY, we'll turn our attention to the last point on our moral compass—COMPASSION. The two values are closely related since compassion for those who are suffering creates a sense of responsibility to act. Yet responsibility requires us to moderate how we act to keep compassion from going too far. Let's venture on to the last two chapters and discover the balancing beauty of compassion.

Chapter 21

What Is Compassion?

Why compassion is not about eliminating suffering

We've been on this journey to
define what our guiding principles
are and to see how to use them to
live well, together. Theoretically it
all sounds noble, but actually living
a life guided by truth, respect, and
responsibility is going to take some
effort. So it's a good thing that the
last stop on our moral compass is
with COMPASSION.

The Moral Compass- Compassion

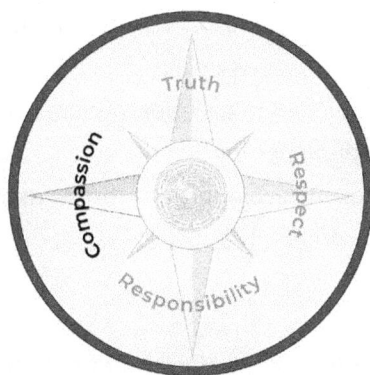

If RESPECT is *why* we
agree to treat each other with
care, dignity, and fairness; and
RESPONSIBILITY is *how* we go about doing it; COMPASSION is the
inspiration that helps us act to help others, especially when life is hard. In
this chapter, we'll see that compassion is where we discover a compelling
drive to care for one another and to harness that energy to help each
other through life's ups and downs. Compassion may surprise you
though. As much as it helps us connect to overcome suffering, it also gives
us the objectivity we need to be sure we're caring in a way that honors our

251

commitment to responsibility—even if that means letting suffering persist sometimes.

Would you rather have sympathy, empathy, or compassion?

If you were dealing with a difficult situation or trauma, which would you rather have: sympathy, empathy, or compassion? If you're asking, "Um, what's the difference?", you're not alone. We often use the terms together and even interchangeably because they're all related to how we understand and relate to other people. Do you ever put yourself in someone else's shoes to see how they might think or feel about something? Of course you do. We've been talking about how we live our lives figuring out what seems like a reasonable and responsible way to act. To figure that out we take a look inward to see what we think and feel about a situation, and we take a look outward to anticipate how other people might think and feel about a situation. All day, we look at different perspectives, understand thoughts and feelings, and then choose how to act as we navigate life and relationships. When the situation is challenging, sympathy, empathy, and compassion offer different approaches for how we understand and relate to each other. Now let's look at each approach more closely to see why we might choose one over the other.

Sympathy

Sympathy is **feeling bad for** someone, from an emotional distance. It may have its place with people we aren't close to, but if we mean to be comforting, sympathy can feel shallow, detached, and even demoralizing.[1] It can come across like "I'm over here, looking at you over there and I'm feeling sorry for you, with a tinge of pity."

Empathy

Empathy is **feeling emotions with** someone. It's a more personal and genuine attempt to understand someone's suffering, but it means going a step further to actually *feeling* emotions along with the other person. On the plus side, sharing someone's positive emotions is a great way to have more joy in your life. (We'll come back to that in the next chapter.) On the other hand, when it comes to sharing someone else's suffering, empathy gets complicated for a couple reasons:

1. Empathy has limits

With our friends, family, and people we identify with, it may feel natural to connect, share, and support them through hard times. But when it comes to people beyond our groups and close contacts, empathy often falls short. That's because empathy evolved to help us *care for* our in-group and *compete against* our out-groups.[2] The way empathy works biologically makes it pretty unlikely someone will think, "You know, I don't understand this person and I don't agree with their choices. Let me jump in and really feel their pain with them."

2. Feeling someone else's pain is hard

Taking on someone else's emotions can be a lot for the empathizer. While empathy is often healthy and it helps us to understand, support, and forgive each other, researchers find that empathy can lead to issues when it gets to be too much.

> Feeling someone else's emotions can become distressing, so rather than wanting to help, empathy can prompt people to withdraw.[3]

> People may, with the help of those cognitive distortions we saw in chapter 2, turn empathy into a sense of guilt, where the empathizer compares how good they have it with the person who is hurting. This can lead people to take on a distorted sense of responsibility for the person's situation, and to initiate actions that are more about the empathizer's own sense of guilt than they are about truly being helpful.[4]

When people care for others all the time (like nurses) or are
constantly engaged with traumatic events (like watching the news),
empathizing can become overwhelming, causing people to go numb
or causing their own health to suffer.[5]

What we can learn from this discussion of sympathy and empathy is
that while we need a way to understand other perspectives and emotions,
and we need a way to reach out to people who are suffering, we need
to find a way to do it with both sincerity and healthy boundaries. This
is where we find the beauty of compassion, because compassion comes
from a different place than sympathy and empathy. Just like we saw with
RESPECT, *compassion comes from a neutral place of universal human
dignity, so it reaches beyond our groups, beyond our own emotions, and it
inspires us to do something at a human-to-human level.*

What is compassion?

Compassion is **feeling concern for** a fellow human being who is
suffering, along with a desire to act.[6] Where empathy is feeling emotions
with someone you can relate to, compassion is feeling concern *for a
fellow human being*. This is more than a subtle difference in wording.
Compassion allows us to step back from group and personal preferences
to connect as humans, in the awareness that we're all vulnerable in this
thing we call life. We all have bodies that bleed and hearts that break.
Compassion is an acknowledgment of our mutual humanity, as if to say:

> **The human in me sees the human in you, and no matter how
> different we are, I can see that you're suffering.**

Some people extend compassion to other living beings, like animals.
Since we're talking about people and societies, we'll focus on human
compassion. Human to human, the neutral stance of compassion allows

us to connect and care for another person without being judgmental about who is deserving—because every human deserves core dignity.

Compassionate action

In saying that compassion takes judgmentalism out of the picture, that doesn't mean we should have limitless tolerance and disregard people's responsibility for the situations they get themselves into. Let's take a look again at the definition of compassion, and focus on its second part:

> Compassion is feeling concern for a fellow human being who is suffering, **along with a desire to act**.

Because it comes from a neutral place of shared humanity, *compassion helps us to be objective about what can and should be done*. Instead of focusing on relieving our own emotions (like we might tend to do with empathy) compassion lets us step back and consider what a reasonable action would be. It's about finding a caring, yet fair and responsible way to respond to someone's hardship. Because let's be realistic, as much as we can have compassion for someone's pain, sometimes we can't—or shouldn't—eliminate their suffering. *What? That doesn't sound very compassionate!* Well then, let's consider a few examples about why this is true:

1. Discomfort leads to growth

Studies show that people who have undergone trauma, like accidents, violence, and disasters, grow more and find more meaning in life when they *don't avoid the distress* related to the trauma.[7] Instead, learning how to live despite hardship takes practice and skill. And through the process of being exposed to emotional discomfort, we build those skills and become stronger and more resilient, not unlike how exposure to illnesses builds our body's immunity to future illnesses.[8] This doesn't mean we welcome more trauma. I'm not saying you should climb to the roof top and yell, "Bring it on!" But for the hardships that will inevitably occur, we learn to live more fully by *facing* unpleasant feelings than we do by *hiding* from them. Thinking back to the Hedonic Treadmill from chapter 1, we balance the ups with the downs in life, and come back to a baseline state of happiness. We can't ebb *and* flow without *both* the pleasure *and* the discomfort.

> Consequences are natural outcomes of choices.

2. Personal accountability matters

Sometimes a person is in a tough spot because they've made choices that put themselves there and the sting of consequences is how they learn to make better choices. As we saw in the chapter on responsibility (chapter 19), having choice without consequences doesn't work—it undermines our efforts to build self-respect and if we want fairness in society, we need accountability.

3. Sometimes, there's not much you can do

We're bound to face experiences in life where we want to ease suffering, but there isn't that much we can personally do. Nonetheless, the human-to-human acknowledgment of compassion is still a powerful gift that we can offer. As bestselling author and Buddhist nun Pema Chödrön writes in *Welcoming the Unwelcome*, when we are free from our own reactions and come from a place of benevolence, "even if there's nothing dramatic we can do to help, other people will feel our support, which actually helps a lot."[9]

Why compassion is important

Compassion helps us balance multiple needs—sincerity, boundaries, fairness, and responsibility. It helps us to see a fellow human who is hurting and inspires us to want to help, but it also helps us keep perspective about what the right thing to do actually is. Instead of focusing on our own emotions and opinions, compassion helps us bring respect and responsibility into the equation so we can balance what's caring with what's fair and good for long-term well-being.

Compassion offers us a range of ways we can respond to suffering, given the circumstances and our own abilities. We might be inspired to connect and resonate for a moment in shared humanity, or we might offer a kind gesture. We might donate to a relief fund or lend a hand personally. If we're able, we might even start an organization to address the bigger issue on a broader scale. The important thing is that *compassion helps us respond to our human drive to do something when we see suffering, while it helps us objectively decide what the right response is.*

Compassion as a common value

The world belief systems we saw in chapter 12 universally called on people to be compassionate. They acknowledged that life would have challenges, and compassion was how people could help each other through the hard times. We saw themes around:

Meeting each other in a place of goodwill– Acting with benevolence, lovingkindness, gentleness, peace, and love.

Facing life's challenges with resilience– Having gratitude for the good in one's life. Having courage and persevering through the hard times.

Helping others who are in need– Being generous, charitable, and helping others become able to care for themselves.

Resolving differences– Listening, seeking understanding, and acting with forgiveness and mercy.

Throughout the belief systems, compassion lends a softness that helps ease the harshness we may experience in life; yet at the same time, compassion has an undercurrent that reflects the strength that's needed to face challenges with courage.

> Compassion draws on our strength to persevere so we can help each other through the hard times.

The Compassion Continuum

So we've seen that compassion helps us connect with each other with sincerity, but within healthy boundaries that honor fairness and responsibility. It's time to take our discussion a step further: When we see that someone is suffering, how do we know how much and what to do? Let's put COMPASSION on a continuum, like we did for TRUTH, RESPECT, and RESPONSIBILITY, to help us see where the lines are between helping and hurting.

The Compassion Continuum

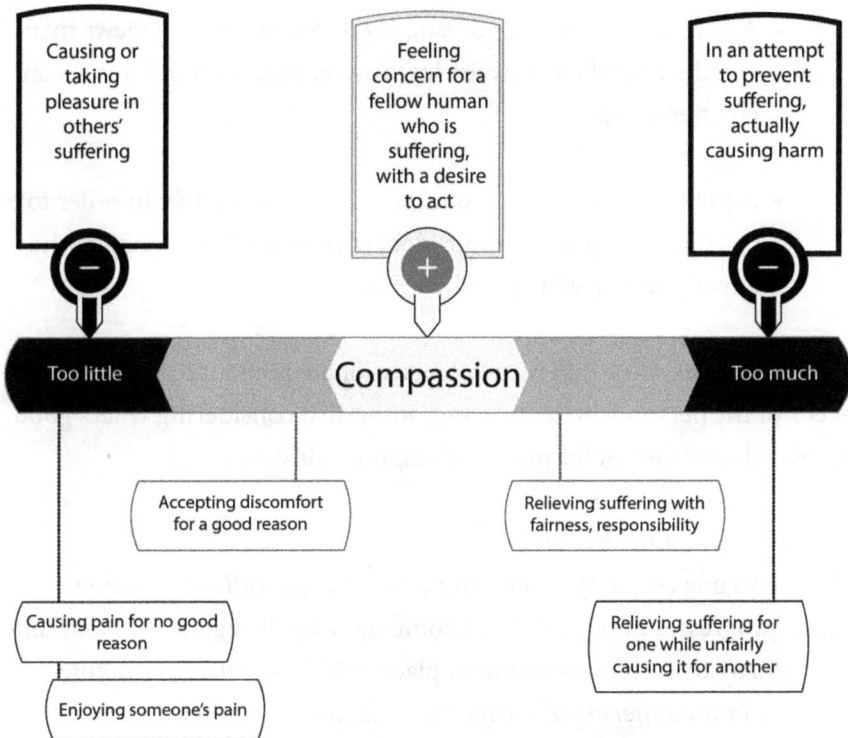

Causing or taking pleasure in others' suffering

Feeling concern for a fellow human who is suffering, with a desire to act

In an attempt to prevent suffering, actually causing harm

− + −

Too little   **Compassion**   Too much

Accepting discomfort for a good reason

Relieving suffering with fairness, responsibility

Causing pain for no good reason

Relieving suffering for one while unfairly causing it for another

Enjoying someone's pain

GOOD, MORAL COMPASSION

Starting at the middle of the continuum, we have *good, moral compassion,* where *we have concern for a fellow human who is suffering, and objectively determine how we should act to help.* Let's look at some examples of compassion that recognize the human behind the suffering, and balance caring with fairness and responsibility:

- A parent tells their teen they can't go out Saturday because they didn't finish their homework. Even though the parent feels bad that the teen is sad and mopey, they still hold firm on the consequence so their child learns to be more responsible.

- A neighbor, who holds drastically different political views than you do, has fallen on some ice. You see past your differences and go offer to help.

- A politician who wants to forgive student loan debt in order to be compassionate also considers what is fair to the people who already sacrificed to pay their loans.

These examples show that being compassionate is about focusing on the needs of the person who is suffering, while also considering what's good for overall well-being, fairness, and responsibility.

TOO LITTLE COMPASSION

Moving to one end of the continuum, we have *too little compassion*, which progresses in severity from someone who disregards the suffering of others to an even more immoral place, which is **causing or taking pleasure in the suffering of others**. For example:

- A parent creates an unreasonably harsh consequence for a teen who made a mistake, not because it's really teaching the teen something, but because the parent is satisfying their own hurt and anger.

- When a YouTuber tricks a homeless man by giving him toothpaste-filled Oreos, so he can post a video of the mean act for his followers.[10]

- When someone intentionally coughs in someone's face during the COVID pandemic because they're angry at the other person's choice to wear a mask.[11] Or when people mock and take pleasure in the death of someone who refused the vaccine and then contracted COVID.[12]

Having a callous disregard or grim pleasure in others' suffering is anti-compassionate. When we refuse to see there are real people who are hurting, we are missing the human vulnerability that is in all of us.

TOO MUCH COMPASSION

Moving to the other end of the continuum, we have *too much compassion*, where *we are so concerned with relieving suffering, that we lose objectivity and inadvertently cause suffering.* We may be trying to help someone, but our good intentions cause negative outcomes. Or, we may help one person or group with such focus, we don't recognize the harm we're causing another. Some examples from our current times include:

- Residents and businesses in some liberal US cities are pushing back against policies that are compassionate toward the homeless but create unfair and unsafe conditions for others.[13] Communities argue that having to step around used drug needles, dealing with rising trash heaps, and increases in crime are just some examples where compassionate tolerance of one group's behavior is causing harmful conditions for others. As one city commissioner puts it, "We're choosing to tolerate the intolerable," and it's damaging the community.[14]

- During the COVID pandemic, schools were closed in the name of protecting the vulnerable and protecting children themselves. In 2022, after analyzing a number of studies, *The New York Times* reported that, "Extended school closures appear to have done

much more harm than good, and many school administrators
probably could have recognized as much by the fall of 2020."[15]
Extended school closures caused lasting harm to children, not
just in learning loss, but in mental health, social development,
child abuse prevention, education inequality, and other factors.[16]
Despite evidence of this early in the pandemic, policies continued
to focus on preventing suffering in one area while inadvertently
causing it in another.

In each of these examples, having compassion for vulnerable humans
was the right thing to do. *But widening the viewport to see how
compassionate actions for one group could also affect another group
would allow advocates, policymakers, and the community to have more
objectivity.* It opens the dialog to find ways to balance compassion with
fairness and the well-being of society overall.

> Compassion, like responsibility, has to be balanced with our
> shared values of fairness and accountability.

Navigating the gray areas

Obviously, callous disregard for suffering is immoral, but when is it
right to live with some discomfort, or to insist that someone is held
accountable even though it hurts? When is good intent to relieve suffering
in one area actually not in a person or society's best interest? Like we saw
with responsibility, our options aren't between two extremes of *should*

or *shouldn't* we act. ***Our options lie in the vast alternatives of when, how much, and in what way we should act.***

To find the right way to be compassionate, we might ask ourselves:

- Who is suffering? What is their perspective? What do they need?

- Is what I want to do about making me feel better or is it about getting the person/group who is suffering what they need?

- Objectively, what would be fair and responsible? Does the action take away someone's personal accountability?

- Are there other people or groups who will be negatively impacted short-term or long-term?

A path forward

Whether we're deciding what to do for an errant teen, an employee who is consistently distracted by personal problems, or a social policy that seems like it's ignoring our needs for the sake of other people, at all levels of our lives we face questions about what the right amount of compassion looks like. Compassion helps us find balance between relieving suffering and being fair and responsible to the bigger picture of well-being. As the world belief systems showed, benevolence and lovingkindness can help us through the hard times. ***Compassion inspires us to care about our fellow humans, and it also helps us channel our desire to act in a truly helpful way.***

Journaling

Have you ever found it hard to empathize with someone? Or, have you ever empathized so much it was hard on you?

Are there situations where you think someone should work through their discomfort or do you believe it's better to avoid all pain?

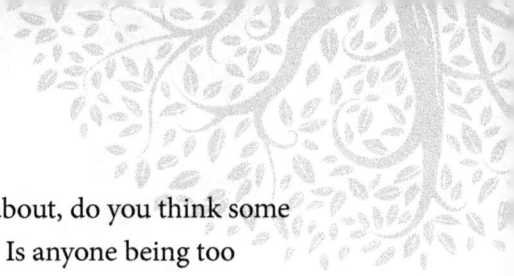

Thinking of an issue that you feel strongly about, do you think some people aren't being compassionate enough? Is anyone being too compassionate?

Up Next

In this chapter we dug into the suffering side of connecting with our fellow humans. In the next chapter, we'll turn to brighter topics, like how feeling positive emotions with each other and seeing progress toward our vision of a better world amplifies our possibilities for joy.

Chapter 22

The Bright Side

How a little perspective changes everything

Your mind will take the shape of what you frequently hold in thought,
for the human spirit is colored by such impressions.

—Marcus Aurelius, *Meditations* 5.16[1]

If this quote from Stoic philosopher Marcus Aurelius is correct, a mind
that constantly holds images of suffering and victimization is bound to be
colored in hues of a dark hopelessness. But what if even in the sadness of
suffering we can find bright shades that will color our minds with hope?
Fortunately, compassion and our entire empathic process do just that.
We're wired to connect and respond to suffering, but we're also lifted
through that connection. Compassion gives life depth, elevating us out of
an existence made up of a series of tasks and struggles, to a place where
we find meaning in the bad and joy in the good. In this final chapter,
let's look at the positive side of the empathic process and discover some
techniques to experience more joy with other people than we could
possibly do alone.

The hidden gift of compassion

Compassion and empathy are an integral part of being human. In fact, in *The Compassionate Instinct*, UC Berkeley researcher Dacher Keltner argues that compassion has been so important over the course of human evolution that it has evolved into our biology:

> Compassion and benevolence, this research suggests, are an evolved part of human nature, rooted in our brain and biology, and ready to be cultivated for the greater good.[2]

The short version of how this happened is that back in hunter-gatherer times, the humans who cared for and responded to suffering in their young, had young who survived to pass on those caring genes. And the tribes full of people who looked out for each other had a better chance of surviving than the tribes full of people who were more selfish and less cooperative. So perhaps it's no wonder, based on how it helped us survive, that a compassionate instinct became wired-in to our very humanness. What may be surprising though, is that compassion isn't just good for the person on the receiving end. Compassion also delivers physical and mental benefits for the person who offers it. According to Keltner:[3]

- Helping others triggers activity in the brain in the same places we receive rewards and experience pleasure, which means acting with compassion for others can give us "the same pleasure we get from the gratification of personal desire."

- When we feel threatened, our heart rate and breathing increase as we prepare for fight or flight. But when we respond to another's suffering with compassion, our heart rate decreases as we prepare "to approach and soothe."

- When people do small acts with compassionate love, like offering "warm smiles, friendly hand gestures, [or] affirmative forward leans," their bodies release oxytocin, which generates feelings of internal warmth and pleasure; and that motivates them to be even more compassionate.

So it truly seems that doing good feels good—for both the person on the receiving end and the person offering compassion. *If we're looking for some bright hues amidst suffering, the act of compassion is its own source of light.*

Sharing joy in others' joy

Given that the empathic process is ingrained in our biology, we might as well see how to work with it in a positive and healthy way. From the last chapter, we know that it's important to have healthy boundaries so we don't become overwhelmed by empathic distress. But did you know, the empathic process has a positive side too? Researchers studied how people experience empathy in real-life and they discovered that *people empathize with other people's positive emotions (like excitement and enthusiasm) three times more frequently* than their negative emotions (like disgust, anger, and fear.)[4] Since we tend to empathize with people who are close to us, this research means that when we share in our family's, friends', and other close connections' joys, we get to experience more joy. And when we are more joyful, they get to share in ours. I'm not sure what the math equation looks like for this, but it must be something where joy times joy equals a whole lot more joy.

> Take joy in others' joy and you get joy to infinity.[5]

Of course, having more joy doesn't mean we won't experience sorrow. Remember that hedonic adaptation issue from chapter 1? We adapt quickly to joys and sorrows so that we can recover to a healthy baseline. But couldn't we all use some more joys to offset the sorrows? This research on empathy shows us that sources of positivity are a lot closer at hand than we might realize. Sharing joy with others is one simple way to brighten our outlook.

A little perspective goes a long way

Even if our friends and family are having moments of joy, there's still lots of bad stuff happening in the world. We started this book with the question, "Does it ever feel like the world's gone sideways?" Watching the news or scanning the headlines could certainly make it seem like we're sliding sideways and downward. Yet if we look at the issues through a perspective of compassion—with objectivity—we might discover rays of light that lead us toward a more hopeful attitude.

If you want to feel better about the world, watch one of Hans Rosling's TED Talks, which use surprising data and a fair bit of humor to show how the state of the world is actually improving. In his book *Factfulness: Ten Reasons We're Wrong About the World—And Why Things are Better Than You Think*, Rosling explains that despite evidence, people resist the idea that life on Earth isn't in a downward spiral. He explains:

> My guess is you *feel* that me saying that the world is getting better
> is like me telling you that everything is fine, or that you should look
> away from these problems and pretend they don't exist: and that feels
> ridiculous, and stressful.[6]

Rosling argues he's instead encouraging people to see that for any issue, there's a state and a direction. When you look at the issue over time, the state of a situation can be "bad" while the direction it's going can be toward getting "better." By being objective about a situation that is both "bad and better," we can feel encouraged that things are improving.

Rosling thoughtfully explains that we aren't denying or betraying those who are suffering by seeing the good:

> I'm a very serious "possibilist." That's something I made up. It means someone who neither hopes without reason, nor fears without reason, someone who constantly resists the overdramatic worldview. As a possibilist, I see all this progress, and it fills me with conviction and hope that further progress is possible.[7]

Rosling's statement is in line with how we defined the true virtuousness of compassion in the last chapter: We can care for our fellow humans while realistically and objectively figuring out how we can keep making life better.

Little wins motivate big wins

There's another reason that we need to pay attention to the bits of progress that lead us toward our goals. Holding the goal out in the distance isn't the secret to getting where we're trying to go. Best-selling author James Clear, in *Atomic Habits*, points out that "Winners and losers have the same goals."[8] (*Wow, pause and think about that for a second.*) He goes on to explain that having a goal doesn't often translate into overnight success. The person who achieves their goal gets there by making continuous small improvements. The changes may be so incremental that it seems like nothing is happening—until those small changes cross a threshold that reveals something has been happening all along.

By celebrating the small wins, we see that we are moving toward the goal, and that keeps us motivated. As an example, if someone is going through a long process of physical therapy after an injury, when they make a small improvement we don't say, "Whatever. Not important. Tell me when you're fully healed and then I'll be happy." (*At least, I hope any compassionate person wouldn't.*) Instead, we encourage them: "I know this is hard but you're doing great. Every little bit counts." Similarly, as we face these issues that seem overwhelmingly large, we can remember that small wins keep us motivated toward achieving bigger wins, so let's enjoy those positive moments together. And if you're facing a daunting personal goal, then a little self-compassion may be in order. The same concept applies whether we're working on internal change or external change—each step in the right direction counts.

> Celebrating the small wins keeps people motivated, and it gives us the opportunity to share in each other's joy.

A moment of gratitude

With all these opportunities for positivity, what can we do to notice and enjoy them? One powerful technique to bring more attention to the positive moments in our lives is through gratitude. This isn't a new idea. In fact, the world belief systems we saw in chapter 12 included lots of old-school wisdom about appreciating what one has. For example, the Bible says, "Rejoice always, pray without ceasing, give thanks in all circumstances." (1 Thess. 5:16-18)[9] Gratitude may be rooted in ancient wisdom, but modern science has also proven that it has notable benefits.

Sonya Lyubomirsky, who you may recall from chapter 1, has studied the impact of gratitude on people's lives. In *The How of Happiness*, she describes gratitude like this:

Gratitude is many things to many people. It is wonder; it is appreciation; it is looking at the bright side of a setback; it is fathoming abundance; it is thanking someone in your life; it is thanking God; it is "counting blessings." It is savoring; it is not taking things for granted; it is coping; it is present-oriented. Gratitude is an antidote to negative emotions, a neutralizer of envy, avarice, hostility, worry, and irritation.[10]

Lyubomirsky has shown that the simple practice of gratitude (and I'll show you a quick and easy technique in just a minute) has been shown not just to correlate, but actually *to create well-being in* people's lives with effects such as:

- Improving optimism and satisfaction with life
- Boosting physical health, such as by reducing headaches, acne, coughing, and nausea
- Experiencing more positive emotions like interest, excitement, joy, and pride
- Helping people feel more connected with others
- Improving the quality of sleep

If I didn't have you at improving optimism, surely the better-quality sleep sold you on gratitude!?!

How can gratitude do so much? The reasons that gratitude has such a positive impact on well-being may sound familiar—they reflect some of the themes we've seen throughout this book about how to create well-being, such as knowing one's worth, seeing how our actions have an impact, growing through discomfort, and feeling connected to others.

8 Ways Gratitude Boosts Positivity[11]

1. We savor the good– Gratitude helps us pay attention to the good so we can more fully enjoy it.

2. It boosts self-worth– Gratitude helps us see how much people have done for us and how much we've accomplished.

3. It helps us cope with stress– Gratitude helps us find the good—the lesson, the silver-lining, the growth—even in trauma and stress.

4. It encourages moral acts– Gratitude helps us to be aware of kind acts and to want to reciprocate.

5. It helps build social bonds– Gratitude helps us feel more connected to people, both in existing relationships and when we're nurturing new ones.

6. It's an antidote to envy– Gratitude encourages us to be grateful for what we have instead of comparing ourselves to others.

7. It reduces negative emotions– While in a state of gratitude, negative emotions like jealousy and anger dissolve.

8. It helps keep our satisfaction "fresh"– Gratitude helps reset our appreciation for the good things in our lives instead of taking them for granted.

And maybe, just maybe, you can uncover more themes as you practice gratitude. So here is a simple way to go about practicing it, if you choose to do so.

How to practice gratitude

Are you ready to reap the benefits of gratitude? To practice gratitude, based on Lyubomirsky's research, the steps are very simple.

> **Once a week, ask yourself, "What are a few small or large things from the past week that I'm grateful for?"**

It helps to set a reminder and take a moment each week to answer this question. If you want to journal about the things you're grateful for, there are a few pages at the end of this chapter, or you can print some journaling pages from RootedInDecency.com. But if writing's not your thing, you could also contemplate, tell a friend, or express your gratitude in another way, like doing something creative. The important thing is to practice gratitude regularly, but not so often that it feels like a chore.

In the studies described in *The How of Happiness*, after just six weeks of writing down things they were grateful for one time per week, respondents in "the gratitude group reported significantly bigger increases in their happiness levels" than the control group.[12] So why not give it a try? If you want to try some other scientifically proven techniques to boost your outlook, Lyubomirsky's *The How of Happiness* includes a number of activities that can help.

A path forward

If we look around in life, we're bound to find suffering. In fact, evolution has helped us become attuned to it, while biological processes drive us to respond to it. But remember this isn't a bad thing. Those biological processes actually help the person who is being compassionate as well as the person receiving compassion. The entire empathic process has an upside: It helps us connect and share life with each other. We support each other in the hard times and we celebrate with each other in the good times. Despite all the hardship in the world, empathy has been shown to give us three times more occasions to feel positive emotions with people in our daily lives than to feel negative ones. *We can enjoy these bright hues by looking for the good, acknowledging the positive progress, and celebrating the little wins. Being grateful for the good things—both big and small—gives us the hope we need to keep trying to make things better.* So perhaps we can give ourselves permission to enjoy the journey.

Journaling

Looking back in time, what are some ways life is better today than it used to be?

Have you ever had a long-term goal? How did you keep yourself motivated while you worked toward it?

What do you think of the idea of being a "possibilist"—someone who neither hopes without reason, nor fears without reason, and finds hope in progress?

See the next two pages for gratitude journaling prompts, or print gratitude journaling pages from RootedInDecency.com.

Up next

Well you did it! You've reached the end of the book. In the conclusion, we'll take a brief look back at where we've journeyed and sum up some key learnings.

Gratitude Journaling

What are a few small or large things from the past week that you're grateful for?

Week 1:

Week 2:

Week 3:

Week 4:

Week 5:

Week 6:

Conclusion

Well here we are at the end of this book. Congrats on taking on a topic that's important for each of us and all of us. We started in chapter 1 by looking at how people really find lasting happiness amidst so much instability today. We discovered that a good life doesn't come from external sources; instead, modern science showed us that the secret to lasting happiness comes from within.

Key sources of lasting happiness and well-being:

- **Honest self-awareness** about our thoughts, feelings, and environment.

- **Internal self-respect** that comes from knowing we are good people who are valued in our relationships with others.

- **Personal responsibility** which includes building a strong sense of agency to make choices and create our own outcomes.

- **Appreciating the positives** in life and recovering from the tough times.

The more we looked within, we saw that today's culture encourages extremes in how we think, feel, and connect that fight against those sources of happiness and stability. But we also saw that we can counter those cultural forces by developing our sense of self-respect, based in the knowledge that we are making decent, moral choices that we can be proud of. *Being rooted in decency offers stability even when life feels like it's gone sideways.*

When we looked outward, we saw that we aren't just individuals, we're individuals who live in societies. Early humans learned how to balance what they wanted for themselves with the way they needed to behave with others, in order to be part of a society that would help them thrive. Not only did humans value the same core behaviors across time and geography, our very biology evolved to help us know what was helpful and what was harmful to our well-being. When society isn't behaving in line with those core values, we feel it in our bodies. *We know when the ground rules we depend on for stability and security aren't being honored, and that's far more unsettling than we may have consciously realized.*

The Moral Compass

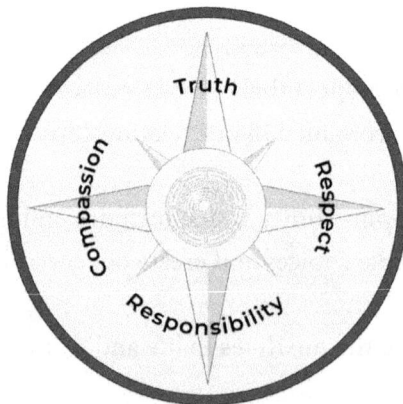

We went on to look at thousands of years of human wisdom and found that the core values that maintain social order and foster trust, cooperation, and fairness can be distilled down into four key points on our moral compass.

The guiding values on our moral compass:

- **Truth**– Being honest with ourselves and others, in our words, actions, and intentions.

- **Respect**– Having self-respect and treating others with the care and dignity we'd like in return.

- **Responsibility**– Voluntarily putting boundaries on our behavior, doing our duties to create well-being, and owning the outcomes of our actions.

- **Compassion**– Sharing the good moments and helping each other through the hard times, with objectivity and responsibility.

We don't have to be perfectly good all the time, but we need shared expectations that ensure most of the time, we're choosing paths that honor these values. *Unless we live life rooted in decency, we don't stand a chance at benefiting from fairness, justice, and freedom.*

The surprising parallels between ancient and modern

Now that we're at a point where we can reflect back on all we've learned during our journey through this book, if we compare those key sources for happiness from chapter 1 (noted at the start of the conclusion) and the guiding values from our moral compass from part three (recounted on this page), you might have noticed that they're very similar. Modern science and ancient moral wisdom inadvertently lead us to the same conclusion: *Well-being and happiness are linked, and the path to achieving them is by living life in line with good moral principles.* So, if you were hoping for a quick answer about how to find inner peace in a world gone sideways, here it is:

> Choose to live a life rooted in decency. It's good for you as an individual and it's good for us as a society. The way to be a decent person is to live a life guided by Truth, Respect, Responsibility, and Compassion, which also happens to be the secret to lasting happiness and well-being.

∿

Chapter Highlights

If you want to remember where some of your favorite "a-ha" moments were throughout the book, here are some brief summaries to help you find them.

Part One

In part one, we looked within to see why we may personally be feeling off-balance in today's culture. We discovered some ideas about how thinking (mind), feeling (body), and connecting (spirit) work together to bring us an internal sense of stability and well-being.

1. Finding Lasting Happiness

Thanks to the **Hedonic Treadmill**, we quickly adapt to both the good things and bad things that are bound to happen in life. That means we'll never "just" be happy, but it also means we're better able to roll with the ebbs and flows of life. Whether we're trying to find happiness, manage stress, or achieve a transcendent well-being, the way to get there is through **honest self-awareness, appreciating the positive, internal self-respect, and personal responsibility**.

2. Mindless Thinking

Instead of reacting automatically, **thinking mindfully** helps us leverage that powerful human strength to evaluate, reason, and consciously engage with what's going on around us. By checking our **cognitive distortions** we can break out of automatic thinking cycles that inflate negativity and hopelessness. The **Triple-column Technique** is one approach to help us identify distortions and engage more rationally.

3. The Body's Language

Denying or suppressing "negative" emotions robs us of valuable information. To use the signals the body is sending us, we can **notice emotions like we notice the other five senses**, taking in the information they offer and then flowing back to equilibrium. The **Three-minute Breathing Space Technique** is one way to pause and notice feelings in a grounded and balanced way.

4. Spirited Connection

Endlessly scrolling through sensational headlines and hate-filled social media posts may feed our sense of outrage, but like Alan Watts' comparison to "orgasm without release," it won't offer the fulfillment we're seeking. Instead, opportunities to **experience awe and wonder in everyday life**—through beauty, threat, ability, and human goodness—are more likely to help us feel **elevated and connected to something greater than ourselves**.

5. Self-Respect vs. Self-Esteem

If we really want to feel good about ourselves, we need to embrace the **positive-negative-positive cycle** that comes with honestly looking at our behavior. Another way of putting it: Just because we don't want to feel bad about a choice, that doesn't mean it was a good choice. A **healthy conscience sends us signals** about whether we are living up to our own principles—and by listening to it, **we can build self-respect that isn't easily shaken** no matter what is going on around us.

Part Two

In part two, we expanded our scope outward to see how we're not just individuals, but individuals who live in societies. Being a decent person has benefits for our inner lives, but it's also essential to the way we live life with other people. Humans need each other, so whether we're cooperating or competing, the quality of our lives is better when we treat each other decently.

6. You Be You—Unless You're a Jerk

Society has evolved to be anti-jerk because our ancestors figured out that we gain something by **cooperating and connecting** with other people. Today, most of us still choose to control our own behavior so that we can enjoy the benefits of being part of society. Through **bonding and bridging social capital**, society helps us reach beyond what we can do alone. Ultimately, expanding outside our own self-focused sphere helps us to be **healthier, happier, and to find more meaning in life**.

7. Competing Moral Priorities

If you've wondered why someone can think they're right while you clearly think they're wrong, the two of you may have different moral priorities. In a given moral decision, we may weigh a combination of **Haidt's Six Moral Foundations**: Care/Harm, Fairness/Cheating, Liberty/Oppression, Loyalty/Betrayal, Authority/Subversion, Sanctity/Degradation. As we feel our way through the decision, and we consider what our group thinks, we may be blind to other people's perspectives. But realizing this offers us a way to **see people we disagree with not as "bad" people, but as people with different priorities.**

8. Us Versus Them

The issue with today's divisiveness is that it leverages biology to turn politics into a tribal battle for survival. Stoking outrage based in **moral disgust** creates a culture that feels like we're constantly under threat. But, **we don't have to buy the outrage other people are selling**. Instead, we can use our **Check Accuracy Warning** light to be more aware of biases and to **counter extreme thinking**. And we can even leverage our ability to easily shift our group identities based on some other **common goal or common interest**—like wanting a more stable, peaceful society.

9. The Contagion of Cruelty and Kindness

We tend to decide an action is correct based on what other people are doing, especially those in our group. Thanks to Cialdini's research on **social proof**, if we want people not to do something, it needs to appear to be uncommon and unacceptable. Shrugging off **bad behavior leads to more bad behavior**. On the other hand, **kindness is equally contagious**, so go ahead and do something nice for someone. You can increase both your and their **jen ratios** with a little extra positivity, and a little less negativity.

10. The Myth of Perfection

None of us are perfect, so we can just go ahead and liberate ourselves from the idea that we need to be. Sometimes though, **we figure out who we want to be, by seeing who we don't want to be.** So as we learn to be rooted in decency, we can let go of old habits that no longer serve us and take comfort in knowing that **each moment is a moment to choose** a new way of being with ourselves and of being with each other. **Right now is a great time to make a good choice.**

Part Three

With parts one and two of the book having established that being a decent person is good for us as individuals and as a society, part three took on the subject of what being a decent person really looks like. In a time when people seem to disagree about what "right" behavior is, we stepped back to explore where morality came from, what common values people can agree on, and how we can apply guiding principles in our daily lives.

11. Right and Wrong

Morality grew out of a need for **ground rules** about how we live and cooperate together. Behaviors that helped well-being were valued by society and became **virtues**. Behaviors that harmed well-being became **vices**. While religion was part of the evolution of morality, **people can be moral without being religious**, which is a good thing considering how many humans aren't religious these days. **The way we define right and wrong isn't arbitrary or strictly personal**—it's based on which behaviors help people flourish together.

12. Shared Values

The seven major enduring belief systems we examined—Hinduism, Judaism, Confucianism, Buddhism, Christianity, Islam, and the Greek Philosophers—all share **common themes in their moral codes**. The systems emphasize the need to **live with good values as a way of life**, to **take responsibility for our own well-being**, and to treat others with care and in ways that promote **trust, fairness, and cooperation**. Individuals **enjoy the benefits (or suffer the consequences)** of their own actions.

13. Defining a Moral Compass

The world belief systems hold great wisdom about which behaviors we humans have valued over time and across geographies. But since that's kind of a lot to process, we took the moral codes and distilled them down into four main values that we can use as guiding principles in daily life.

We revealed a new **moral compass** that contains four main points: **Truth, Respect, Responsibility, and Compassion.**

14. What Is Truth

Being truthful means that we **speak and act in a way that represents things as they are in factual reality.** The way we live together means we sometimes choose to bend the truth because it helps us cooperate and compete more kindly. We can navigate the gray areas around telling the right amount of truth, in the right way, by considering **intent, accuracy,** and the **consequences** we're having on our other principles.

15. Trust Me

The **truth still matters** today and always because society runs on trust, and **you can't have trust without truth.** A lack of truth **affects our ability to make good decisions** and it leaves **smudges** on our interactions that impact our **relationships** and our **own sense of self-worth.**

16. Willfully Deceived

The idea of a **"post-truth" era** is really just a climate where the truth exists, but people are willing to put that truth aside so that they can choose to believe what they are comfortable believing. When we allow a culture of lies to stand, we are teaching people that they have nothing to lose by trying to lie to us. And sometimes, we are **willing participants in our own deceit** because we don't want to question our beliefs. By using the **4 Tips for Managing Cognitive Dissonance,** we can be careful not to rationalize away our own morality just because we don't like unpleasant truths.

17. What Is Respect

When we treat someone or something with respect, it isn't necessarily because we admire or even agree with them, but **we do value the principle that people should be treated with appropriate care and dignity.** We can devalue people through too little respect, and we can also cause harm with too much respect that leads us to blindly obey people or ideologies. We can live together with fairness and justice by committing to our unwritten agreement that: **I will treat you with the care and dignity you deserve, and in return, I expect you will treat me with the care and dignity I deserve as a fellow human.**

18. Working Against Ourselves

In the name of respect for their own groups, some groups in society are **justifying being disrespectful**—degrading, violent, and even dehumanizing—to others. **Public shaming** is just one tool in the arsenal, and instead of holding people accountable, it's turning society into a **despot** with unchecked power. There's hope though! With **4 Ways to Improve Respect**, we can decide what we really want, address actions and consequences civilly and without the shame, and we can step behind a veil of ignorance to do a better job of restoring true fairness and justice in society.

19. What Is Responsibility

Being responsible is about **choosing to act in a way that promotes well-being for ourselves and for our relationships**, so it's a powerful force that helps us **manage the give-and-take** that makes social life possible. **Responsibility empowers us** to have control over our own lives, but it also **demands that we accept accountability** for the consequences we create. We can be irresponsible, and we can be too responsible; so managing the gray areas of responsibility comes down to creating **public justifications** of **when, how much, and under what circumstances** boundaries, duties, and accountability are reasonable for both individual and shared well-being.

20. Life After Victimhood

Identity politics began as a way to address historic wrongs where our society wasn't living up to its ideals of **fair and equal give-and-take.** Today though, it's morphed into a **competitive victimhood** that is counterproductive to its own aims. The **collective blame culture** goes against our principles of responsibility, respect, and honesty. And by identifying with suffering, identity politics can lock its own members in a perpetual **mindset of victimization**. Instead, we can choose to step away from divisive victim culture and divisive nostalgia so that we may **define a new American story** based in common values.

21. What Is Compassion

Compassion is **feeling concern for a fellow human being** who is suffering, **along with a desire to act**. Yet because it comes from a neutral place of shared humanity, compassion helps us to be **objective about what can and should be done**, even if that means allowing discomfort and the pain of consequences. We can lack compassion or we can have too much compassion, where we inadvertently cause suffering because we aren't being objective. Dealing with the gray areas of compassion means we are inspired to care for fellow humans, but we **channel that desire to act in a truly helpful way**.

22. The Bright Side

Compassion is such an important asset for humans that we've evolved to be **wired to offer it and to get physical and mental benefits from doing so**. The empathic process helps us **connect and share in each other's joys** too, not just in our suffering. So go ahead and share some joy, **notice the things you're grateful for**, and **celebrate the small wins**, because that's what gives us hope and helps us persevere through life's ups and downs. Compassion gives life depth and meaning.

With that, we're done for now. I invite you to explore RootedInDecency.com for journaling and mindfulness activities that can help you on your own path.

Acknowledgments

I'd like to thank my family and friends for listening to countless discussions of "a-ha" moments and not a small amount of moral philosophy at the dinner table. In particular, thanks to Cole for her insights and enthusiastic discussions; to Gregory for being so supportive; and to Ci for showing each morning that he cared what I was working on. Thanks to all my friends who read early versions and gave me such valuable feedback and encouragement. To the book's fantastic editor, Elizabeth Zack, thank you for your guidance and insight. Thanks to the whole team that supported this effort as I channeled my inner Aristotle. And to the creators of the works referenced throughout the book, thank you for sharing your wisdom, and allowing me to present it in a new light.

Notes

Introduction

1. Robert Sapolsky, *Behave: The biology of humans at our best and worst* (Penguin 2017). For more on this, see chapter 8 of this book, *Rooted in decency*.

2. See chapter 12 of this book, *Rooted in decency*.

3. Sonja Lyubomirsky, *The how of happiness: A new approach to getting the life you want* (Penguin 2007). For more on this, see chapter 1 of this book, *Rooted in decency*.

Part One- Looking Inward

1. Pew Research Center, *In U.S., decline of Christianity continues at rapid pace,* 2019, October 17. https://www.pewforum.org/2019/10/17/in-u-s-decline-of-christianity-continues-at-rapid-pace/

2. Huston Smith, *The world's religions* (Harper One 1991, Originally published 1958), p.101.

3. _____.

Chapter 1: Finding Lasting Happiness

1. Sonja Lyubomirsky, *The how of happiness: A new approach to getting the life you want* (Penguin 2007).

2. _____, p. 37.

3. Dacher Keltner, *Born to be good: The science of a meaningful life* (WW Norton 2009), p. 13.

4. Lyubomirsky, *The how of happiness*, p. 50.

5. _____, pp. 41-42.

6. _____, p. 48.

7. _____, p. 22.

8. Paul Napper & Anthony Rao, *The power of agency: The 7 principles to conquer obstacles, make effective decisions, and create a life on your own terms* (St. Martin's Press 2019), p. 3.

9. _____, p. 6. Emphasis from original source.

10. _____, p.15. Emphasis from original source.

11. Scott Barry Kaufman, *Transcend: The new science of self-actualization* (Penguin Random House 2020), p. xxvi.

12. _____, p. 60.

13. _____, p. xxvi.

Chapter 2: Mindless Thinking

1. Shelley Carson & Ellen Langer, Mindfulness and self-acceptance, *Journal of Rational-Emotive & Cognitive-Behavior Therapy*, 24(1), 2006, 29–43. https://doi.org/10.1007/s10942-006-0022-5

2. _____, p. 30.

3. _____, p. 30.

4. Adapted from Mark Williams, John Teasdale, Zindel Segal, & Jon Kabat-Zinn, *The mindful way through depression: Freeing yourself from chronic unhappiness* (The Guilford Press 2007).

5. _____.

6. Adapted from David Burns, *Feeling good: The new mood therapy* (Harper 2012, Originally published 1980) and Greg Lukianoff & Jonathan Haidt, *The coddling of the American mind: How good intentions and bad ideas are setting up a generation for failure* (Penguin 2018). Burns discusses cognitive distortions with respect to how individuals inflate negative perceptions of themselves. Lukianoff and Haidt expand those concepts to societal distortions.

7. Lukianoff & Haidt, *The coddling of the American mind,* p. 89.

8. _____, p. 89. Emphasis from original source.

9. Charles Sykes, *How the right lost its mind* (St. Martin's Press 2017), p. 180.

10. Discussion of CBT and triple-column approach from Burns, *Feeling good.*

11. For data on effectiveness see Burns, *Feeling good,* Kindle p. 674.

Chapter 3: The Body's Language

1. Adapted from Robert Sapolsky, *Behave: The biology of humans at our best and worst* (Penguin 2017).

2. _____, pp. 4-5.

3. Mark Williams, John Teasdale, Zindel Segal & Jon Kabat-Zinn, *The mindful way through depression: Freeing yourself from chronic unhappiness* (The Guilford Press 2007).

4. _____, p. 35.

5. Karla McLaren, *The language of emotions: What your feelings are trying to tell you* (Sounds True 2010).

6. Dacher Keltner, *Born to be good: The science of a meaningful life* (W.W. Norton 2009).

7. Williams, et. al., *The mindful way.*

8. Harvard Health, *Exercising to relax,* Harvard Medical School, 2020, July 7. https://www.health.harvard.edu/staying-healthy/exercising-to-relax.

9. Williams, et. al., *The mindful way,* p. 182. Detail on the Three-Minute Breathing Space Technique on p. 183.

10. _____, p. 183.

Chapter 4: Spirited Connection

1. Pew Research Center, *In U.S., decline of Christianity continues at rapid pace,* 2019, October 17. https://www.pewforum.org/2019/10/17/in-u-s-decline-of-christianity-continues-at-rapid-pace/

2. _____. Between 2009 and 2019, the percentage of US adults who say they attend religious services a few times a year or less increased from 47% to 54%. Those attending monthly or more declined from 52% in 2009 to 45% in 2019.

3. Robert Sapolsky, *Behave: The biology of humans at our best and worst* (Penguin 2017).

4. _____, p.127.

5. _____, p. 127.

6. Hans Rosling, Ola Rosling, & Anna Rosling Rönnlund, *Factfulness: Ten reasons we're wrong about the world - and why things are better than you think* (Flatiron Books 2018).

7. Susan Weinschenk, *The dopamine seeking-reward loop*, Psychology Today, 2018, February 28. https://www.psychologytoday.com/us/blog/brain-wise/201802/the-dopamine-seeking-reward-loop.

8. Maria Popova, *Orgasm without release: Alan Watts presages our modern media gluttony in 1951*, Brain Pickings, 2014, March 11. https://www.brainpickings.org/2014/03/11/alan-watts-media-gluttony/

9. Sapolsky, *Behave*, p. 44.

10. _____, pp. 69-70.

11. Dacher Keltner, *Born to be good: The science of a meaningful life* (W.W. Norton, 2009).

Chapter 5: Self-Respect vs. Self-Esteem

1. Ilona de Hooge, Moral emotions and prosocial behaviour: It may be time to change our view of shame and guilt, *Handbook of Psychology of Emotions: Recent Theoretical Perspectives and Novel Empirical Findings*, Vol 2, 2013, pp. 255-276.

2. _____.

3. Jim Taylor, *Parenting: The sad misuse of self-esteem*, Psychology Today, 2010, Feb 22. https://www.psychologytoday.com/us/blog/the-power-prime/201002/parenting-the-sad-misuse-self-esteem

4. Po Bronson & Ashley Merryman, *NurtureShock: New thinking about children* (Twelve 2009), Kindle loc. 272-273.

5. Roy Baumeister, et. al., Does high self-esteem cause better performance, interpersonal success, happiness, or healthier lifestyles? *Psychological Science in the Public Interest*, 4(1), 2003, May, 1–44. https://doi.org/10.1111/1529-1006.01431

6. Roy Baumeister, Rethinking Self-Esteem, *Stanford Social Innovation Review*, Winter, 2005, p. 36.

7. Shelley Carson & Ellen Langer, Mindfulness and self-acceptance, *Journal of Rational-Emotive & Cognitive-Behavior Therapy*, 24(1), 2006, 29–43. https://doi.org/10.1007/s10942-006-0022-5

8. Bronson & Merryman, *NutureShock*, Kindle loc. 293-301.

9. de Hooge, Moral emotions and prosocial behaviour.

10. Claudine Clucas, Understanding self-respect and its relationship to self-esteem, *Personality and Social Psychology Bulletin*, 46(6), 2019, 839–855. https://doi.org/10.1177/0146167219879115

11. Supported by ideas in Clucas 2019, Taylor 2010, Carson & Langer 2006. Three different approaches to reviewing self-esteem, self-respect, and self-acceptance all suggest that seeing how one's actions lead to consequences (and taking ownership for them), is essential to a more positive and realistic view of oneself.

12. Clucas, Understanding self-respect.

Part Two: Looking Outward

1. Plato, *The republic of Plato* (Jowett, Trans.) (Oxford 1888, Online in 2017 by The Gutenberg Project: https://www.gutenberg.org/files/55201/55201-h/55201-h.htm), 362c.

2. _____, 353e-354a.

3. Jonathan Haidt, *The righteous mind: Why good people are divided by politics and religion* (Pantheon Books 2012).

Chapter 6: You Be You— Unless You're a Jerk

1. Hannah Dobrogosz, *People Are Sharing The "Unwritten Rules" Of Society*, BuzzFeed, 2021, March 15. https://www.buzzfeed.com/hannahdobro/unwritten-rules-to-live-by

2. Supported by discussions in Jonathan Haidt, *The righteous mind: Why good people are divided by politics and religion* (Pantheon Books 2012) and Dacher Keltner, *Born to be good: The science of a meaningful life* (WW Norton 2009).

3. Keltner, *Born to be good*, p. 63.

4. Thomas Paine, *The rights of man: The French Revolution- Ideals, arguments and motives* (Musaicum 2017, Originally published 1791), Kindle loc. 2032-2036.

5. References to social capital and its benefits, see Robert Putnam, *Bowling alone: Revised and updated: The collapse and revival of American community* (Simon & Schuster 2020, Originally published 2000). Quote from p.23.

6. Putnam offers Tupelo, Mississippi as an example. In 1940, it was "one of the poorest counties in the poorest state" in the US. After efforts to develop as a community and promote cooperation, Tupelo became a "national model of community and economic development." Putnam, *Bowling Alone*, p. 323.

7. _____, p. 326.

8. _____, p. 327.

9. Robert Waldinger, *What makes a good life? Lessons from the longest study on happiness*, TED, 2015, November, https://www.ted.com/talks/robert_waldinger_what_makes_a_good_life_lessons_from_the_longest_study_on_happiness/transcript?language=en

10. Haidt, *The righteous mind*, pp. 229-230.

11. Jonathan Sacks, *Morality: Restoring the common good in divided times* (Basic Books 2020), p. 18.

12. Dalai Lama, Desmond Tutu, & Douglas Abrams, *The book of joy* (Penguin 2016).

13. Colleen Doyle Bryant, *Truth be told quotes* (LoveWell Press 2020, Originally published 2018), p. 18.

Chapter 7: Competing Moral Priorities

1. Moral dilemma scenarios as well as discussion and descriptions of moral foundations are adapted from Jonathan Haidt, *The righteous mind: Why good people are divided by politics and religion* (Pantheon Books 2012).

2. Haidt, *The righteous mind*, p. 318.

3. From Marcus Aurelius, *Meditations*, 7.26, as printed in *The daily stoic* by Holiday and Hanselman (Portfolio/Penguin 2016), p.82.

Chapter 8: Us Versus Them

1. Robert Sapolsky, *Behave: The biology of humans at our best and worst* (Penguin 2017).

2. Discussion of oxytocin and mirror neurons from Sapolsky, *Behave* and Jonathan Haidt, *The righteous mind: Why good people are divided by politics and religion* (Pantheon Books 2012).

3. Po Bronson & Ashley Merryman, *NurtureShock: New thinking about children* (Twelve 2009), Kindle loc: 737.

4. Sapolsky, *Behave*, p. 393.

5. _____, p. 398.

6. Supported by Sapolsky, *Behave,* and Haidt, *The righteous mind.*

7. Sapolsky, *Behave*, p. 41.

8. _____, p. 41.

9. Julian Zelizer, *Burning down the house: Newt Gingrich, and the rise of the new Republican party* (Penguin 2020), p. 302.

10. GOPAC Memo, 1990, "Language a Key Mechanism of Control", original document shown in the Internet Archive: https://archive.org/details/286852-stolberg/mode/2up . Article clarifying publication date: Michael Oreskes, "For G.O.P. Arsenal, 133 Words to Fire", *New York Times*, 1990, September 9. https://www.nytimes.com/1990/09/09/us/political-memo-for-gop-arsenal-133-words-to-fire.html

11. Zelizer, *Burning down the house,* pp. 302-303.

12. NPR, *What Florida's parental rights in education law means for teachers,* 2022, April 5. https://www.npr.org/2022/04/04/1090946670/ what-floridas-parental-rights-in-education-law-means-for-teachers

13. Emily Brooks, *'Groomer' debate inflames GOP fight over Florida law,* The Hill, 2022, April 8. https://thehill.com/news/ house/3262988-groomer-debate-inflames-gop-fight-over-florida-law/

14. David Brooks, *The second mountain: The quest for a moral life* (Random House 2019), p. 35.

15. Robert Putnam, *Bowling alone: The collapse and revival of American community* (Revised and updated) (Simon & Schuster 2020), p. 342.

Chapter 9: The Contagion of Cruelty and Kindness

1. Jimmy Kimmel Live, *Celebrities Read Mean Tweets #7,* YouTube, 2014, May 22. https://www.youtube.com/watch?v=imW392e6XR0

2. Kelly Tyko, Target shopper wearing '$40,000 Rolex' destroys face mask display, while Costco shopper protests mask policy. *USA Today,* 2020, July 6. https://www.usatoday.com/story/money/2020/07/06/ mask-rant-shoppers-protest-face-coverings-target-costco/5382837002/

3. Blake Morgan, A surge in unruly behavior has forced companies to discipline their customers, *Forbes,* 2021, June 3. https://www.forbes.com/ sites/blakemorgan/2021/06/03/a-surge-in-unruly-behavior-has-forced-companies-to-discipline-their-customers/?sh=727fcfcd67c6

4. For a few examples see:

- Rebecca Klapper, Death threats to members of Congress have doubled this year, Capitol Police say. *Newsweek,* 2021, May 18. https:// www.newsweek.com/death-threats-members-congress-have-doubled-this-year-capitol-police-say-1592587

- Michelle Mello, et al. Attacks on Public Health Officials During COVID-19. *JAMA,* 2020;324(8):741–742. https://doi.org/10.1001/ jama.2020.14423

- Bill Whitaker, *Federal judges call for increased security after threats jump 400% and one judge's son is killed*, CBS News, 2021, February 21. https://www.cbsnews.com/news/federal-judge-threats-attack-60-minutes-2021-02-21/

5. Robert Cialdini, *Influence: The psychology of persuasion* (New and expanded) (Harper Business 2021, Originally Published 1984), p. 129-130. Emphasis from original source.

6. Susan Liautaud with Lisa Sweetingham, *The power of ethics: How to make good choices in a complicated world* (Simon & Schuster 2021), p. 69. Emphasis from original source.

7. David Brooks, *The second mountain: The quest for a moral life* (Random House 2019), p. 10.

8. Dacher Keltner, *Born to be good: The science of a meaningful life* (W.W. Norton, 2009).

9. _____, p. 6.

10. Huston Smith, *The world's religions* (Harper One 1991, Originally published 1958).

11. Keltner and Smith both use the word "jen" which is the same as "ren" which is the pinyin form of the Chinese character (仁). In Chinese, the "r" is pronounced with a sound similar to a "j", so some English translations spell it jen.

12. Daniel Gardner, *Confucianism: A very short introduction* (Oxford University Press 2014), p. 22.

13. Smith, *The world's religions*, p. 159.

Chapter 10: The Myth of Perfection

1. Dalai Lama & Desmond Tutu with Douglas Abrams, *The book of joy* (Penguin, 2016), pp. 91-92.

2. Debbie Ford, *The dark side of the light chasers: Reclaiming your power, creativity, brilliance, and dreams* (Riverhead Books 2010, Originally published 1998), Kindle loc. 346-348.

3. Colleen Doyle Bryant, *Be proud* (LoveWell Press 2011).

4. Adapted from Colleen Doyle Bryant, *Truth be told quotes* (LoveWell Press 2020, Originally published 2018). https://truthbetoldquotes.com/quotes-teens/quote-good-character.html

Part 3: Setting a Course

1. Susan Liautaud with Lisa Sweetingham, *The power of ethics: How to make good choices in a complicated world* (Simon & Schuster 2021), p. 24.

Chapter 11: Right and Wrong

1. Cate Shortland (Director), *Black Widow* [Film] (Marvel 2021).

2. David Brooks, *The second mountain: The quest for a moral life* (Random House 2019), p. 11. Brooks goes on to argue that viewing morality as an individual choice has been harmful to society.

3. For detail on the evolution of morality, see:
   • Jonathan Haidt, *The righteous mind: Why good people are divided by politics and religion* (Pantheon Books 2012).
   • Dacher Keltner, *Born to be good: The science of a meaningful life* (WW Norton 2009), Chapter 4.
   • Jonathan Sacks, *Morality: Restoring the common good in divided times* (Basic Books 2020), Chapter 19.

4. Haidt, *The righteous mind*, p. 253.

5. Sacks, *Morality*, p. 280.

6. M. V. Nadkarni, Ethics in Hinduism, *Ethics For Our Times: Essays in Gandhian Perspective* (Oxford University Press 2011) https://doi.org/10.1093/acprof:oso/9780198073864.001.0001 and Swami Ramsukhdas, *Srimad Bhagavadgita* (S.C. Vaishya, Trans.), (Gita Press Gorakhpur 1997, Originally published 1989).

7. Sacks, *Morality*, p. 232.

8. Phil Zuckerman, *Society without God: What the least religious nations can tell us about contentment* (New York University Press 2020), p. 10.

9. _____, p. 26.

10. Ara Norenzayan, Does religion make people moral? *Behaviour*, 151(2/3) 2014, 365-384. Quote from p. 377. http://www.jstor.org/stable/24526014

11. _____, p. 379.

12. Zuckerman, *Society without God.*

13. Pew Research Center, *In U.S., decline of Christianity continues at rapid pace,* 2019, October 17. https://www.pewforum.org/2019/10/17/in-u-s-decline-of-christianity-continues-at-rapid-pace/

14. Zuckerman, *Society without God*, p. 3.

15. _____, pp. 1-2.

Chapter 12: Shared Values

1. Conrad Hackett & David McClendon, *Christians remain world's largest religious group*, Pew Research Center, 2017, April 5. https://www.pewresearch.org/fact-tank/2017/04/05/christians-remain-worlds-largest-religious-group-but-they-are-declining-in-europe/

2. Tim Dowley, *Introduction to world religions* (C. H. Partridge, Ed.) (Fortress Press 2018), etextbook p. 88-89.

3. _____.

4. Section on Hinduism compiled from:

- Swami Bhaskarananda, *The essentials of Hinduism: A comprehensive overview of the world's oldest religion* (Viveka 2002).
- M. V. Nadkarni, Ethics in Hinduism, *Ethics for our times: Essays in Gandhian perspective* (Oxford University Press 2011). https://doi.org/10.1093/acprof:oso/9780198073864.001.0001
- Huston Smith, *The world's religions* (Harper One 1991, Originally published 1958).

5. Nadkarni, Ethics in Hinduism, no page numbers in DOI online copy of the chapter.

6. Bhaskarananda, *The essentials of Hinduism*, Kindle loc. 653-655.

7. _____, Kindle loc. 1490.

8. Quote from: *Mahabharata*, Udyoga Parvan 39.57 as noted in Bakker, F. (2013). Comparing the Golden Rule in Hindu and Christian Religious Texts. *Studies in Religion/Sciences Religieuses*, 42(1), 38-58. https://doi.org/10.1177/0008429812460141

9. Section on Judaism compiled from:

- Rabbi Sid Schwarz, Judaism and Social Justice: Five core values from the rabbinic tradition, *Religions: A Scholarly Journal*, 2012(2). https://doi.org/10.5339/rels.2012.justice.10
- Smith, *The world's religions.*
- Rabbi Joseph Telushkin, *The book of Jewish values: A day-by-day guide to ethical living* (Bell Tower 2000).

10. Jonathan Sacks, *The ten utterances: Excerpts from the Koren-Sacks Shavuot Machzor*, Rabbi Sacks Legacy Trust, 2016, May 31. https://rabbisacks.org/ten-utterances/

11. _____.

12. Telushkin, *The book of Jewish values*, p. 74. Emphasis from original source.

13. English Standard Version Bible, The Bible Gateway, 2021. https://www.biblegateway.com/

14. Section on Confucianism compiled from:

- Confucius, *Analects: With selections from traditional commentaries* (E. Slingerland, Trans.) (Hackett 2003, Originally published n.d.).
- Daniel K. Gardner, *Confucianism: A very short introduction* (Oxford University Press 2014).
- Smith, *The world's religions.*

15. Smith, *The world's religions*, p. 163.

16. Ren is Chinese pinyin for the character (仁) which is pronounced with a "j" sound in English, hence the translations as both ren or jen.

17. Etymology reference from Daniel K. Gardner, *Confucianism: A very short introduction.*

18. Confucius, *Analects.*

19. Section on Buddhism complied from:

- Rupert Gethin, *Sayings of the Buddha* (Oxford University Press 2008).

- Thich Nhat Hanh, *The heart of the Buddha's teaching: Transforming suffering into peace, joy, and liberation* (Harmony Books 2015, Originally published 1998).
- Smith, *The world's religions.*

20. Nhat Hanh, *The heart of the Buddha's teaching*, p. 11.

21. Gethin, *Sayings of the Buddha*, p. 138.

22. Dharmatrata (Ed.), *Udanavarga: A collection of verses from the Buddhist Canon.* W. Rockhill (Trans.) Trubner, 1883.

23. Section on Aristotle compiled from:

- Aristotle, *The Nicomachean Ethics* (Oxford world's classics) (D. Ross, Trans., & L. Brown, Ed.) (Oxford University Press 2009, Originally published c. 350 BCE).
- Richard Kraut, Aristotle's ethics, In E. N. Zalta (Ed.), *The Stanford encyclopedia of philosophy* (Metaphysics Research Lab, Stanford University 2018). https://plato.stanford.edu/archives/sum2018/entries/aristotle-ethics/

24. Jon Miller, A distinction regarding happiness in ancient philosophy, *Social Research*, 77(2), 2010 Summer, 595–624. Quote from p. 599. http://www.jstor.org/stable/40972231

25. Aristotle, *The Nicomachean Ethics*, II.6.

26. _____, II.9.

27. _____, V.1.

28. Section on Christianity compiled from:

- Richard B. Hays, *The moral vision of the New Testament* (Harper One 1996).
- Smith, *The world's religions.*

29. Section on Islam compiled from:

- M. Cherif Bassiouni, *The social system and morality of Islam*, Middle East Institute, 2012, January 24. https://www.mei.edu/publications/social-system-and-morality-islam

- Justin Parrot, *The guiding principles of faith: Sincerity, honesty, and good will in Islam*, Yaqeen Institute for Islamic Research, 2018, July 19. https://yaqeeninstitute.org/read/paper/the-guiding-principles-of-faith-sincerity-honesty-and-good-will-in-islam
- Justin Parrot, *Can a "good Muslim" be a "bad person"? Aligning faith and character*, Yaqeen Institute for Islamic Research, 2019 July 3. https://yaqeeninstitute.org/read/paper/can-a-good-muslim-be-a-bad-person-aligning-faith-and-character
- Ahmad Rashid Salim, *Islam explained: A short introduction to history, teachings, and culture* (Rockridge Press 2020).
- Smith, *The world's religions.*

30. Bassiouni, *The social system and morality of Islam.*
31. Parrot, *Can a "good Muslim" be a "bad person"?*, p. 28.
32. Parrot, *The guiding principles of faith*, p.4.
33. Parrot, *Can a "good Muslim" be a "bad person"?*, p. 9.

Chapter 14: What Is Truth

1. Sources for definition and discussion of degrees of truth:
   - My experience writing books and teaching resources on honesty: see Bryant, n.d.-a in the references list or: https://talkingtreebooks.com/category/teaching-traits/honesty-worksheet-teaching-resources.html
   - The world belief systems in chapter 12 of this book, *Rooted in decency.*
   - *General sources on truth*:
   - Robert Feldman, *The liar in your life: The way to truthful relationships* (Twelve 2009).
   - Sam Harris, *Lying* (Four Elephants Press 2013).
   - Lee McIntyre, *Post-truth* (MIT Press 2018).
   - Pamela Meyer, *Liespotting: Proven techniques to detect deception* (St. Martin's Press 2010).
2. Danny Clemens, *'He's a decent family man': Watch the moment John McCain defended Barack Obama on 2008 campaign trail*, ABC7 Chicago, 2018, August 26. https://abc7chicago.com/mccain-defends-obama-arab-2008-campaign-john/4058948/

3. Harris, *Lying*, p. 13, Emphasis from original source.

Chapter 15: Trust Me

1. Bobby Allyn, *Former Theranos CEO Elizabeth Holmes to be sentenced on Sept. 26*, NPR, 2022, January 12. https://www.npr.org/2022/01/12/1072612059/former-theranos-ceo-elizabeth-holmes-to-be-sentenced-on-sept-26 and John Carreyrou, SEC charges Theranos CEO Elizabeth Holmes with fraud, *Wall Street Journal*, 2018, March 14. https://www.wsj.com/articles/sec-charges-theranos-and-founder-elizabeth-holmes-with-fraud-1521045648?mod=article_inline&page=1&pos=8

2. Aaron Blake, Analysis | Sidney Powell's Tucker Carlson-esque defense: 'reasonable people' wouldn't take her wild voter-fraud claims as fact, *Washington Post*, 2021, March 23. https://www.washingtonpost.com/politics/2021/03/23/sidney-powells-tucker-carlson-esque-defense/

3. Robert Feldman, *The liar in your life: The way to truthful relationships* (Twelve 2009).

4. Pamela Meyer, *Liespotting: Proven techniques to detect deceptio*n (St. Martin's Press 2010), p. 9.

5. Feldman, *The liar in your life*, p. 24.

6. _____, p. 25.

7. Robert Putnam, *Bowling alone: The collapse and revival of American community* (Revised and updated) (Simon & Schuster 2020, Originally published 2000).

8. _____, p. 135.

9. Feldman, *The liar in your life*, p. 24.

Chapter 16: The Post-Truth Con

1. Ryan Holiday & Stephen Hanselman, *The daily stoic: 366 meditations on wisdom, perseverance, and the art of living* (Portfolio/Penguin 2016), p. 78.

2. Oxford University Press, *Oxford Word of the year 2016*, Oxford Languages, (n.d.). https://languages.oup.com/word-of-the-year/2016/

3. _____.

4. Lee McIntyre, *Post-truth* (MIT Press 2018), Kindle p. 15.

5. For detailed documentation of the role of lobbies, politicians, media, etc. in creating a post-truth climate see:
  - McIntyre, *Post-truth.*
  - Charles Sykes, *How the right lost its mind* (St. Martin's Press 2017).

6. Po Bronson & Ashley Merryman, *NurtureShock: New thinking about children* (Twelve 2009).

7. ____, Kindle loc. 1164.

8. ____, Kindle loc. 1208.

9. For techniques that teach children to be honest see: Colleen Doyle Bryant, *How to teach kids to be honest*, Talking with Trees Books, (n.d.-b). https://talkingtreebooks.com/blog/posts/teaching-kids-to-be-honest-truthful.html

10. Pamela Meyer, *Liespotting: Proven techniques to detect deception* (St. Martin's Press 2010), p. 22.

11. Robert Feldman, *The liar in your life: The way to truthful relationships* (Twelve 2009), p. 55.

12. Cognitive Dissonance sections compiled from:
  - Elliot Aronson & Carol Tavris, The role of cognitive dissonance in the pandemic, *The Atlantic*, 2020, July 12. https://www.theatlantic.com/ideas/archive/2020/07/role-cognitive-dissonance-pandemic/614074/
  - Joel Cooper, Cognitive dissonance: Where we've been and where we're going, *International Review of Social Psychology*, 32(1), 2019, 7, 1-11. http://doi.org/10.5334/irsp.277
  - Eddie Harmon-Jones (Ed.), *Cognitive Dissonance: Reexamining a Pivotal Theory in Psychology* (Second Edition) (American Psychological Association 2019).

13. Aronson & Tavris, The role of cognitive dissonance in the pandemic.

14. ____.

15. Elliot Aronson, Dissonance, Hypocrisy, and the Self-Concept in Eddie Harmon-Jones (Ed.), *Cognitive Dissonance: Reexamining a Pivotal Theory in Psychology* (American Psychological Association 2019), p.144.

16. Aronson & Tavris, The role of cognitive dissonance in the pandemic.

17. Joel Cooper, Cognitive dissonance: Where we've been and where we're going.

18. Aronson & Tavris, The role of cognitive dissonance in the pandemic. Emphasis from original source.

Chapter 17: What Is Respect

1. Robin S. Dillon, Respect, In E. N. Zalta (Ed.), *The Stanford encyclopedia of philosophy* (Metaphysics Research Lab, Stanford University 2018). https://plato.stanford.edu/archives/spr2018/entries/respect/

2. Sources for definition and discussion of degrees of respect:

   • My experience writing books and teaching resources on respect: see Bryant, n.d.-d in the references list or: https://talkingtreebooks.com/category/teaching-traits/respect-worksheets-teaching-resources.html

   • The world belief systems in chapter 12 of this book, *Rooted in decency.*

   • *General sources on respect, human dignity, fairness:*

   • Dillon, Respect.

   • Jonathan Glover, *Humanity: A moral history of the twentieth century* (Second Edition) (Yale Univ. Press 2012, Originally published 1999).

   • Immanuel Kant, *The metaphysics of morals* (M. Gregor, Ed. & Trans.) (Cambridge University Press 1996, Originally published 1797).

   • John Rawls, *Justice as fairness: A restatement* (E. Kelly, Ed.) (Belknap Press 2001).

   • Jonathan Sacks, *Morality: Restoring the common good in divided times* (Basic Books 2020).

3. Brian Duignan, John Rawls, *Encyclopedia Britannica*, 2022, February 17. https://www.britannica.com/biography/John-Rawls

4. Rawls, *Justice as fairness*, §2.2.

5. _____.

6. Jonathan Haidt, *Wired to be Inspired*, Greater Good Science Center, 2005, March 1. https://greatergood.berkeley.edu/article/item/wired_to_be_inspired

7. For specifics accounts of student protests, see Greg Lukianoff & Jonathan Haidt, *The coddling of the American mind: How good intentions and bad ideas are setting up a generation for failure* (Penguin 2018) and Justin Folk (Director), *No Safe Spaces* [Film] (Atlas 2019).

8. Tom Jackman, Police Union says 140 officers injured in Capitol Riot, *Washington Post*, 2021, January 27. https://www.washingtonpost.com/local/public-safety/police-union-says-140-officers-injured-in-capitol-riot/2021/01/27/60743642-60e2-11eb-9430-e7c77b5b0297_story.html

9. Brian Duignan, United States Capitol attack of 2021, *Encyclopedia Britannica*, 2022, January 6. https://www.britannica.com/event/United-States-Capitol-attack-of-2021

10. Jonathan Glover, *Humanity*, p. 404.

Chapter 18: Working Against Ourselves

1. Jonathan Sacks, *Morality: Restoring the common good in divided times* (Basic Books, 2020), p. 217.

2. Charles Sykes, *How the right lost its mind* (St. Martin's Press 2017), pp. 181-182.

3. Dennis Prager, Trump, Conservatives, and the 'principles' question, *National Review*, 2016, September 6. https://www.nationalreview.com/2016/09/never-trump-supporters-dont-realize-hillary-clinton-worse-option-donald-trump/

4. Sykes, *How the right lost Its mind*, pp. 12-13.

5. Colleen Doyle Bryant, *Truth be told quotes* (LoveWell Press 2020, Originally published 2018), p. 20.

6. I searched the phrase "should be ashamed of" (including quotation marks) in Google News Tab, Feb 19, 2022.

7. David Morgan & Susan Cornwell, *Cheney ousted by U.S. house Republicans, but will seek re-election*, Reuters, 2021, May 12. https://www.reuters.com/world/us/liz-cheney-vote-us-house-republicans-reach-watershed-over-trump-2021-05-12/

8. Justin Folk (Director), *No Safe Spaces* [Film] (Atlas 2019), at 0:55:26.

9. June Price Tangney, Jeffrey Stuewig, & Debra J. Mashek, What's moral about the self-conscious emotions?, In J. Tracy, R. Robins, & J. Tangney (Eds.), *The self-conscious emotions: Theory and research* (pp. 21-37) (The Guilford Press 2007).

10. Brené Brown, *I thought it was just me: Women reclaiming power and courage in a culture of shame* (Gotham 2007), p. 20.

11. Tangney, et.al., What's moral about the self-conscious emotions?

12. Jeffrey Stuewig & June Price Tangney, Shame and guilt in antisocial and risky behaviors, In J. Tracy, R. Robins, & J. Tangney (Eds.), *The self-conscious emotions: Theory and research* (pp. 371-388) (The Guilford Press 2007), p. 373.

13. Mark Lilla, *The once and future liberal: after identity politics* (Harper 2017), p. 129.

14. Daron Acemoglu & James A. Robinson, *The narrow corridor: States, societies, and the fate of liberty* (Penguin Books 2020), (Originally published 2019).

15. _____, p. 7.

16. John Rawls, *Justice as fairness: A restatement*, (E. Kelly, Ed.) (Belknap Press 2001).

17. Brown, *I thought it was just me*, p. 59.

Chapter 19: What Is Responsibility

1. Sources for definition and discussion of degrees of responsibility:
   • My experience writing books and teaching resources on responsibility: see Bryant, n.d.-e in the references list or: https://talkingtreebooks.com/category/teaching-traits/responsibility-worksheets-teaching-resources.html
   • The world belief systems in chapter 12 of this book, *Rooted in decency*.
   • *General sources on responsibility*:
   • Susan Liautaud & Lisa Sweetingham, *The power of ethics: How to make good choices in a complicated world* (Simon & Schuster 2021).

- Marion Smiley, Collective Responsibility, In E. N. Zalta (Ed.), *The Stanford encyclopedia of philosophy* (Metaphysics Research Lab, Stanford University 2017). https://plato.stanford.edu/archives/sum2017/entries/collective-responsibility/
- Matthew Talbert, Moral Responsibility, In E. N. Zalta (Ed.), *The Stanford encyclopedia of philosophy* (Metaphysics Research Lab, Stanford University 2019). https://plato.stanford.edu/archives/win2019/entries/moral-responsibility/
- Garrath Williams, *Responsibility*, Internet encyclopedia of philosophy: A peer-reviewed academic resource, (n.d.). https://iep.utm.edu/responsi/

2. For Confucius, see Huston Smith, *The world's religions* (Harper One 1991, Originally published 1958), p. 182. For Hinduism, see Swami Bhaskarananda, *The essentials of Hinduism* (Viveka 2002), Kindle loc. 1522.

3. Colleen Doyle Bryant, *Truth be told quotes* (LoveWell Press 2020, Originally published 2018).

4. Dacher Keltner, *Born to be good: The science of a meaningful life* (WW Norton 2009).

5. Talbert, Moral responsibility.

6. Jennifer Wolfe, *When parents scream at school board meetings, how can I teach their children?* CNN, October 14, 2021. https://www.cnn.com/2021/10/14/opinions/parents-weaponize-school-board-meetings-wolfe/index

7. See chapter 7 of this book, *Rooted in decency,* or original source: Jonathan Haidt, *The righteous mind: Why good people are divided by politics and religion* (Pantheon Books 2012).

8. Valencia Higuera, *What is Helicopter Parenting?* Healthline, 2019, September 12. https://www.healthline.com/health/parenting/helicopter-parenting

9. John Rawls, *Justice as fairness: A restatement,* (E. Kelly, Ed.) (Belknap Press 2001), §1.4.

10. Liautaud & Sweetingham, *The power of ethics*, p.12. Emphasis in original source.

Chapter 20: Life After Victimhood

1. John Rawls, *Justice as fairness: A restatement* (E. Kelly, Ed.) (Belknap Press 2001), §13.2.

2. Mark Lilla, *The once and future liberal: After identity politics* (Harper 2017), p. 9.

3. Amy Chua, *Political tribes: Group instinct and the fate of nations* (Penguin 2018).

4. _____, p. 183.

5. _____, p.184.

6. Lilla, *Once and future liberal,* p. 67.

7. Scott Barry Kaufman, Unraveling the mindset of victimhood, *Scientific American*, 2020, June 29. https://www.scientificamerican.com/article/unraveling-the-mindset-of-victimhood/

8. Jordan B. Peterson, *How Anti-racism is Hurting Black America* [Video], YouTube, 2022, April 4, in video at 1:10:55. https://youtu.be/u9quq9NGUcM

9. Chua, *Political Tribes*, p.9.

10. Kaufman, Unraveling the mindset of victimhood.

11. Noa Schori-Eyal, Yechiel Klar, & Yarden Ben-Ami, Perpetual ingroup victimhood as a distorted lens: Effects on attribution and categorization, *European Journal of Social Psychology*, 2017, 47(2), 180–194. Quote on p. 181. https://doi.org/10.1002/ejsp.2250

12. Ibram X. Kendi, *How to be an anti-racist* (One World 2019), p. 97.

13. Jonathan Sacks, *Morality: Restoring the common good in divided times* (Basic Books, 2020), pp. 197-198.

14. Chua, *Political tribes*, p. 173.

Chapter 21: What Is Compassion

1. Shane Sinclair, et.al., Sympathy, empathy, and compassion: A grounded theory study of palliative care patients' understandings, experiences, and preferences. *Palliative Medicine*, 2017, 31(5), 437–447. https://doi.org/10.1177/0269216316663499

2. Supported by Jonathan Haidt, *The righteous mind: Why good people are divided by politics and religion* (Pantheon Books 2012) and Robert Sapolsky, *Behave: The biology of humans at our best and worst* (Penguin 2017).

3. Olga Klimecki & Tania Singer, Empathic distress fatigue rather than compassion fatigue? Integrating findings from empathy research in psychology and social neuroscience. In B. Oakley, et.al. (Eds.), *Pathological Altruism* (Kindle pp. 368-383) (Oxford University Press 2012).

4. Lynn E. O'Connor, et.al., Empathy-based pathogenic guilt, pathological altruism, and psychopathology. In B. Oakley, et. al. (Eds.), *Pathological Altruism* (Kindle pp. 10-30) (Oxford University Press 2012).

5. Elisa Gabbert, Is compassion fatigue inevitable in an age of 24-hour news? *The Guardian*, 2018, August 2. https://www.theguardian.com/news/2018/aug/02/is-compassion-fatigue-inevitable-in-an-age-of-24-hour-news and Olga Klimecki & Tania Singer, Empathic distress fatigue rather than compassion fatigue?

6. Sources for definition and discussion of degrees of compassion:
   - The world belief systems in chapter 12 of this book, *Rooted in decency*.
   - *General sources on empathy and compassion:*
   - Gregory J. Depow, Zoë Francis, & Michael Inzlicht, The Experience of Empathy in Everyday Life. *Psychological Science*, 2021, 32(8), 1198–1213. https://doi.org/10.1177/0956797621995202.
   - Dacher Keltner, The compassionate instinct, In D. Keltner, J. Marsh, & J. A. Smith (Eds.), *The compassionate instinct: The science of human goodness* (The Greater Good Science Center 2010).
   - Klimecki & Singer, Empathic distress fatigue rather than compassion fatigue.

- O'Connor, et.al., Empathy-based pathogenic guilt in *Pathological Altruism*.

- Sinclair, et.al., Sympathy, empathy, and compassion in *Palliative Medicine*.

7. Scott Barry Kaufman, *Transcend: The new science of self-actualization* (Penguin Random House 2020).

8. Greg Lukianoff & Jonathan Haidt, *The coddling of the American mind: How good intentions and bad ideas are setting up a generation for failure* (Penguin 2018).

9. Pema Chödrön, *Welcoming the Unwelcome: Wholehearted living in a brokenhearted world* (Shambhala 2019), p. 3.

10. CBS Baltimore, *YouTuber Kanghua Ren sentenced to jail for feeding toothpaste-filled oreos to homeless man*, 2019, June 5. https://baltimore.cbslocal.com/2019/06/05/ youtuber-sentenced-jail-feeding-toothpaste-filled-oreos-homeless-man/

11. Bianca Buono, *She coughed in someone's face and her video went viral. Now she's lost her job.* 12news.com, 2021, September 9. https:// www.12news.com/article/news/health/coronavirus/coughing-karen-of-scottsdale-loses-job-after-grocery-store-video-goes-viral/75-65859a72-fb8a-472a-a38f-5f79be7159b3

12. Nicholas Goldberg, When an anti-vaxxer dies of COVID, is that cause for glib, ironic satisfaction? *Los Angeles Times*, 2022, January 6. https://www.latimes.com/opinion/story/2022-01-06/ kelly-ernby-antivax-covid-death

13. Sara Cline, *Liberal US cities change course, now clearing homeless camps*, ABC News, 2022, March 11. https://abcnews.go.com/Health/ wireStory/face-liberal-us-cities-target-homeless-camps-83382340

14. Jeff Gianola, *Month after homeless camp sweep, neighbors say situation is worse*, KOIN.com, 2022, March 2. https://www.koin.com/ is-portland-over/lets-be-honest-homeless-camp-cleanups-do-nothing/

15. David Leonhardt, 'Not good for learning', *New York Times*, 2022, May 5. https://www.nytimes.com/2022/05/05/briefing/school-closures-covid-learning-loss.html

16. Russel Viner, et. al., School Closures During Social Lockdown and Mental Health, Health Behaviors, and Well-being Among Children and Adolescents During the First COVID-19 Wave: A Systematic Review, *JAMA Pediatrics,* 2022;176(4):400–409. doi:10.1001/jamapediatrics.2021.5840

Chapter 22: The Bright Side

1. Ryan Holiday & Stephen Hanselman, *The daily stoic: 366 meditations on wisdom, perseverance, and the art of living* (Portfolio/Penguin 2016), p. 103.

2. Dacher Keltner, The compassionate instinct, In D. Keltner, et. al. (Eds.), *The compassionate instinct,* pp. 8-15, (The Greater Good Science Center 2010), Quote from p. 9.

3. _____, pp. 10-11.

4. Gregory J. Depow, Zoë Francis, & Michael Inzlicht, The Experience of Empathy in Everyday Life. *Psychological Science,* 2021, 32(8), 1198–1213. https://doi.org/10.1177/0956797621995202

5. In the interest of reference integrity, I've written this quote several times before, including in a blog: https://talkingtreebooks.com/blog/posts/find-joy-in-others-joy.html and in my book for teens, *Truth be told quotes* (LoveWell Press 2020).

6. Hans Rosling, Ola Rosling, & Anna Rosling Rönnlund, *Factfulness: Ten reasons we're wrong about the world—and why things are better than you think* (Flatiron Books 2018), p. 68.

7. _____, p. 69.

8. James Clear, *Atomic habits: An easy & proven way to build good habits & break bad ones* (Avery 2018), p. 24.

9. English Standard Version Bible, The Bible Gateway, 2021. https://www.biblegateway.com/

10. Sonja Lyubomirsky, *The how of happiness: A new approach to getting the life you want* (Penguin 2007), p. 89.

11. Adapted from Sonja Lyubomirsky, *The how of happiness,* pp. 92-95.

12. _____, p. 92.

References

Acemoglu, D., & Robinson, J. A. (2020). *The narrow corridor: States, societies, and the fate of liberty.* Penguin Books. (Originally published in 2019)

Allyn, B. (2022, January 12). *Former Theranos CEO Elizabeth Holmes to be sentenced on Sept. 26.* NPR. https://www.npr.org/2022/01/12/1072612059/former-theranos-ceo-elizabeth-holmes-to-be-sentenced-on-sept-26

Aristotle. (2009). *The Nicomachean ethics* (D. Ross, Trans., & L. Brown, Ed.). Oxford University Press. (Originally published c. 350 BCE)

Aronson, E. (2019). Dissonance, hypocrisy, and the self-concept. In E. Harmon-Jones (Ed.), *Cognitive Dissonance: Reexamining a Pivotal Theory in Psychology.* (pp. 141-158). American Psychological Association.

Aronson, E., & Tavris, C. (2020, July 12). The role of cognitive dissonance in the pandemic. *The Atlantic.* https://www.theatlantic.com/ideas/archive/2020/07/role-cognitive-dissonance-pandemic/614074/

Bakker, F. (2013). Comparing the Golden Rule in Hindu and Christian religious texts. *Studies in Religion/Sciences Religieuses*, 42(1), 38-58. https://doi.org/10.1177/0008429812460141

Bassiouni, M. C. (2012, January 24). *The social system and morality of Islam.* Middle East Institute. https://www.mei.edu/publications/social-system-and-morality-islam

Baumeister, R. F., Campbell, J. D., Krueger, J. I., & Vohs, K. D. (2003). Does high self-esteem cause better performance, interpersonal success, happiness, or healthier lifestyles? *Psychological Science in the Public Interest*, 4(1), 1–44. https://doi.org/10.1111/1529-1006.01431

Baumeister, R. (2005). Rethinking self-esteem. *Stanford Social Innovation Review*, Winter, 34-41.

Bhaskarananda, S. (2002). *The essentials of Hinduism: A comprehensive overview of the world's oldest religion*. Viveka.

Blake, A. (2021, March 23). Analysis | Sidney Powell's Tucker Carlson-esque defense: 'reasonable people' wouldn't take her wild voter-fraud claims as fact. *Washington Post*. https://www.washingtonpost.com/politics/2021/03/23/sidney-powells-tucker-carlson-esque-defense/

Bronson, P., & Merryman, A. (2009). *NurtureShock: New thinking about children*. Twelve.

Brooks, D. (2019). *The second mountain: The quest for a moral life*. Random House.

Brooks, E. (2022, April 8). 'Groomer' debate inflames GOP fight over Florida law. The Hill. https://thehill.com/news/house/3262988-groomer-debate-inflames-gop-fight-over-florida-law/

Brown, B. (2007). *I thought it was just me: Women reclaiming power and courage in a culture of shame*. Gotham.

Bryant, C. D. (2011). *Be proud*. LoveWell Press.

Bryant, C. D. (2020). *Truth be told quotes*. LoveWell Press. (Originally published 2018)

Bryant, C. D. (n.d.-a). *Honesty worksheets and teaching resources*. Talking with Trees Books. https://talkingtreebooks.com/category/teaching-traits/honesty-worksheet-teaching-resources.html

Bryant, C. D. (n.d.-b). *How to teach kids to be honest*. Talking with Trees Books. https://talkingtreebooks.com/blog/posts/teaching-kids-to-be-honest-truthful.html

Bryant, C. D. (n.d.-c). *Minimizing jealousy in children: Take joy in others' joy.* Talking with Trees Books. https://talkingtreebooks.com/blog/posts/find-joy-in-others-joy.html

Bryant, C. D. (n.d.-d). *Respect worksheets and teaching resources.* Talking with Trees Books. https://talkingtreebooks.com/category/teaching-traits/respect-worksheets-teaching-resources.html

Bryant, C. D. (n.d.-e). *Responsibility worksheets and teaching resources.* Talking with Trees Books. https://talkingtreebooks.com/category/teaching-traits/responsibility-worksheets-teaching-resources.html

Bryant, C. D. (n.d.-f). *Right now is a great time to make a good choice.* Talking with Trees Books. https://talkingtreebooks.com/blog/posts/teaching-kids-make-good-choices.html

Buono, B. (2021, September 9). *She coughed in someone's face and her video went viral. Now she's lost her job.* 12news.com. https://www.12news.com/article/news/health/coronavirus/coughing-karen-of-scottsdale-loses-job-after-grocery-store-video-goes-viral/75-65859a72-fb8a-472a-a38f-5f79be7159b3

Burns, D. (2012). *Feeling good: The new mood therapy.* Harper. (Originally published 1980)

Carreyrou, J. (2018, March 14). SEC charges Theranos CEO Elizabeth Holmes with fraud. *Wall Street Journal.* https://www.wsj.com/articles/sec-charges-theranos-and-founder-elizabeth-holmes-with-fraud-1521045648

Carson, S. H., & Langer, E. J. (2006). Mindfulness and self-acceptance. *Journal of Rational-Emotive & Cognitive-Behavior Therapy,* 24(1), 29–43. https://doi.org/10.1007/s10942-006-0022-5

CBS Baltimore. (2019, June 5). *YouTuber Kanghua Ren sentenced to jail for feeding toothpaste-filled oreos to homeless man.* https://baltimore.cbslocal.com/2019/06/05/youtuber-sentenced-jail-feeding-toothpaste-filled-oreos-homeless-man/

Chödrön, P. (2019). *Welcoming the Unwelcome: Wholehearted living in a brokenhearted world.* Shambhala.

Chua, A. (2018). *Political tribes: Group instinct and the fate of nations.* Penguin.

Cialdini, R. B. (2021). *Influence: The psychology of persuasion* (New and expanded). Harper Business. (Originally published 1984)

Clear, J. (2018). *Atomic habits: An easy & proven way to build good habits & break bad ones.* Avery.

Clemens, D. (2018, August 26). *'He's a decent family man':* *Watch the moment John McCain defended Barack Obama on* *2008 campaign trail.* ABC7 Chicago. https://abc7chicago.com/ mccain-defends-obama-arab-2008-campaign-john/4058948/

Cline, S. (2022, March 11). *Liberal US cities change course, now clearing homeless camps.* ABC News. https://abcnews.go.com/Health/wireStory/ face-liberal-us-cities-target-homeless-camps-83382340

Clucas, C. (2019). Understanding self-respect and its relationship to self-esteem. *Personality and Social Psychology Bulletin*, 46(6), 839–855. https://doi. org/10.1177/0146167219879115

Confucius. (2003). *Analects: With selections from traditional commentaries* (E. Slingerland, Trans.). Hackett. (Originally published n.d.)

Cooper, J. (2019). Cognitive dissonance: Where we've been and where we're going. *International Review of Social Psychology*, 32(1), 7. http://doi.org/10.5334/ irsp.277

deHooge, I. (2013). Moral emotions and prosocial behaviour: It may be time to change our view of shame and guilt. *Handbook of Psychology of Emotions: Recent Theoretical Perspectives and Novel Empirical Findings,* Vol 2, pp. 255-276. https://www.researchgate.net/publication/264084735

Depow, G. J., Francis, Z., & Inzlicht, M. (2021). The experience of empathy in everyday life. *Psychological Science*, 32(8), 1198–1213. https://doi. org/10.1177/0956797621995202

Dharmatrata (Ed.). (1883). *Udanavarga: A collection of verses from the Buddhist Canon.* W. Rockhill (Trans.). Trubner.

Dillon, R. S. (2018). Respect. In E. N. Zalta (Ed.), *The Stanford encyclopedia of philosophy*. Metaphysics Research Lab, Stanford University. https://plato. stanford.edu/archives/spr2018/entries/respect/

Dobrogosz, H. (2021, March 15). *People are sharing the "unwritten rules" of society that we should all follow, and I hope you're taking notes.* BuzzFeed. https://www.buzzfeed.com/hannahdobro/unwritten-rules-to-live-by

Dowley, T. (2018). *Introduction to world religions.* (etextbook). (C. H. Partridge, Ed.). Fortress Press.

Duignan, B. (2022, January 6). United States Capitol attack of 2021. *Encyclopedia Britannica.* https://www.britannica.com/event/United-States-Capitol-attack-of-2021

Duignan, B. (2022, February 17). John Rawls. *Encyclopedia Britannica.* https://www.britannica.com/biography/John-Rawls

English Standard Version Bible. (2021). The Bible Gateway. https://www.biblegateway.com/

Feldman, R. S. (2009). *The liar in your life: The way to truthful relationships.* Twelve.

Folk, J. (Director). (2019). *No Safe Spaces* [Film]. Atlas.

Ford, D. (2010). *The dark side of the light chasers: Reclaiming your power, creativity, brilliance, and dreams.* Riverhead Books. (Originally published 1998)

Gabbert, E. (2018, August 2). Is compassion fatigue inevitable in an age of 24-hour news? *The Guardian.* https://www.theguardian.com/news/2018/aug/02/is-compassion-fatigue-inevitable-in-an-age-of-24-hour-news

Gardner, D. K. (2014). *Confucianism: A very short introduction.* Oxford University Press.

Gethin, R. (2008). *Sayings of the Buddha* (Oxford World's Classics). Oxford University Press.

Gianola, J. (2022, March 2). *Month after homeless camp sweep, neighbors say situation is worse.* KOIN.com. https://www.koin.com/is-portland-over/lets-be-honest-homeless-camp-cleanups-do-nothing/

Glover, J. (2012). *Humanity: A moral history of the twentieth century* (Second Edition). Yale Univ. Press. (Originally published 1999)

Goldberg, N. (2022, January 6). When an anti-vaxxer dies of COVID, is that cause for glib, ironic satisfaction? *Los Angeles Times.* https://www.latimes.com/opinion/story/2022-01-06/kelly-ernby-antivax-covid-death

GOPAC. (1990). *Language a Key Mechanism of Control*. Original document shown in the Internet Archive: https://archive.org/details/286852-stolberg/mode/2up

Hackett, C., & McClendon, D. (2017, April 5). *Christians remain world's largest religious group*. Pew Research Center. https://www.pewresearch.org/fact-tank/2017/04/05/christians-remain-worlds-largest-religious-group-but-they-are-declining-in-europe/

Haidt, J. (2005, March 1). *Wired to be inspired*. Greater Good Science Center. https://greatergood.berkeley.edu/article/item/wired_to_be_inspired

Haidt, J. (2012). *The righteous mind: Why good people are divided by politics and religion*. Pantheon Books.

Harmon-Jones, E. (Ed.). (2019). *Cognitive dissonance: Reexamining a Pivotal Theory in Psychology* (Second Edition). American Psychological Association.

Harris, S. (2013). *Lying*. Four Elephants Press.

Harvard Health. (2020, July 7). *Exercising to relax*. Harvard Medical School. https://www.health.harvard.edu/staying-healthy/exercising-to-relax

Hays, R. B. (1996). *The moral vision of the New Testament*. Harper One.

Higuera, V. (2019, September 12). *What is Helicopter Parenting?* Healthline. https://www.healthline.com/health/parenting/helicopter-parenting

Holiday, R., & Hanselman, S. (2016). *The daily stoic: 366 meditations on wisdom, perseverance, and the art of living*. Portfolio/Penguin.

Jackman, T. (2021, January 27). Police Union says 140 officers injured in Capitol Riot. *Washington Post*. https://www.washingtonpost.com/local/public-safety/police-union-says-140-officers-injured-in-capitol-riot/2021/01/27/60743642-60e2-11eb-9430-e7c77b5b0297_story.html

Jimmy Kimmel Live. (2014, May 22). *Celebrities Read Mean Tweets #7* [Video]. YouTube. https://www.youtube.com/watch?v=imW392e6XRo

Kant, I. (1996). *The metaphysics of morals* (M. Gregor, Ed. & Trans.). Cambridge University Press. (Originally published 1797)

Kaufman, S. B. (2020) *Transcend: The new science of self-actualization*. Penguin Random House.

Kaufman, S. B. (2020, June 29). Unraveling the mindset of victimhood. *Scientific American*. https://www.scientificamerican.com/article/unraveling-the-mindset-of-victimhood/

Keltner, D. (2009). *Born to be good: The science of a meaningful life*. WW Norton.

Keltner, D. (2010). The compassionate instinct. In D. Keltner, J. Marsh, & J. A. Smith (Eds.), *The compassionate instinct*. (pp. 8-15). The Greater Good Science Center.

Kendi, I. X. (2019). *How to be an anti-racist*. One World.

Klapper, R. (2021, May 18). Death threats to members of Congress have doubled this year, Capitol Police say. *Newsweek*. https://www.newsweek.com/death-threats-members-congress-have-doubled-this-year-capitol-police-say-1592587

Klimecki, O., & Singer, T. (2012). Empathic distress fatigue rather than compassion fatigue? Integrating findings from empathy research in psychology and social neuroscience. In B. Oakley, A. Knafo, G. Madhavan, & D. S. Wilson (Eds.), *Pathological Altruism* (pp. 368-383). Oxford University Press.

Kraut, R. (2018). Aristotle's ethics. In E. N. Zalta (Ed.), *The Stanford encyclopedia of philosophy*. Metaphysics Research Lab, Stanford University. https://plato.stanford.edu/archives/sum2018/entries/aristotle-ethics/

Lama, D., Tutu, D., & Abrams, D. (2016). *The book of joy*. Penguin.

Leonhardt, D. (2022, May 5). 'Not good for learning'. *New York Times*. https://www.nytimes.com/2022/05/05/briefing/school-closures-covid-learning-loss.html

Liautaud, S., & Sweetingham, L. (2021). T*he power of ethics: How to make good choices in a complicated world*. Simon & Schuster.

Lilla, M. (2017). *The once and future liberal: After identity politics*. Harper.

Lukianoff, G., & Haidt, J. (2018). *The coddling of the American mind: How good intentions and bad ideas are setting up a generation for failure*. Penguin.

Lyubomirsky, S. (2007). *The how of happiness: A new approach to getting the life you want*. Penguin.

McIntyre, L. (2018). *Post-truth*. MIT Press.

McLaren, K. (2010). *The language of emotions: What your feelings are trying to tell you.* Sounds True.

Mello, M. M., Greene, J. A., & Sharfstein, J. M. Attacks on public health officials during COVID-19. *JAMA*, 2020;324(8):741–742. https://doi.org/10.1001/jama.2020.14423

Meyer, P. (2010). *Liespotting: Proven techniques to detect deception.* St. Martin's Press.

Miller, J. (2010). A distinction regarding happiness in ancient philosophy. *Social Research*, 77(2), 595–624. http://www.jstor.org/stable/40972231

Morgan, B. (2021, June 3). A surge in unruly behavior has forced companies to discipline their customers. *Forbes.* https://www.forbes.com/sites/blakemorgan/2021/06/03/a-surge-in-unruly-behavior-has-forced-companies-to-discipline-their-customers/?sh=727fcfcd67c6

Morgan, D., & Cornwell, S. (2021, May 12). *Cheney ousted by U.S. house Republicans, but will seek re-election.* Reuters. https://www.reuters.com/world/us/liz-cheney-vote-us-house-republicans-reach-watershed-over-trump-2021-05-12/

Nadkarni, M. V. (2011). Ethics in Hinduism. *Ethics for our times: Essays in Gandhian perspective.* Oxford University Press. https://doi.org/10.1093/acprof:oso/9780198073864.001.0001

Napper, P., & Rao, A. (2019). *The power of agency: The 7 principles to conquer obstacles, make effective decisions, and create a life on your own terms.* St. Martin's Press.

Nhat Hanh, T. (2015). *The heart of the Buddha's teaching: Transforming suffering into peace, joy, and liberation.* Harmony Books. (Originally published 1998)

Norenzayan, A. (2014). Does religion make people moral? *Behaviour*, 151(2/3), 365-384. http://www.jstor.org/stable/24526014

NPR. (2022, April 5). *What Florida's parental rights in education law means for teachers.* https://www.npr.org/2022/04/04/1090946670/what-floridas-parental-rights-in-education-law-means-for-teachers

O'Connor, L. E., Berry, J. W., Lewis, T. B., & Stiver, D. J. (2012). Empathy-based pathogenic guilt, pathological altruism, and psychopathology. In B. Oakley, A. Knafo, G. Madhavan, & D. S. Wilson (Eds.), *Pathological Altruism* (pp. 10-30). Oxford University Press.

Oreskes, M. (1990, Sept. 9). For G.O.P. Arsenal, 133 Words to Fire. *New York Times.* https://www.nytimes.com/1990/09/09/us/political-memo-for-gop-arsenal-133-words-to-fire.html

Oxford University Press. (n.d.). *Oxford Word of the year 2016.* Oxford Languages. https://languages.oup.com/word-of-the-year/2016/

Paine, T. (2017). *The rights of man: The French Revolution- Ideals, arguments and motives.* Musaicum Books. (Originally published 1791)

Parrot, J. (2018, July 19). *The guiding principles of faith: Sincerity, honesty, and good will in Islam.* Yaqeen Institute for Islamic Research. https://yaqeeninstitute.org/read/paper/the-guiding-principles-of-faith-sincerity-honesty-and-good-will-in-islam

Parrot, J. (2019, July 3). *Can a "good Muslim" be a "bad person"? Aligning faith and character.* Yaqeen Institute for Islamic Research. https://yaqeeninstitute.org/read/paper/can-a-good-muslim-be-a-bad-person-aligning-faith-and-character

Peterson, J. [Jordan B. Peterson]. (2022, April 4). *How anti-racism is hurting Black America* [Video]. YouTube. https://youtu.be/u9quq9NGUcM

Pew Research Center. (2019, October 17). *In U.S., decline of Christianity continues at rapid pace.* Pew Research. https://www.pewforum.org/2019/10/17/in-u-s-decline-of-christianity-continues-at-rapid-pace/

Plato. (1888). *The Republic of Plato* (B. Jowett, Trans.). Oxford. (Original work published c. 375 BCE). Online in 2017 by The Gutenberg Project: https://www.gutenberg.org/files/55201/55201-h/55201-h.htm

Popova, M. (2014, March 11). *Orgasm without release: Alan Watts presages our modern media gluttony in 1951.* Brain Pickings. https://www.brainpickings.org/2014/03/11/alan-watts-media-gluttony/

Prager, D. (2016, September 6). Trump, conservatives, and the 'principles' question. *National Review.* https://www.nationalreview.com/2016/09/never-trump-supporters-dont-realize-hillary-clinton-worse-option-donald-trump/

Putnam, R. D. (2020). *Bowling alone: The collapse and revival of American community* (Revised and updated). Simon & Schuster. (Originally published 2000)

Ramsukhdas, S. (1997). *Srimad Bhagavadgita* (S.C. Vaishya, Trans.). Gita Press Gorakhpur. (Originally published 1989)

Rawls, J. (2001). *Justice as fairness: A restatement* (E. Kelly, Ed.). Belknap Press.

Rosling, H., Rosling, O., & Rönnlund, A. R. (2018). *Factfulness: Ten reasons we're wrong about the world - and why things are better than you think*. Flatiron Books.

Sacks, J. (2016, May 31). *The ten utterances: Excerpts from the Koren-Sacks Shavuot Machzor*. Rabbi Sacks Legacy Trust. https://rabbisacks.org/ten-utterances/

Sacks, J. (2020). *Morality: Restoring the common good in divided times*. Basic Books.

Salim, A. R. (2020). *Islam explained: A short introduction to history, teachings, and culture*. Rockridge Press.

Sapolsky, R. (2017). *Behave: The biology of humans at our best and worst*. Penguin.

Schori-Eyal, N., Klar, Y., & Ben-Ami, Y. (2017). Perpetual ingroup victimhood as a distorted lens: Effects on attribution and categorization. *European Journal of Social Psychology, 47*(2), 180–194. https://doi.org/10.1002/ejsp.2250

Schwarz, S. I. (2012). Judaism and social justice: Five core values from the rabbinic tradition. *Religions: A Scholarly Journal, 2012*(2). https://doi.org/10.5339/rels.2012.justice.10

Shortland, C. (Director). (2021). *Black Widow* [Film]. Marvel.

Sinclair, S., Beamer, K., Hack, T. F., McClement, S., Raffin Bouchal, S., Chochinov, H. M., & Hagen, N. A. (2017). Sympathy, empathy, and compassion: A grounded theory study of palliative care patients' understandings, experiences, and preferences. *Palliative Medicine, 31*(5), 437–447. https://doi.org/10.1177/0269216316663499

Smiley, M. (2017). Collective responsibility. In E. N. Zalta (Ed.), *The Stanford encyclopedia of philosophy*. Metaphysics Research Lab, Stanford University. https://plato.stanford.edu/archives/sum2017/entries/collective-responsibility/

Smith, H. (1991). *The world's religions*. Harper One. (Originally published 1958)

Stuewig, J., & Tangney, J. P. (2007). Shame and guilt in antisocial and risky behaviors. In J. Tracy, R. Robins, & J. Tangney (Eds.), *The self-conscious emotions: Theory and research* (pp. 371-388). The Guilford Press.

Sykes, C. (2017). *How the right lost its mind*. St. Martin's Press.

Talbert, M. (2019). Moral responsibility. In E. N. Zalta (Ed.), *The Stanford encyclopedia of philosophy*. Metaphysics Research Lab, Stanford University. https://plato.stanford.edu/archives/win2019/entries/moral-responsibility/

Tangney, J. P., Stuewig, J., & Mashek, D. (2007). What's moral about the self-conscious emotions? In J. Tracy, R. Robins, & J. Tangney (Eds.), *The self-conscious emotions: Theory and research* (pp. 21-37). The Guilford Press.

Taylor, J. (2010, February 22). *Parenting: The sad misuse of self-esteem*. Psychology Today. https://www.psychologytoday.com/us/blog/the-power-prime/201002/parenting-the-sad-misuse-self-esteem

Telushkin, J. (2000). *The book of Jewish values: A day-by-day guide to ethical living*. Bell Tower.

Tyko, K. (2020, July 6). Target shopper wearing '$40,000 Rolex' destroys Face Mask Display, while Costco Shopper protests Mask Policy. *USA Today*. https://www.usatoday.com/story/money/2020/07/06/mask-rant-shoppers-protest-face-coverings-target-costco/5382837002/

Viner R., Russell S., Saulle R., Croker, H., Stansfield, C., Packer, J. Nicholls, D., Goddings, A., Bonell, C., Hudson, L., Hope, S., Ward, J., Schwalbe, N., Morgan, A., Minozzi, S. School closures during social lockdown and mental health, health behaviors, and well-being among children and adolescents during the first COVID-19 wave: A systematic review. *JAMA Pediatrics*. 2022;176(4):400–409. doi:10.1001/jamapediatrics.2021.5840

Waldinger, R. (2015, November). *What makes a good life? Lessons from the longest study on happiness.* TED. https://www.ted.com/talks/robert_waldinger_ what_makes_a_good_life_lessons_from_the_longest_study_on_happiness/ transcript?language=en

Weinschenk, S. (2018, February 28). *The dopamine seeking-reward loop.* Psychology Today. https://www.psychologytoday.com/us/blog/ brain-wise/201802/the-dopamine-seeking-reward-loop

Whitaker, B. (2021, February 21). *Federal judges call for increased security after threats jump 400% and one judge's son is killed.* CBS News. https://www. cbsnews.com/news/federal-judge-threats-attack-60-minutes-2021-02-21/

Williams, G. (n.d.). *Responsibility.* Internet encyclopedia of philosophy: A peer-reviewed academic resource. https://iep.utm.edu/responsi/

Williams, M., Teasdale, J., Segal, Z., & Kabat-Zinn, J. (2007). *The mindful way through depression: Freeing yourself from chronic unhappiness.* The Guilford Press.

Wolfe, J. (2021, October 14). *When parents scream at school board meetings, how can I teach their children?.* CNN. https://www.cnn.com/2021/10/14/opinions/ parents-weaponize-school-board-meetings-wolfe/index

Zelizer, J. E. (2020). *Burning down the house: Newt Gingrich, and the rise of the new Republican party.* Penguin.

Zuckerman, P. (2020). *Society without God: What the least religious nations can tell us about contentment.* New York University Press.

About the Author

Colleen Doyle Bryant is the author of five books and more than 50 learning resources about making good choices for the right reasons. Her Talking with Trees series for elementary students and Truth Be Told series for teens are used in curricula to teach good character traits and social emotional skills like honesty, respect, responsibility, and kindness. More than 100,000 of her good values teaching resources are downloaded each year by parents and teachers around the world. Colleen has a degree in sociology from Duke University.
Learn more at ColleenDoyleBryant.com

More by the Author

Talking with Tree Series
Written for children grades K-4, the Talking Trees use old-school wisdom, a little humor, and a lot of heart to help younger students learn important life lessons about honesty, respect, responsibility, empathy, and more good traits. Find books and teaching materials at **TalkingTreeBooks.com.**

Truth Be Told Quotes
Designed for high school teens, *Truth Be Told Quotes* presents important lessons for young adult life in a modern, image-based format. The book and teaching resources encourage growth around connecting choices and consequences, developing good character, resolving conflict, managing emotions, and more important life lessons. Find books, videos, and teaching resources at **TruthBeToldQuotes.com.**

Find printable journaling pages, book club
resources and more at:

RootedInDecency.com

www.ingramcontent.com/pod-product-compliance
Lightning Source LLC
Chambersburg PA
CBHW072050020426
42334CB00017B/1451